How Is Architecture Political?

ARCHITECTURE EXCHANGE:
Engagements with Contemporary Theory and Philosophy

Series Editor: Joseph Bedford, Associate Professor, School of Architecture, Virginia Tech, USA

The purpose of this series of Architecture Exchange books is to deepen intellectual exchange between architecture and other fields of contemporary theory. We are perhaps too familiar with the disappointment that can follow even the best of academic conferences when after 'no more time for questions' attendees disperse into the night. The ambition of this series of books is quite simply to prolong that curtailed moment of questioning, to extend the time and space of debate, and to see what ideas, fissures and fault lines emerge that might reveal new understanding.

In each book, a prominent contemporary theorist is invited to share their work with a group of 'architects' (more precisely, architects, architectural educators, architectural historians and architectural theorists). The architects are invited to spend several months reading from the theorist's body of work to prepare thoughts on how that body of work might have consequences for architecture. The exchange proper is then catalysed by an event in which everyone comes together to present their thoughts and respond to one another. But instead of dispersing into the night, the debate continues in the months that follow: through conversations between each participant and the editors to further unpack the connections and conflicts that began to arise; through the further development of their arguments in print and additional commentary printed as marginalia.

The resulting book presents the work of a contemporary thinker to architectural audiences and explores its relevance to architecture through a specifically dialogical exposition that seeks simultaneously to introduce new theoretical ideas to architecture, to introduce the enduring problematics of architecture to readers in contemporary theory, and to encourage students of architecture (of all ages) to explore new ways of viewing their discipline.

How Is Architecture Political?

Engaging Chantal Mouffe

Edited by
JOSEPH BEDFORD

BLOOMSBURY ACADEMIC
LONDON • NEW YORK • OXFORD • NEW DELHI • SYDNEY

BLOOMSBURY ACADEMIC
Bloomsbury Publishing Plc, 50 Bedford Square, London, WC1B 3DP, UK
Bloomsbury Publishing Inc, 1359 Broadway, 12th Floor, New York, NY 10018, USA
Bloomsbury Publishing Ireland, 29 Earlsfort Terrace, Dublin 2, D02 AY28, Ireland

BLOOMSBURY, BLOOMSBURY ACADEMIC and the Diana logo
are trademarks of Bloomsbury Publishing Plc

First published in Great Britain 2024
This paperback edition published 2025

Copyright © Joseph Bedford and Contributors, 2024

Joseph Bedford has asserted his right under the Copyright, Designs and Patents Act, 1988, to be identified as Editor of this work.

For legal purposes the Acknowledgements on p. ix constitute an extension of this copyright page.

Series Design by Twelve Studio

All rights reserved. No part of this publication may be: i) reproduced or transmitted in any form, electronic or mechanical, including photocopying, recording or by means of any information storage or retrieval system without prior permission in writing from the publishers; or ii) used or reproduced in any way for the training, development or operation of artificial intelligence (AI) technologies, including generative AI technologies. The rights holders expressly reserve this publication from the text and data mining exception as per Article 4(3) of the Digital Single Market Directive (EU) 2019/790.

Bloomsbury Publishing Inc does not have any control over, or responsibility for, any third-party websites referred to or in this book. All internet addresses given in this book were correct at the time of going to press. The author and publisher regret any inconvenience caused if addresses have changed or sites have ceased to exist, but can accept no responsibility for any such changes.

A catalogue record for this book is available from the British Library.

A catalog record for this book is available from the Library of Congress.

ISBN: HB: 978-1-3502-6306-2
PB: 978-1-3502-6310-9
ePDF: 978-1-3502-6307-9
eBook: 978-1-3502-6308-6

Series: Architecture Exchange

Typeset by Integra Software Services Pvt. Ltd.

For product safety related questions contact productsafety@bloomsbury.com.

To find out more about our authors and books visit www.bloomsbury.com and sign up for our newsletters.

Contents

List of Figures		vi
List of Contributors		vii
Acknowledgements		ix
1	How Is Architecture Political? *Joseph Bedford*	1
2	How to Envisage the Political Dimension of Architecture *Chantal Mouffe* Interview	13 20
3	Can Architecture Be Political? *Pier Vittorio Aureli* Interview	33 46
4	Polis-Oikos *Reinhold Martin* Interview	59 67
5	Mobilizing Dissent: The Possible Architecture of the Governed *Ines Weizman* Interview	84 97
6	Agonistic Practice *Sarah Whiting* Interview	109 122
7	The Politics of Architecture *Roundtable and Q&A*	136
8	Architecture's Challenges to Chantal Mouffe *Joseph Bedford*	149
Afterword: Chantal Mouffe		160
Bibliography		164
Index		175

Figures

1 Andrea Palladio, Plan of Villa Emo in Fanzolo (1555–61), Original Woodcut from I quattro libri dell'architettura di Andrea Palladio. Public Domain — 37
2 Photographs of Karl Marx Hof by Martin Gerlach Jr. (1879–1944). Images courtesy of Wien Museum Online Sammlung. CCO Public Domain — 40
3 Photograph of the 'May Brigade' (1931). Image Source: Wikimedia Commons. Creative Commons Public Domain. CC-PD-Mark — 45
4 Peter Paul Rubens's copy of The Battle of Anghiari (1603) (Louvre, Paris). Image Source: Wikimedia Common. CC-BY-SA-4.0 — 52
5 City Cathedral. Iskander Galimov, 1989. Image courtesy of Iskander Galimov — 90
6 St. Peters. Iskander Galimov, 1988. Image courtesy of Iskander Galimov — 90
7 Russian Centre in Bologna, Italy. Iskander Galimov in collaboration with Michail Fadeyev, 1989 — 91
8 Competition for Prince-Albrecht-Areal. West Berlin. Christian Enzmann and Bernd Ettel, 1983–4. Image courtesy of Christian Enzmann and Bernd Ettel — 92
9 Axonometry submitted to urban design competition for Bersarin Platz, Christian Enzmann and Bernd Ettel, 1984. Image courtesy of Christian Enzmann and Bernd Ettel — 93
10 Photograph of model submitted to urban design competition for Bersarin Platz, Christian Enzmann and Bernd Ettel, 1984. Image courtesy of Christian Enzmann and Bernd Ettel — 94
11 Alfredo Jaar, The Skoghall Konsthall, 2000. Image courtesy of Alfredo Jaar — 113
12 Dogma, Simple Heart (2002–9). Image courtesy of Dogma — 117
13 BIG, Superkilen (2012). Image courtesy of BIG and Iwan Baan — 118

Contributors

Pier Vittorio Aureli is Professor at the École Polytechnique Fédérale de Lausanne (EPFL), Switzerland, where he directs the Laboratory Theory and Project of Domestic space and teaches courses on History and Theories of Architecture, and a co-founder of Dogma alongside Martino Tattara. Aureli previously taught at the Architectural Association in London, Yale School of Architecture, Berlage Institute in Rotterdam, and Columbia University in New York. He is the author of *The Project of Autonomy: Politics and Architecture within and against Capitalism* (2008), *The Possibility of an Absolute Architecture* (2011), *Less Is Enough. On asceticism and architecture* (2013), *The City as a Project* (2014) and *Architecture and Abstraction* (2023).

Joseph Bedford is an Associate Professor of History and Theory at Virginia Tech, USA. He is the director of the Architecture Exchange, a platform that fosters discourse and exchange. He is the author of *Is There an Object-Oriented Architecture* (2020), *How Is Architecture Political?* (2024) and *How Does Architecture Distribute the Sensible?* (2025) as well as numerous book chapters and articles in journals such as *JAE*, *ARQ*, *AA Files*, *ATR*, *OASE*, *Log* and *NYRA*. He is the series editor of this *Architecture Exchange* book series with Bloomsbury Press as well as the e-flux Architecture series *Theory's Curriculum*. He was educated at Cambridge University, The Cooper Union and Princeton University, where he received, respectively, his bachelors, masters and doctorate degrees.

Reinhold Martin is a historian of architecture and media and a professor at Columbia University in New York, USA. He is a founding co-editor of the journal *Grey Room* and former director of the Temple Hoyne Buell Center for the Study of American Architecture at Columbia University. His books include *The Organizational Complex: Architecture, Media, and Corporate Space* (2003), *Utopia's Ghost: Architecture and Postmodernism, Again* (2010), *The Urban Apparatus: Mediapolitics and the City* (2016) and *Knowledge Worlds: Media, Materiality, and the Making of the Modern University* (2021).

Chantal Mouffe is Professor of Political Theory at the Centre for the Study of Democracy at the University of Westminster in London, UK. She is one of the leading figures in post-marxism, bringing post-structuralist philosophy to bear upon the political traditions of the Left, redefining Left politics in terms of Radical Democracy. She is the author of *Gramsci and Marxist Theory* (1979), *Hegemony and Socialist Strategy: Towards a Radical Democratic Politics* (1985) with Ernesto Laclau, *The Challenge* of Carl Schmitt (1999), *The Democratic Paradox* (2000), *On the Political* (2005), *Agonistics: Thinking the World Politically* (2013) and *For a Left Populism* (2018).

Ines Weizman is Head of the PhD Programme at the School of Architecture, Royal College of Art, London and Professor of Architectural Theory and Design at the Academy of Fine Arts, Vienna. She also directs the Center for Documentary Architecture (CDA), an interdisciplinary research collective of architectural historians, filmmakers, and digital technologists. Among her books are Architecture and the Paradox of Dissidence (2014) and Before and After: Documenting the Architecture of Disaster, co-authored with Eyal Weizman (2014), *Dust & Data: Traces of the Bauhaus across 100 Years (2019), Documentary Architecture: Dissidence through Architecture (2020) and 100+ Neue Perspektiven auf die Bauhaus-Rezeption'* (2021).

Sarah M. Whiting is the Dean and Josep Lluís Sert Professor of Architecture at Harvard Graduate School of Design, USA. She is a founding partner of WW Architecture, along with Ron Witte and the founding editor of *Point*, a book series aimed at shaping contemporary discussions in architecture and urbanism. Prior to Harvard, Whiting has had a long career as an architectural educator in several schools including most recently as Dean and William Ward Watkin Professor of Architecture at Rice School of Architecture. In addition to her work as an academic leader, Whiting has also been an intellectual leader within the field, most notably, shaping the paradigmatic shift in the discourse towards a projective approach to architecture in the early 2000s.

Acknowledgements

Several people and institutions supported this book to help make it a reality. First and foremost, the book would not have been possible without the generosity of Chantal Mouffe and the other contributors, Pier Vittorio Aureli, Reinhold Martin, Ines Weizman, and Sarah Whiting, who gave far more to this publication over the course of its development than is usual.

The project was conceived with Jessica Reynolds in the earlier years of the Architecture Exchange, and the one-day exchange was organized and co-hosted by myself, Jessica Reynolds, Shumi Bose and Umberto Bellardi Ricci. They not only helped host the day of the exchange, but also joined in a reading group focused on Mouffe's work in the year leading up to the event. We had several wonderful sessions at one another's various London flats. Jessica and Shumi also joined in conducting some of the interviews in the days following the exchange, and their probing questions augment the interview sections of the book. I am also grateful to Jan-Werner Müller at Princeton University who invited me to present a paper on the work of Chantal Mouffe during the same year at his conference at Princeton on "Architecture, Urban Space, and Democracy." But more than that invitation, I am grateful to Jan for his teaching in the three seminars in political theory that I took with him at Princeton.

The one-day exchange was made possible also thanks to the generous support of Brett Steele, the then director of the Architectural Association who lent the AA premises as the venue. Manijeh Verghese was also incredibly supportive in arranging the logistics. The financial support that enabled the event to happen was kindly provided by the Arts Council England.

Following the event Madelyn Walker, Matthew Knight, Ryan Jacobs, Archi Dasgupta and Tooba Jalal helped compile the manuscript for the book, and Corinna Anderson and Jonah Rowen did first round edits on the manuscript. The final round of copy editing of the manuscript was done by Arianna Corradi. And Arianna Corradi also compiled the index for the book.

Finally, I am incredibly grateful to Liza Thompson, Lucy Harper, Ben Piggott and Katrina Calsado at Bloomsbury Press for guiding this book through. I am also grateful to the University of Minnesota Press for permission to reprint Reinhold Martin's 'Polis-Oikos' text which, while written for this book, was published first in *The Urban Apparatus: Mediapolitics and the City* (Minneapolis, MN: University of Minnesota Press, 2016).

1

How Is Architecture Political?

Joseph Bedford

Chantal Mouffe's political theory has long been of interest to architecture. Mouffe was first invited to give a talk to an audience of architects in 1997 at the Architectural Association in London.[1] The journal of architecture, art and media *Grey Room* sought an interview with Mouffe in one of their first issues in 2001.[2] Since then, she has been engaged in a series of conversations by the German architect Markus Miessen, published in the book *The Space of Agonism*, and has continued to give lectures in schools of architecture on the topic of agonism and public space.[3] A wide range of thinkers in the field of architecture have engaged her writings, as have those in adjacent fields such as urbanism and geography.[4] Yet, no sustained dialogue between her theory and architecture has been attempted until this moment.

The exchange that follows embarked upon that more sustained dialogue. It began as a one-day event in London at the Architectural Association and continued through post-event interviews and through the further development of ideas in print for this publication. It took place between Chantal Mouffe and four representative thinkers, historians, educators and practitioners in the field of architecture from both sides of the Atlantic: Pier Vittorio Aureli, Reinhold Martin, Ines Weizman and Sarah Whiting. In it, the participants attempted to understand architecture through Chantal Mouffe's work, but also to deepen the larger dialogue between architectural theory and political theory, and to reflect together on the question: how is architecture political?

Chantal Mouffe is one of the most important, prolific, and provocative political theorists of our time. Because architectural theory has had a long-standing relationship to the body of post-structuralist theory which helped her to define her approach, there is an immediate common ground between her theory and architectural theory. Architecture, moreover, also shares the same history of economic, social and political changes surrounding the fate of socialism that has been the central problematic of her career. It shares the same fateful impact of the rise of centralized planning and welfare state patronage and its subsequent decline. And it shares the same experience of grappling with the effects of the post-Fordist transformation of industrial economies, the same spatial displacements of globalization and the same impacts of the market primacy of neoliberal economics.

Mouffe's work can be understood as part of an effort to reposition the politics of the Left after the crisis of Marxist thought. Born and schooled in Belgium, she had been a student of the Marxist theorist Louis Althusser in Paris at a time when Althusser was attempting to reread Marx's writings through the lens of new ideas about language and ideology. After beginning her academic career teaching philosophy at the National University of Colombia, in Bogota, Mouffe eventually settled in Britain where she and her partner Ernesto Laclau became key players in the intellectual debates of the New Left.[5] Together, they co-authored the seminal text *Hegemony and Socialist Strategy: Towards a Radical Democratic Politics* in 1985,[6] a book that launched the discourse of 'post-Marxism' by conjoining for the first time the anti-essentialist, post-structuralist philosophy of Jacques Derrida and Jacques Lacan with socialist thought.

From the linguist Ferdinand de Saussure came the idea of signification as a network of differences. From Derrida came the idea that networks of signs were unstable, centreless and dynamic. From Lacan came the idea of the self as an empty vessel lacking any natural content, and whose inability to bare such a lack, leads them to identify with systems of signs in the hope of covering up the lack that fundamentally defines them. To these theories of language and subjectivity, they drew the consequence for politics that the instability of sign systems rendered unstable both the truth about the world and the nature of the self, and made the social world a restless and ever-changing struggle for symbolic order. This was ultimately so because symbolic order was never natural, but was only historical and thus contingent. The proposed transformation of the Left from a materialist discourse of redistribution to an identity-based discourse of recognition, which the book outlined, became the centre point of a heated debate about the future of the Left; one which still rages on today.

Prior to this joint endeavour with Laclau, Mouffe had already drawn a great many elements of her theory from her close reading of the work of Antonio Gramsci.[7] Already, Gramsci's writings led Mouffe both towards the central importance of cultural analysis and ideology, towards the importance of the politics of the private sphere, 'the social' and civil society, and towards the idea that political organization at all these 'levels' was more important than the so-called 'laws of history' or the so-called 'economic determinations' behind 'class struggle'. To be sure, Gramsci himself remained committed to class politics as the ultimate goal of political struggles, but his introduction of the politics of culture and society as central to the strategy of the Left was decisive for Mouffe, and helped her break away from the economic reductivism and essentialism she perceived still in Althusser's thought.

Hegemony and Socialist Strategy in effect conjoined these Gramscian ideas with a number of ideas from post-structuralism. The enormous impact that *Hegemony and Socialist Strategy* had on intellectual debates on the Left was due first and foremost to its timely yet highly controversial critique of Marxism. Secondly, its impact was due to the seductive possibility of the theoretical framework which the book offered, which developed into what became known as 'discourse theory' and which offered a method for analysing all kinds of concrete political situations.[8] Thirdly, its impact was due to its defence of the importance of political struggles that were not based upon demands for economic redistribution but for recognition of identity groups, such as women, Blacks, gays and lesbians, or demands for action on particular causes, such as environmentalist, anti-war and anti-nuclear causes – all of which the book grouped under 'new social movements'. And fourthly and finally, its impact was due to its promise that liberalism could become a viable project for the Left: if liberalism were more fully connected to the politics that lay at the heart of democracy; if liberalism recognized the fundamental principle of the equality of 'the people' as well as liberty for all as co-defining the West's political modernity; and if liberalism was fully committed to the institutions of open and truly representative debate. They called this newly reformed liberalism, 'radical democracy'.

After the publication of *Hegemony and Socialist Strategy* Mouffe and Laclau would pursue two distinct paths. Laclau's work developed further the conceptual architecture of the discourse theory that they had constructed together. He did so by responding to the critics of the theoretical ideas which they had advanced in *Hegemony and Socialist Strategy*, by making various modifications of its theoretical framework. As part of these intellectual debates, he went on to develop the idea that they had always intended to present a tension between particularism and universalism, and that he had intended to keep in play the universal dimension as an important moment within all social struggles. He also worked on redefining populism as *the* central strategy for the Left.[9]

Mouffe, by contrast, forged a reputation as a political philosopher, by developing an extensive body of articles that critiqued the various forms of liberalism that stood as competing models to the more politicized liberalism which they advocated for under the banner of radical democracy, and by engaging in a wide range of debates in the process about topics such as postmodernism, citizenship, globalization, the rise of the right, the resurgence of nationalism, art and public space. The collected volumes that brought together these articles – *The Return of the Political* in 1993, *The Democratic Paradox* in 2000 and *Agonistics: Thinking the World Politically* in 2013 – became central works in many fields and were widely reviewed and discussed in journals of political science, political theory, sociology, philosophy, foreign affairs, critical theory, feminist studies, and in many countries and languages.[10]

Mouffe and Laclau remained in close agreement with one another, however, as their different trajectories developed and their two paths can be seen as complementary to one another, representing a division of labour between the elaboration and defence of their theoretical system by Laclau, and the comparative account of the merits of their project of radical democracy by Mouffe. While Mouffe did not occupy herself as much with the philosophical disagreements that Laclau was to become embroiled with, she nonetheless has always continued to reiterate the basic theoretical framework of *Hegemony and Socialist Strategy* in her subsequent writing and has used it as the basis of a set of principles from which her subsequent arguments have followed.[11]

It was through a series of articles engaging critically with the writings of John Rawls, Charles Taylor, Michael Sandel, Michael Walzer, Alasdair MacIntyre and Jürgen Habermas in particular that Mouffe refined the concrete implications of the ideas within *Hegemony and Socialist Strategy* for the making of a more fruitful pluralist, liberal and democratic political theory for our age; one that could potentially redefine the project of the Left.[12] In this work, she deepened her critique of various liberalisms by drawing upon, above all, the work of Niccolò Machiavelli and Carl Schmitt, to insist on the primacy of politics and its irreducibility to reason, nature, human nature and morality.

Where in the 1980s, Mouffe had called for democracy to become more inclusive to plural forms of identities, from the 1990s onwards, her work evolved to become in equal measure a defence of Western democracy itself and its institutions against the threat of a general disengagement from politics and the failure of neoliberal and centrist discourse to represent real progressive alternatives. The spectre that haunted the West after the cold war, from the emergence of ethnic tensions in the former soviet east, to the return of various fundamentalisms, to the rise of the nationalist Right, became as much an object of critique in her recent work as positivism, bureaucratism and economic reductionism had been in her earlier work. These various ghosts are the result, for Mouffe, of the failure to properly institute political conflict, and of the transformation of politics into moral discourses.

Since the publication in 2005 of *On the Political*, Mouffe has consolidated her agonistic model into a highly robust intellectual framework, with a set of concepts that because of their abstract nature can be tested against a wide range of fields, including architecture. Thus far in our introduction I have briefly traced the historical evolution of Mouffe's thought in her reading of Derrida, de Saussure, Freud, Lacan, Gramsci and Schmidt, and have seen where a number of ideas came from historically, but I have not yet introduced to the reader the concepts themselves. In order to prepare the reader for the exchange that follows, it is worth defining some of the more salient concepts from the wide range of Mouffean terminology, including earlier poststructuralist concepts like *articulation, discourse, discursive formations, overdetermination, nodal points, empty signifiers, the subject, subject positions, lack* and later Gramscian and Schmidtian concepts like *politics and the political, we/they, friend/enemy, constitutive outside, antagonism and agonism*.

Let me begin with the concept of *discourse*, arguably one of the most important to her thought, philosophically and connected to that the concepts of *articulation, nodal points, empty signifiers, subject positions*, and so on that are part of the larger 'discourse theory' behind her work.

Discourse, for Mouffe, is not just solely a concept that is about words or language, rather as she understands it, is a concept that also includes within it every level of reality from actions and institutions to material things. As she and Laclau put it in 1985: 'the practice of articulation ... cannot consist of purely linguistic phenomena; but must instead pierce the entire material density of the multifarious institutions, rituals and practices through which a discursive formation is structured.'[13] In this view, all the non-linguistic aspects of the world are equally identifiable as a discourse. Bricks, footballs, rockets, brushing one's teeth and getting married are also linked together in the same patterns that constitute the same structures that pre-determine behaviour and actions.

As a guide, one might imagine discourse as being a kind of network or web. Quite literally, one might picture the texture of a spider's web, with nodes and connection points, that can be rewoven in different ways. For Mouffe, this web of discourse is also best thought of as being non-hierarchical with no overarching centre or origin point. In a sense the image of the spider's web breaks down. In the web of discourse, there are patterns, structures and formations. There are even some points in the network that serve as particularly important nodes, but there is no controlling agent at the centre.

Next, I can introduce the concept of *articulation*. The concept of articulation focuses one's attention on the way that the elements of a discourse are connected together and the way that they can be disconnected and reconnected in new ways. Think of the way that one uses the term 'articulated' to speak of an articulated truck or lorry – sometimes just called an 'artic'. In an articulated vehicle, the tractor is hooked up to one or more trailers using a pivot bar. They are connected and move together but the connection can always be decoupled and the tractor coupled to different trailers. Articulation could be said to simply mean that the words we use, and the ideas, actions and things to which they are bound, are linked together in patterns of relationships that in their relatively stable structures over time constitute the discourse. Because a discourse is here conceived of as a kind of web of linkages and disconnections, it is also pictured from a historical vantage point as being formed and reforming in different ways over time; hence Mouffe's preference on occasion for the distinctly Foucauldian term, discursive formation, to give to the idea of discourse the sense that it can be changed.

Perhaps the best illustration of what it might mean to make a substantial rearticulation of the web of discourse – one that has the kind of political significance that can form an entirely new hegemonic bloc – is the linking together of the patriotic themes of duty to the nation, family and tradition, on the one hand, with individualistic themes of competition, entrepreneurship and freedom, on the other, that took place within the rise of Thatcherism in Britain in the late 1970s, and correspondingly Reaganism in the United States in the early 1980s.[14] Ideas of tradition and freedom might on the surface of things not fit very well together. The former once belonged to conservatism and the latter to liberalism in their nineteenth-century forms. Yet in the specific historical conjuncture of the late twentieth century, it became possible to combine them through certain kinds of rhetorical acrobatics in order to construct a new discourse that aligned different elements of conservative and liberal thought and to constitute a powerful mesh of ideas that could capture the hearts and minds of a wider voting bloc than previous political discourses.

This example also shows how, within democratic societies where winning hearts and minds at the ballot box is crucial for power, representation and symbolism is crucial and rhetorical systems can be constructed even if they seem naturally contradictory. At the symbolic level of discourse, relations between words, ideas, actions and things can be formed, even though they contain internal contradictions, or antagonisms. To help us picture this, one might also think of this network or web of discourse as a sheet (or quilt) that floats above the material and natural basis of reality but which does not entirely and directly correspond to it. It is linked to it at certain points which fix the fabric in place, but at other points it billows and folds freely. You might then also picture this sheet as a kind of bed sheet that is too big for the bed, and which does not map to its surface one-to-one. As a result, it is doomed to be continuously wrinkled and creased.

This image of discourse as a bed sheet that is too big for the bed can help as we turn next to the concept of *overdetermination*. Overdetermination simply means that the quantity of symbolic meaning is in excess of the material reality to which it might relate and because of this excess, human beings are, as it were, pitted in a constant struggle with one another over which symbols best map the material reality. Imagine an unhappy couple in a marriage bed fighting with one another over where the inevitable wrinkles in the bed sheet should be and where the smooth parts of the sheet are. The network or web of words, ideas, actions and things can be reformed, and folded in different ways, with some nodes being brought close to others for a time, yet the situation can never be resolved such that one might finally determine once and for all what things in nature truly meant. Things are simply overdetermined. Discourse is constituted by the very fact that there are too many factors explaining any causal event, too many claims on the definition of anything, too many discourses by which anything might be interpreted, and it is because everything is overdetermined that nothing in the social world should be understood as having natural, causally predictable or rational explanation.

This image of a flabby bed sheet, which is just another way of picturing meaning as excessive such that it cannot be made to correspond one-to-one to reality, is offered here as a visual aid to imagine what could also have been said in the more technical, post-structuralist terminology that was developed from an earlier body of linguistics, to say that meaning is not constituted positively by a fixed relationship between signs and nature, but is constituted negatively by the differential relationships between all signs in a discourse. In terms of Saussurean linguistics, if the sign takes its meaning only by way of all the other signs from which it is not, then all meaning is a product of relationships of difference. The constant play and slippages between signs that Derrida emphasized are equivalent to the frustrated attempt of someone to smooth out the bed sheet only to find that the creases have moved elsewhere.

The image of the sheet (or quilt) might help us understand two more concepts that are linked to Mouffe's underlying discourse theory, that of *nodal points* and *empty signifiers*. Firstly, the concept of a nodal point is at once a point of articulation, like the node in our spider's web where two, three or more threads are joined together. It is thus a privilege point of connection within a network or field. Yet following the overarching anti-essentialism of Mouffe's discourse theory, a nodal point should not be thought of necessarily as a place within a discourse with a natural or necessary content that permanently fixes it in place. Rather it remains a contingent relationship. The threads of meaning could in principle be disconnected (*disarticulated*) from one another and reconnected (*rearticulated*) to other threads of meaning. As an example, if a powerful discursive formation were to emerge that could challenge the hegemonic hold of neoliberal ideology, it would likely involve the decoupling of the relationship between freedom and tradition and the relinking of each to other important meanings that would form other powerful realignments that could gather a larger organization of political will behind it.

Crucial here then is the idea that the points that seem to be most politically important within discourse should themselves be understood as empty, as vacuous place holders or hubs that gather a density of relationships around them. Mouffe even assumes that some nodal points organize the field of signification around them as successfully as they do precisely *because* they have no positive meaning in themselves that could be settled upon and fixed. For example, a certain point in a discourse, like the idea of democracy, can in fact be in itself undefinable. Its power comes not from its essence but simply from its central place at the heart of a dense network of other discursive points. And it is often for this reason that abstract nouns and philosophical ideas loom large in the game of rhetoric that discourse theory engages: not only the abstract concept of democracy, but also concepts like freedom, universality, necessity, identity, tradition, history, truth, nature, meaning, nation, country, peace, security, place, belonging, humanity, the self, the human, etc.

Let I will conclude the section of this brief introduction to key concepts in discourse theory with those concepts which address the place of the human being within discourse, namely the concept of the *subject,* and with it the idea of *subject positions,* and that of *lack.*

Central to Mouffe's intellectual framework is the idea that individuals are also entangled within this network of relations and that they too have no positive content of their own, being just like everything else in reality, similarly constituted by relationships of difference with respect to all other elements in the network. Here, as already noted, Mouffe's intellectual debt is to Lacan's theory of the subject. Because individual human beings have no positively given natural content of their own, their identities are given to them by their position within the larger field of discourses that they inhabit. For this reason, the *subject* is also by definition a *subject position.*

Subject positions are not freely chosen by an individual. Rather they are inherited from one's childhood in particular cultures and contexts and unconsciously acquired through participation in society. Subject positions are multiple and overlapping with one another such that the individual is split internally by them. This creates a dislocation within the self, which is experienced as a fundamental *lack*. From this basis, Mouffe has derived a psychology in which all individuals desire to cover over this fundamental lack and hide their internally dislocated and contradictory nature, by identifying with this or that group, and seeking to stabilize that identification by way of some clear division with respect to other groups that helps them constitute their identity. That is, the very tribal and group-like nature of human beings, they argue, is fundamental, and follows from the fundamental ontology of the social world as an unstable centreless discourse.

Here I can begin to fold into my survey of Mouffe's key concepts those that belong to her later reading of figures such as Carl Schmidt, and which she came to understand in terms of her earlier debts to post-structuralism. As Mouffe argued in her 2005 book *On the Political,* a number of concepts such as *politics/the political* the *we/they, friend/ enemy*, and *antagonism/agonism*, are crucial to understanding politics. As we will see, they build upon earlier ideas about the identity of the subject being constructed by way of the formation of lines of division with others precisely because difference was the only way that identity was given within an anti-essentialist framework.

For Mouffe, in her later work, the political was taken as a concept from Schmidt as a means of understanding all of human reality as fundamentally politically constituted at an ontological level. If 'politics' as a term was used to refer to the more everyday business of rhetoric and the discursive manoeuvring that take place on the streets, in the halls of government, in lobbying practices and in the public sphere, the phrase 'the political' was used to refer to the underlying nature of existence itself as being structured politically from the outset. The phrase 'the political' was intended by Mouffe to conjure a Machiavellian or 'might is right' view of politics in which there is no outside realm of truth or nature to which any social order would appeal in order to prove itself to be right. Instead, 'the political' refers to the way that order is simply constituted by the pure force and decision of the sovereign ruler – and as Schmidt put it in a kind of circular logic that required no grounding, the sovereign *is* simply that person who decides.

Despite human affairs seeming on the surface of things to be somewhat peaceful, and despite war being mercifully less frequent for many of us than it might otherwise be, this state of affairs is haunted in this view by the ever-present possibility that individuals or groups might form into enemies with one another and violence and warfare might break out in a struggle to assert a new order through force. If we feel peace mostly and on a daily basis it is only because order remains enforced by sovereign power that has already decided. But there is nothing natural or foundational about that decision; it is simply an assertion of will. For Mouffe, we are often led to forget about the ontological nature of this ever-present possibility of the friend/enemy distinction re-emerging and are on a daily basis persuaded to become caught up in matters of aesthetics, economics and morality but the truly underlying basis of the social order is the kind of all-out-conflict that involved sovereign power and the assertion of order by force.

There are levels to the way that Mouffe imagines this. At a basic level of psychology and the formation of identities, as we have said, individuals gain their identity from the distinctions they draw from the others from who they are different. They form groups and distinguish themselves from one another. Such groupings are described by Mouffe as we/they relations. Yet not all we/they relations are necessarily those which tend towards aggressive forms of conflict and enmity. They have the possibility of becoming so when they are fuelled and exaggerated by antagonisms.

Finally, then, I arrive at the penultimate concept, and one of the key concepts organizing all of Mouffe's theory of discourse tying it to a theory of politics, that of the idea of *antagonism*. Antagonisms are the result of particular articulations of the discourse that create a temporary fixity or temporary structure within it. Because the discourse itself has no centre or origin, and because it is in principle contingent and open to play, and because the subjects that are part of it cannot bear such a lack of structure, they form antagonisms as a means to give order to the discursive field. An antagonism is a particular nodal point, often a particularly empty one, which serves to divide the field into camps. The division of society into groups is organized, in Mouffe's view, around two opposing attempts to define a particular nodal point in the field. She insists that antagonisms cannot be eradicated, because they are structural to the nature of the social field as such, and the fact that the social field is defined by the absence of necessity and by a surplus of overdetermined significations.

Antagonisms are therefore an inevitable consequence of a social field that cannot be determined and that thus implies permanent restlessness and conflict. Antagonisms might move location and emerge around different points in the network, but they will always be there, and it is in the nature of discourses and the nature of subjects to temporarily fissure and to be reformed over conflicting groups, because such fissures enable those groups and the lacking subjects who form them to conceal their lack and feel whole. Because discourse is without centre, origin or stable structure, discourse becomes inherently a field of struggle for power. It is not destined to evolve in any particular way. Antagonism, then, is precisely that wrinkle in the fabric of discourse that we cannot ever smooth out. It emerges in locations where we/they relations become more aggressive and begin to harden into friend/enemy relations.

Finally, linked to the concept of antagonism is the concept which has become the most important to Mouffe in the later phase of her work; that of *agonism*. If antagonisms name a type of we/they relationship that has become oppositional, non-communicative, aggressive and that is at risk of breaking out into violence, then agonism for her names another form that the we/they relationship can take, in which differing parties can understand themselves as mutually linked to one another despite their disagreements. In an agonistic relationship, enemies are substituted by adversaries. Like all the great adversarial relationships in history – from Sherlock Holmes and Professor Moriarty, Superman and Lex Luther, to Robin Hood and the Sheriff of Nottingham – adversaries are opponents that ultimately respect each other's legitimate right to exist, and even recognize their mutual dependence upon one another. Despite pretences, they do not really wish to violently vanquish one another, but will ultimately always allow each other to live, and to withdraw in respectful defeat to fight another day. For Mouffe then, the task of Radical Democracy is to institute conflict in such ways that antagonisms are domesticated into agonism; to constitute agonic battlefields in which opponents fight with one another over their differences while recognizing the legitimacy of the other in the fight and ultimately respecting the battlefield itself as a framework that structures and constrains their encounter.

With this basic overview of the historical development of Mouffe's ideas and our basic introduction to some of the key terms and ideas, the reader should be able to proceed and enter into the debate that unfolded between her and the four architectural practitioners, historians and theorists who responded to her work: Pier Vittorio Aureli, Reinhold Martin, Ines Weizman and Sarah Whiting.

Within what follows, the reader will encounter a wide range of issues and topics within the realm of architectural practice, history and theory that were brought into dialogue with Mouffe's intellectual framework, such that both could be mutually tested against each other.

These issues and topics included among them the question of whether architecture should be understood as an authored representational and symbolic language or as an anonymous, material, and technical infrastructure if one is to best grasp its politics in the present moment. They included the question of how architecture relates to its audience and processes of identification; whether through the legibility, meaning and recognition of its forms, or through the role of forms in dividing and organizing relationship. Relating to this, they included also the question of whether architectural design itself has a politics, or whether the politics of architecture lays more properly in the politics of its practice, its labour conditions and its professional procedures. Or put another way, whether there is a politics of form and a politics of architectural knowledge and architectural education, as well as a politics of practice. They included the question of whether architecture's politics is best thought about in terms of notions such as the public, public space, the city or the civic, or whether other historical conditions have displaced these notions, such as the emergence of urbanization, the social and biopolitics. They include the question of what scale is most appropriate in order to grasp the central political agency of architecture, whether this be the scale of the building, the scale of the city, the scale of the territory and the region or even the global or planetary. They included the evaluation of how the politics of architectural practices differ from the politics of art practices, and particularly how architecture's specificity might be understood in terms of the economic, material, and professional constraints and regulations that architecture must involve. Yet at the same time, they also included the question of practices within architecture that are more like art, such as paper architecture, autonomy, withdrawal, refusal and critique. Finally, and perhaps above all else, they repeatedly involved questions of housing, as the central cite for discussing how architecture is political.

For all of the agreements and disagreements within the exchange that follows over these questions and others, and for all the miscommunication as well as communication between the different fields of architecture and political theory, what stands out above all is a richness of intellectual dialogue that can be catalyzed by the confrontation between different fields and thinkers. I have attempted to offer a summary of the exchange in the concluding chapter of the book, 'Architecture's Challenge to Chantal Mouffe' to which the reader can turn at any point for a useful roadmap of the different positions being put forward in the book and the key differences between each of the authors.

Mouffe has offered her own succinct summary of her theoretical framework in her own essay which opens this volume, 'How to Envisage the Political Dimension of Architecture' which the reader is invited to turn to next in order to begin. I have already attempted above to lay out a basic historical and theoretical introduction to her ideas, but the reader is also encouraged to consult some of the many excellent introductions to her work as further guides.[15]

The best way to understand how her work has begun to transform, and might continue to transform, architectural thought, however, would be for the reader simply to enter into the dialogue that unfolds throughout the pages of this book. It is a 'dialogue' constituted by initial arguments put forwards by Mouffe, Aureli, Martin, Weizman and Whiting. It is the immediate dialogue that took place between them in the round table at the end of the day. It is also the dialogue that took place between myself and each participant after the one-day event which further unpacked their initial propositions. And it is finally the dialogue that took place here in print form as each person reviewed the manuscript before publication and added their final comments, interjections, questions and queries.

Notes

1   Lecture at the Architectural Association. 'Ethics and the Question of Space, the Environment and Architecture', 17 November 1997.
2   Chantal Mouffe, 'Every Form of Art Has a Political Dimension', *Grey Room*, no. 2 (Winter, 2001): 98–125.
3   Markus Miessen Chantal Mouffe, *The Space of Agonism*, ed. Nikolaus Hirsch and Markus Miessen (London: Sternberg Press, 2013). Despite its title, however, Miessen's publication barely addresses either space or architecture. Chantal Mouffe, 'Democratic Politics and Agonistic Public Spaces', Lecture at Harvard Graduate School of Design (17 April 2012) https://www.youtube.com/watch?v=4Wpwwc25JRU and Chantal Mouffe, 'Intellectual Activist: Agonistics: Thinking the World Politically', Lecture at Columbia University Graduate School of Architecture, Preservation and Planning (27 March 2014) https://www.youtube.com/watch?v=2yHX_6FGsvs
4   Architects who have read her work include Teresa Hoskyns, Doina Petrescu, Urtzi Grau and Cristina Goberna, Peggy Deamer and Manuel Shvartzberg, Teddy Cruz and Dirk van den Heuvel. In urbanism, her discourse theory and agonistic theory have been widely taken up in an effort to rethink urban planning theory, by figures such as Pia Bäcklund, Raine Mäntysalo, Sophie Bond, Michael Gunder, Jean Hillier, John Ploger. In geography, Doreen Massey has especially engaged with her work and that of Ernesto Laclau.
5   For a good historical treatment of Mouffe's development and in particular the influences of the various contexts of France, Latin America and Britain on her development, see Warren Breckman, *Adventures of the Symbolic Post-Marxism and Radical Democracy* (New York: Columbia University Press, 2015), 197–8. See also Ralph Miliband, 'The New Revisionism in Britain', *New Left Review* 150 (1985): 26.
6   Chantal Mouffe and Ernesto Laclau, *Hegemony and Socialist Strategy: Towards a Radical Democratic Politics* (New York: Verso, 1985).
7   Key texts by Mouffe in this formative period include the essays 'Gramsci today', and 'Hegemony and Ideology in Gramsci' published in *Gramsci and Marxist Theory* in 1979.
8   On discourse theory, see Jacob Torfing, *New Theories of Discourse: Laclau, Mouffe, and Žižek* (London: Blackwell, 1999); Marianne W Jorgensen and Louise J Phillips, 'Laclau

and Mouffe's Discouse Theory', in *Discourse Analysis as Theory and Method* (London: Sage, 2002), 24–60; and Jacob Torfing and David Howarth eds., *Discourse Theory in European Politics: Identity, Policy and Government* (London: Palgrave MacMillon, 2005).
9 See in particular, Laclaus's intellectual debates with Judith Butler, Ernesto Laclau, and Slavoj Žižek eds., *Contingency, Hegemony and Universality: Contemporary Dialogues on the Left* (New York: Verso, 2000) and for Laclau's later work on populism, see Ernesto Laclau, *On Populist Reason* (New York: Verso, 2005).
10 Chantal Mouffe, *The Return of the Political* (New York, Verso, 1993); Chantal Mouffe, *The Democratic Paradox* (New York: Verso, 2005) and Chantal Mouffe, *Agonistics: Thinking the World Politically* (New York: Verso, 2013). Of her many books, *On the Political* of 2005 stands out as the clearest summation of her ideas in a single book and is recommended to the reader as the best entry point to her work. Chantal Mouffe, *On the Political* (London: Routledge, 2005).
11 Mouffe did take part in responding to one of these critiques; that of Norman Geras. See 'Post-Marxism?', *New Left Review* 163 (May/June 1987): 40–82; Norman Geras, 'Ex-Marxism without Substance: Being a Real Reply to Laclau and Mouffe', *New Left Review* 169 (May/June, 1988): 34–61; and her reply with Ernesto Laclau and Chantal Mouffe Laclau, 'Post-Marxism without Apologies', *New Left Review* 166 (November-December, 1987): 79–106.
12 See for Chantal Mouffe, 'Rawls: Political Philosophy without Politics', *Philosophy and Social Criticism* 13, no. 2 (1987): 105–23; Chantal Mouffe, 'American Liberalism and Its Critics: Rawls, Taylor, Sandel and Walzer', *Praxis International* 8, no. 2 (July 1988): 193–206; Chantal Mouffe, 'Radical Democracy: Modern or Postmodern?', in *Universal Abandon? The Politics of Postmodernism*, ed. Andrew Ross (Minneapolis, MN: University of Minnesota Press, 1988), 31–46; and Chantal Mouffe, 'Radical Democracy or Liberal Democracy?' *Socialist Review* 20 (April-June, 1990): 57–66 and Chantal Mouffe 'On the Articulation between Liberalism and Democracy', paper presented at the conference of The Legacy of C. B. Macpherson' in Toronto, Canada, in October 1989.
13 Mouffe and Laclau, *Hegemony*, 109
14 For an analysis of this linkage, see Stuart Hall and Martin Jacques eds., *The Politics of Thatcherism* (London: Lawrence & Wishart, 1983).
15 For the best introduction to Mouffe's theoretical framework, see Jules Townshend, 'Laclau and Mouffe's Hegemonic Project: The Story So Far', *Political Studies* 52 (2004): 269–88; Simon Tormey, 'Ernesto Laclau and Chantal Mouffe', in *From Agamben to Žižek: Contemporary Critical Theorists*, ed. Jon Simons (Edinburgh: Edinburgh University Press, 2010), 144–60; Warren Breckman, 'The Post-Marx of the Letter: Laclau and Mouffe between Postmodern Melancholy and Post-Marxist Mourning', in *Adventures of the Symbolic: Postmarxism and Democratic Theory* (New York: Columbia University Press, 2013), 183–216; Jules Townshend, 'Discourse Theory and Political Analysis: A New Paradigm from the Essex School?', *The British Journal of Politics and International Relations* 5, no. 1 (2016): 129–42; and Torfing Jacobs, 'The Dislocated Universe of Laclau and Mouffe: An Introduction to Post-Structuralist Discourse Theory', *Critical Review* 30, nos. 3–4 (2018): 294–315.

2

How to Envisage the Political Dimension of Architecture

Chantal Mouffe

What follows will not answer the question of how architecture is political, because this is not my field of expertise. What I intend to do instead is to suggest how this question could be envisaged from the discursive agonistic approach that I have elaborated in my work. The main tenets of this approach have been developed in several books since *Hegemony and Socialist Strategy*, co-written with Ernesto Laclau.[1] I will begin by recalling them.

Let's start with the distinction between 'politics' and 'the political'. In ordinary language, it is not very common to speak of 'the political' but I think that such a distinction opens important avenues for reflection and various political theorists are making it. Some theorists envisage 'the political' as a space of freedom and public deliberation, while others see it as a space of power, conflict and antagonism. My understanding of 'the political' clearly belongs to the second perspective. More precisely, with 'the political' I refer to the dimension of antagonism which I take to be constitutive of human societies, whereas with 'politics' I refer to the set of practices and institutions through which an order is created, organizing human coexistence in the context of conflictuality that is provided by 'the political'.

According to this 'dissociative' perspective, properly political questions always involve decisions that require us to make a choice between conflicting alternatives; they are not mere technical issues to be solved by experts. The incapacity to think politically that we witness today is to a great extent due to the uncontested hegemony of liberalism. 'Liberalism', in the way I use the term in the present context, refers to a philosophical discourse with many variants, united not by a common essence but by a multiplicity of what Ludwig Wittgenstein calls 'family resemblances'. There are certainly many liberalisms but, save for a few exceptions, the dominant tendency in liberal thought is characterized by a rationalist and individualist approach which is unable to adequately grasp the pluralistic nature of the social world, with the conflicts that pluralism entails; conflicts for which no rational solution could ever exist, hence the dimension of antagonism that characterizes human societies. The typical liberal understanding of pluralism is that we live in a world in which there are indeed many perspectives and values and that, due to empirical limitations, we will never be able to adopt them all, but that, when put together, they could constitute a harmonious and non-conflictual ensemble. This is why this type of liberalism must negate the political in its antagonistic dimension. Indeed, one of the main tenets of this liberalism is the rationalist belief in the availability of a universal consensus based on reason. No wonder that the political constitutes its blind spot. Liberalism has to negate antagonism because, by bringing to the fore the inescapable moment of decision – in the strong sense of having to decide in an undecidable terrain – antagonism reveals the very limit of any rational consensus.

When we examine the different perspectives within contemporary liberal political thought, we can single out two main paradigms, sometimes called 'aggregative' and 'deliberative'. The 'aggregative' envisages politics as the establishment of a compromise between competing forces in society. It applies concepts borrowed from economics to the domain of politics and thus portrays individuals as rational beings driven by the maximization of their own interests, acting in the political world in a basically instrumental way. As a reaction to this instrumentalist model, the 'deliberative' paradigm aims instead at creating a link between morality and politics by replacing instrumental rationality with communicative rationality. Its advocates present political debate as a specific field of application of morality, and believe that it is possible to create in the realm of politics a rational moral consensus by means of free discussion. In this case politics is not apprehended through economics, but through ethics or morality. Both models, however, belong to a rationalist approach, be it on the mode of instrumental rationality or communicative rationality. What is left aside by a rationalist approach is that in politics we are always dealing with a 'we' opposed to a 'them', with antagonism being an ever-present possibility. Moreover, because of its rationalism, liberalism is unable to acknowledge the crucial role played in the field of politics by what I call 'passions', an affective dimension central to the constitution of collective forms of identification. Without identifications it is impossible to grasp the construction of political identities, since these identities are always collective. This is another reason why liberalism, with its methodological individualism, cannot grasp the specificity of the political.

I contend that it is only when we acknowledge 'the political' in its antagonistic dimension that we can pose the central question for democratic politics. This question, *pace* liberal theorists, is not how to negotiate a compromise among competing interests, nor is it how to reach a 'rational', i.e. fully inclusive consensus, a consensus without any exclusion. Despite what many liberals want us to believe, the specificity of democratic politics is not the overcoming of the we/them opposition, but the different ways in which it is established. What democracy requires is drawing the we/them discrimination in a way compatible with the recognition of the pluralism which is constitutive of modern democracy.

With respect to the impossibility of establishing a consensus without exclusion, I have found the notion of the 'constitutive outside' particularly useful. This term has been proposed by Henry Staten to refer to a number of themes developed by Jacques

Derrida around notions like 'supplement', 'trace' and 'difference'.[2] The aim is to highlight the fact that the creation of an identity always implies the establishment of a difference, difference which is often constructed on the basis of a hierarchy. Once we have understood that every identity is relational and that the affirmation of a difference is a precondition for the existence of any identity, i.e. the perception of something 'other' which constitutes its 'exterior', we can understand why politics is concerned with the constitution of a 'we' which can only exist by the demarcation of a 'them'. This does not mean of course that such a relation is necessarily one of friend/enemy, i.e. an antagonistic one. But we should realize that, in certain conditions, there is always the possibility that this we/them relation could become antagonistic. This happens when the 'them' is perceived as putting into question the identity of the 'we' and as threatening its existence. From that moment on, any form of we/them relation, be it religious, ethnic, economic or other, becomes the locus of an antagonism.

As far as collective identities are concerned, we find ourselves in the following situation. Identities are the result of processes of identifications, and they can never be completely fixed. We are never confronted with 'we/them' oppositions expressing essentialist identities pre-existing the process of identification. Moreover, as I have stressed, since the 'them' represents the condition of possibility of the 'we', its 'constitutive outside', the constitution of a specific 'we' always depends on the type of 'them' from which it is differentiated. This is a crucial point because it allows us to envisage the possibility of different types of we/them relations according to the way the 'them' is constructed.

What we can assert from these reflections is that the we/them distinction, which is the condition of possibility for the formation of political identities, can always become the locus of an antagonism. Since all forms of political identities entail a we/them distinction, the possibility of the emergence of antagonism can never be eliminated. It is therefore an illusion to believe in the advent of a society from which antagonism can be eradicated. The political belongs to our ontological condition.

In *Hegemony and Socialist Strategy*, we argued that next to antagonism the concept of hegemony is the other key notion for addressing the question of 'the political'. To acknowledge the dimension of 'the political' as the ever-present possibility of antagonism requires coming to terms with the undecidability and the lack of a final ground which pervades every order. In other words, it requires recognizing the hegemonic nature of every kind of social order, and the fact that every society is the product of a series of practices that attempt at establishing order in a context of contingency. Society, therefore, is not the unfolding of a logic exterior to itself, whatever the source of this logic might be: forces of production, development of the Spirit, laws of history, etc.

Every order is the temporary and precarious articulation of contingent practices that could always be otherwise. Therefore, every order is predicated on the exclusion of other possibilities, and it can be called 'political' because it expresses a particular structure of power relations. There are always other possibilities that have been repressed, and that can be reactivated. Every hegemonic order is susceptible to being challenged by counter-hegemonic practices, i.e. practices that will attempt to disarticulate the existing order so as to install another form of hegemony.

'Hegemonic practices' are articulatory practices through which a certain order is established, and the meaning of social institutions is fixed. The political is linked to those acts of hegemonic institution. It is in this sense that one has to differentiate the social from the political. The social is the realm of sedimented practices, i.e. practices that conceal the originary acts of their contingent political institution and which are taken for granted, as if they were self-grounded. Sedimented social practices are a constitutive part of any possible society; not all social bonds are put into question at the same time. The social and the political have thus the status of what Heidegger called 'existentials', i.e. necessary dimensions of any societal life.

Which We/Them for Democratic Politics?

Once the ever-present possibility of antagonism is acknowledged, one can understand why one of the main tasks for democratic politics consists in defusing the potential antagonism that exists in social relations. If we accept that this cannot be done by transcending the we/them relation, but only by constructing it in a different way, then the following question arises: what could constitute a 'tamed' relation of antagonism, what form of we/them would it imply? How could conflict be accepted as legitimate and take a form that does not destroy the political association? This requires that some kind of common bond exists between the parties in conflict, so that they will not treat their opponents as enemies to be eradicated, and see their demands as illegitimate, which is precisely what happens with the antagonistic friend/enemy relation. However, opponents cannot be seen simply as competitors whose interests can be dealt with through mere negotiation, or reconciled through deliberation, because in that case the antagonistic element would simply have been eliminated. If we want to acknowledge on one side the ineradicability of the antagonistic dimension, while on the other side allowing for the possibility of its 'taming', we need to envisage a third type of relation. This is the type of relation which I have proposed to call 'agonism'.[3] While antagonism is a we/them relation in which the two sides are enemies who do not share any common ground, agonism is a we/them relation where the conflicting parties, although acknowledging that there is no rational solution to their conflict, nevertheless recognize the legitimacy of their opponents; they are 'adversaries' not 'enemies'. This means that, while in conflict, they see themselves as belonging to the same political association, as sharing a common symbolic space within which the conflict takes place.

At stake in the agonistic struggle is the very configuration of power relations around which a given society is structured; it is a struggle between opposing hegemonic projects which can never be reconciled rationally. The antagonistic dimension is a real, always present confrontation, but it is played out under conditions regulated by a set of democratic procedures accepted by the adversaries. An agonistic conception of democracy acknowledges the contingent character of the hegemonic, politico-economic articulations that determine the specific configuration of a society at a given moment. They are precarious and pragmatic constructions which can be disarticulated and transformed as a result of the agonistic struggle among the adversaries. Contrary to the various liberal models, the agonistic approach that I am advocating recognizes that society is always politically instituted, and never forgets that the terrain in which hegemonic interventions take place is always the outcome of previous hegemonic practices, and that it is never a neutral one. This is why the antagonistic approach denies the possibility of a non-adversarial democratic politics, and criticizes those who, by ignoring the dimension of 'the political', reduce politics to a set of supposedly technical moves and neutral procedures.

Public Space

Since we are concerned with architecture here, I would like to indicate how the agonistic model of democratic politics may affect the envisaging of public space. The most important consequence is that the agonistic model challenges the widespread conception which informs, albeit in different ways, most liberal visions of public space as the terrain where consensus can emerge. For the agonistic model, on the contrary, public space is the battleground where different hegemonic projects are confronted, without any possibility of final reconciliation. I have spoken so far of public space, but I should specify that we are not dealing with a single space. According to the agonistic approach, public spaces are always plural and the agonistic confrontation takes place in a multiplicity of discursive surfaces. I also want to insist on a second important point. While there is no underlying principle of unity, and no predetermined centre to this diversity of spaces, there always exist diverse forms of articulation among them; we are not faced with the kind of dispersion envisaged by some postmodernist thinkers, nor are we dealing with the kind of 'smooth' space found in Deleuze and his followers. Public spaces are always striated and hegemonically structured. A given hegemony results from a specific articulation of a diversity of spaces, which means that the hegemonic struggle also consists in the attempt to create a different form of articulation among public spaces.

My approach is clearly very different from the one defended by Jürgen Habermas. When he envisages the political public space, which he calls the 'public sphere', he presents it as the place where deliberation aiming at a rational consensus takes place. To be sure, Habermas now accepts that, given the limitations of social life, it is improbable that such a consensus could effectively be reached, and he sees his ideal situation of communication as a 'regulative idea'. However, according to the perspective that I am advocating for, the impediments to the Habermasian ideal speech situation are not empirical but ontological, and the rational consensus that he presents as a regulative idea is in fact a conceptual impossibility. Indeed, it would require the availability of a consensus without exclusion, of a we without a them, which is precisely something that, as I have shown, is impossible.

Critical Artistic Practices

Let us now examine the relevance of the hegemonic agonistic approach to the field of cultural and artistic practices. I have argued that by bringing to the fore the discursive character of the social, and the multiplicity of discursive practices through which 'our world' is constructed, the hegemonic approach is particularly fruitful when it comes to apprehending the relation between art and politics. This relation should not be envisaged in terms of two separately constituted fields, art on one side and politics on the other, between which a relation would need to be established. According to this approach, there is an aesthetic dimension in the political and there is a political dimension in art. Indeed, from the point of view of the theory of hegemony, artistic and cultural practices play a role in the constitution and maintenance of a given symbolic order – or in challenging it. This is why they necessarily have a political dimension. The political, for its part, concerns the symbolic ordering of social relations, what Claude Lefort calls 'the mise en scène', 'the mise en forme' of human coexistence and this is where its aesthetic dimension lies. This is why I have suggested that to make a distinction between political and non-political art is not useful. Instead of speaking of 'political art', we should rather speak of 'critical art'.

The importance of the hegemonic approach to critical cultural and artistic practices is that it shows that the construction of hegemony is not limited to traditional political institutions, but extends to the multiplicity of places usually called 'civil society'. This is where, as Antonio Gramsci has shown, a particular conception of the world is established, and a specific understanding of reality is defined, which he refers to as 'common sense', that which provides the terrain where specific forms of subjectivity are constructed. And he insisted that the domain of culture plays a crucial role because this is one of the terrains where the 'common sense' is built and subjectivities are created.

The hegemonic approach reveals that artistic practices constitute an important terrain for the construction of political identities. It allows us to grasp the decisive role that those practices could play in the counter-hegemonic struggle because they contribute to the emergence of new forms of subjectivity. An important dimension of the counter-hegemonic struggle is indeed the transformation of common sense, understood as the space where specific forms of subjectivity are constructed. From this perspective, critical art is constituted by a manifold of artistic practices that question the dominant hegemony. Their objective is the transformation of political identities through the creation of new practices and language games that will mobilize affects in a way that allows for the disarticulation of the framework in which current forms of identification are taking place, so as to allow for other forms of identification to emerge.

It is worth indicating that there are different answers to the question of what is critical art, because not all conceptions of radical politics envisage the 'criticality' of artistic practices in the same way. At the moment, we can roughly distinguish two main strategies to visualize radical politics; one I have called 'engagement with', and the other 'withdrawal from'. The second one has been promoted by thinkers like Michael Hardt, Antonio Negri and their followers, who reject any engagement with the state and with existing institutions. They advocate a strategy of 'exodus' and call for the desertion of the places of power. This strategy is justified by the claim that, under the post-Fordist conditions of cognitive capitalism, desertion is the only form of resistance to the immanence of biopower. It should include the institutions of the art world which they see as totally instrumentalized by 'the creative industries'. They have become complicit with capitalism and cannot provide a site of resistance anymore.

Against the view of radical politics as 'exodus', the strategy that the hegemonic approach advocates for is one that, borrowing a notion from Gramsci, I call a 'war of position'. It does not consist in withdrawing from the existing institutions, but in engaging with them in order to bring about a profound transformation of the way that they function. This war of position aims at targeting the nodal points around which the neo-liberal hegemony has been established, in order to disarticulate the key discourses and practices through which it is sustained and reproduced. The war of position consists in a diversity of counter-hegemonic practices and interventions operating in a multiplicity of spaces: economic, legal, political and cultural. The domain of culture plays a crucial role in this war of position because, as we have seen, this is where the 'common sense' is established and subjectivities are constructed.

Critical artistic and cultural practices can contribute to the fostering of an agonistic confrontation that will permit the existing hegemony to be challenged by making visible what the dominant consensus tends to obscure and obliterate. This can be done through a diversity of interventions and an active engagement with a wide range of institutions in a multiplicity of spaces. There are indeed multiple terrains in which artistic practices can unsettle the established common sense and contribute to the emergence of new forms of subjectivity, and the terrain of architecture is certainly one of them.

Notes

1   Ernesto Laclau and Chantal Mouffe, *Hegemony and Socialist Strategy: Towards a Radical Democratic Politics* (London: Verso, 1985); Chantal Mouffe, *The Return of the Political* (London: Verso, 1993); Chantal Mouffe, *The Democratic Paradox* (London: Verso, 2000). Chantal Mouffe, *Agonistics* (London: Verso, 2013).
2   Henry Staten, *Wittgenstein and Derrida* (Oxford: Basil Blackwell, 1985).
3   The idea of 'agonism' is developed in chapter 4 of my book *The Democratic Paradox*.

Interview

Joseph Bedford: I would like to start by asking you about democracy today, both in the West and around the world. The first part of my question is simply, Are Western democracies *really* democratic today? And the second part is: for countries that are not democratic, would the strategy of dissidence be needed as much as the strategy of agonism?

Chantal Mouffe: Because my approach is post-foundationalist, I respond to questions like 'What *really* is democracy?' by asking in return 'Which democracy?' what specific moment or conjuncture? I would say that democracies today are democratic only in name, but not in their values. We still have elections, but the central values of democracy – equality, popular sovereignty and agonistic debate – have been eliminated. A specific conjuncture of democracy that I examine in *On the Political* is the one in which we are told – by people like Anthony Giddens – that we have moved beyond the categories of left and right, and that there is no alternative to neoliberal globalization. This is a specific conjunction within democracy. I call it a post-democratic democracy because agonism is no longer possible, and hence there is no real political choice. I speak of 'post-democracy' because we claim to be democratic in theory, yet we neglect the values of democracy in practice.

With respect to dissidence, I find that it makes sense in totalitarian societies, because in those cases agonism is impossible, and dissidence is the only means of resistance. So, yes, in answer to the second part of your question, I would say that agonism only makes sense within a democratic society. It is democratic societies that my work addresses. I do not address non-democratic societies. I argue that what we need to do in societies that operate under the institution of democracy, in name at least, is to *reintroduce* agonism. This is a matter of forcing liberal democratic societies to put in practice what they claim to be in theory.

Joseph Bedford: According to Ines Weizman however, during our exchange, our current political situation in the West is one which can be described as 'authoritarian capitalism'. This description suggests that the West is already non-democratic and quasi-totalitarian. If Ines's description is correct, would this not precisely imply the need for the strategy of dissidence; of 'withdrawal from' on the assumption that the institutions really are lost, corrupt or unchangeable?

Chantal Mouffe: The notion that capitalism in the West is becoming increasingly authoritarian has some measure of truth to it. I would prefer the term 'authoritarian neoliberalism' though, as the move towards authoritarianism is a feature of neoliberal modes of governance during moments of crisis. Neoliberalism is still a form of capitalism of course, but it is a specific form based on a specific mode of governance. Since the economic crisis of 2008 and the rise of populist movements from the right and the left since 2011, the hegemony of neoliberalism has, however, been under siege. It is because of this siege, and the crisis that neoliberalism faces, that it has become more and more authoritarian in order to defend itself.

We have not fully moved towards authoritarianism yet though. Rather our moment is better described as one in which democracy can no longer enter into a compromise with capitalism. Wolfgang Streeck discusses this in his book *Buying Time: The Delayed Crisis of Democratic Capitalism*.[1] Some people on the left say that in this impasse it is liberal or representative democracy that we need to abandon. This is wrong. On the contrary, I would say that we need to make democracy *really* democratic by returning the element of agonism to it and reintroducing the possibility of conflict to democracy so that different views are represented. The problem is that today democracies are not really representative and there is no possibility of choice. This is the problem we need to address. The only chance of saving democracy now is to push back against neoliberalism and its tendency towards authoritarian forms of governance in moments of crisis.

Joseph Bedford: What is the relationship between the political theory of democracy that you have outlined, and the project of socialism, which has traditionally defined what it means to be on the Left?

Chantal Mouffe: In *Hegemony and Socialist Strategy*, we redefined socialism precisely in terms of the radicalization of democracy. Socialism is not an end point. There is no blueprint, and it is not a form of society that we already know. We argued in *Hegemony and Socialist Strategy* that socialism is the democratization of the economy and of socio-economic conditions. The Left must go beyond economics and recognize that movements like feminism, anti-racism and ecology are also important. Other forms of domination compound class domination. Socialism is an emancipatory project that needs to take all forms of domination into account, and to articulate and establish a chain of equivalence between them. Socialism must be an extension of democracy. It must establish democratic relationships across the economy, but it must extend those democratic relationships to include people of all genders, races and sexual identities.

Joseph Bedford: That relates to Reinhold Martin's question in the roundtable discussion when he described the ideal of socialism as the redistribution of wealth through housing. He said that for him ultimately such a moment of resource redistribution would be his 'moment of truth'.

Chantal Mouffe: Yes, that is one important element, and especially so for architects. The roundtable discussion made it clear to me that the question of housing is a field where architecture can really take on politics. Redistribution, however, is not the only aspect of the Left, there is also recognition. Axel Honneth and Nancy Fraser have both argued for 'redistribution, but also recognition' in a similar way.[2] This is what we were saying in *Hegemony and Socialist Strategy* as well: our socio-economic demands are important, but we also advocate for other initiatives that have to do with fights against other forms of domination in other social relations, such as the subjugation of LGBTQ+ people. For this reason, I prefer to use the term 'radical democracy' in place of the term 'socialism'. It is not that I reject socialism, but I see this as only one part of a much wider project of emancipation.

Joseph Bedford: So, socialism will emerge from democracy rather than democracy emerging from socialism?

Chantal Mouffe: Yes, and there is no blueprint to follow to emerge at a predetermined socialist society, so debate and conflict are essential. You cannot just say, 'This is what you need to do'. That would be an undemocratic way to proceed. There is not just one model to follow. It is different for different places and constituencies and cannot have an endpoint. You cannot say 'Now that it has been realized, society is exactly how it should be'. We have to give primacy to democracy, therefore, because it is an open horizon; an unfinished project. As Derrida put it speaking of democracy, democracy is always a 'democracy to come'. It is always underway and always open-ended. If it were not, it would not be pluralist.

Joseph Bedford: Let me ask you a question about what you referred to as your post-foundationalist approach. You have in this approach rejected that idea that a theory of democracy must be rooted within the ideal of the good, the moral and the ethical. If democracy is to be open-ended in the way that you describe, you say that it cannot be anchored to the foundation of the good as an ideal. Is this correct?

Chantal Mouffe: I argue that one must reject the conflation of the political with the moral, but I do not reject the ethical. The moral is a concept that presumes universality. The ethical by contrast is particular, specific and situated. I insist on what I call the 'ethical-political', in which the ethical must always be put in a contingent form, it is part of a particular conjunction. But the ethical is there for me.

Joseph Bedford: Discussions of foundationalism versus post-foundationalism often have Plato as their reference point. For Plato, there is such a thing as a good chair in the sense of a chair that does what a chair is meant to do well, or a good carpenter who is good because they make better chairs rather than worse chairs. The good is therefore better or worse ways of doing or being, and Plato extrapolates from this to say that judgements are guided by some kind of ideal; a good chair, a good carpenter, a good society, a good city. The good is related to ideals, we might say. Your reference to Derrida saying 'democracy to come', while being open and deferred, nonetheless still suggests to me that some ideal must still be operative within your theory, to distinguish between better and worse forms of democracy. That is, one would hope that whatever is 'to come' from democracy would make a democracy that is truer to itself, richer, and would bring about a better world.

Chantal Mouffe: Yes, but in my book, *Agonistics,* I say, 'It is a good that only exists as good as long as it cannot be realized'. If it is realized, then it will cease to be good. It is paradoxical. We need to distinguish here between the good and truth. There will always be a conflicting conception of the good society. There is no universal, common good, but that does not mean that one should not try to achieve it. There will always be contestations over what the common good is. That is why I describe it as a horizon. We will never arrive at a definitive point at which we will consider that we have finally reached the common good. The common good is not a question of truth.

For people on the Left, including me, it is difficult to accept that we are not the arbiters of the truth. This is always a temptation for people on the Left. According to agonistic politics, we must accept the fact that our opponents have different views, which they have the right to defend. If we do not permit our opponents on the Right to be right, we preclude agonistic struggle from the outset. Instead of seeing others as enemies, I argue that we need to see them as *adversaries*. If you regard opponents as wrong, and they become enemies, you are going to try to eliminate them. Instead, we need to accept the adversary's different view of what constitutes a good society. It might be a view that you do not like, but they have the right to defend it. This is not a question of truth. I think the idea of truth in politics is terrible because it necessarily leads to a politics that inhibits agonistic struggle. Agonistic struggle is impossible if you believe that there is a position of truth in the field of politics.

Joseph Bedford: Would you not say though that the very idea of agonistic struggle, as you present it as essential to democracy better understood, is itself a kind of truth?

Chantal Mouffe: No. Agonistic struggle is not a truth. Rather, agonistic struggle is an ethical-theoretical decision. Because it is a decision, other decisions can always be possible. Acting in politics, or even acting in theory, requires you to take a position. My conception of the common good, the kind of society I am going to fight for, is agonistic, but that kind of society is not a truth, it is a decision. In my theory, I take a non-essentialist position. There are people who would not agree with that.

Joseph Bedford: If I understand correctly, it is a decision rather than a truth because even the idea of agonism is subject to agonism. You are saying that it is agonism all the way down. You cannot anchor agonism or conflict in something non-agonistic or non-conflictual.

Chantal Mouffe: Yes. There are different camps in the terrain of political theory. Political theory does not anchor politics in truth. My political theory is one camp among others. I speak from a particular position, but I accept and respect that there are other positions, such as, for example, that of Habermas. I would never declare that I am in the right, and Habermas is wrong. I am not defending relativism here, however, as that would also eliminate the necessity of conflict. I am defending the idea that while I am not necessarily right, I have a position and it is my task in the conflict to attempt to persuade people and bring them to my view, through pragmatic arguments. If you start from the position that I defend, you will be able to understand a series of phenomenon, I believe, which are not comprehensible from Habermas's position. I hope to persuade him then through the pragmatic way that my theory explains certain phenomena better than his.

I view fighting in politics as always trying to construct hegemony. Yet hegemony is always fragile, nothing is absolutely guaranteed. It may be constructed in a way that is more stable and longer lasting, but it is always susceptible to being disarticulated by a counter-hegemonic move. Hegemony always depends on a certain articulation, or configuration of power relations, but there are always other forces. You can try to construct hegemony and through persuasion win more people to your cause and build institutions that are going to last longer. But it is never definite. There is always something that can open the possibility of contestation.

Joseph Bedford: I would like to attempt, if I may, to bring this discussion of hegemony close to architecture. One architectural example I might suggest for discussion might be the British Houses of Parliament, the 'Palace of Westminster' by Charles Barry and Augustus Pugin; a building which clearly plays a central role in ruling social order and whose design matters in relation to what that ruling order communicates about itself. When the building was redesigned after the fire of 1834 in a gothic revival style, the architects could be said to have accomplished a couple of things ideologically that contributed towards the hegemonic order. Ideologically, they advanced the idea of Britain's national identity as rooted in medieval traditions, even though these traditional ways of life were in the process of being torn apart by the development of the factory system under capitalism and industrialization. Similarly, the gothic style could be contrasted with neoclassical style being championed primarily in France as the marker of enlightenment ideals of universality and the freedoms of the French revolution – I am thinking of Jacques-Germain Soufflot's Pantheon in Paris. In contrast to the neoclassical style at this moment, the gothic style could express the idea that British society was not a revolutionary society. So that stylistic choices by which that building was designed at that moment could be said to function is a means of advancing anti-revolutionary ideas, and obfuscating capitalist exploitation, and that it therefore played a role in the maintenance of a ruling hegemonic order.

Chantal Mouffe: I agree. But the building alone does not construct the ruling hegemonic order. Of course, a building can be an element in the construction of hegemony, but it is inscribed in a multiplicity of other practices. You do not construct a hegemony just by building something, although buildings may act as symbols of a certain form of hegemony. We should also distinguish between hegemony itself and the hegemonic struggle to introduce a different hegemony. The example of the British Houses of Parliament, in the way that you describe it, sounds as though its role was in reinforcing an existing hegemony, but not participating in a struggle to change the hegemony.

Joseph Bedford: That is true, though in the moment of the fire and during the competition perhaps, there was an opening in which a struggle might have taken place but did not. The building is currently in bad condition and members of parliament complain about leaking roofs. As a result, they have recently been discussing the need for a new building. This again might be another opening; one might imagine a group of members of parliament coming forward and arguing that, because the new building is unfit, a new building would be needed and that building could be designed differently. It could be designed in a modernist language, abandoning the romantic nationalist nostalgia of neo-medieval architecture and adopting a style associative of internationalism. The same group might also propose that a new parliament be built in a different city, in the middle of the country, rather than in London, which would also challenge the traditional authority of the role of London as the epicentre of the British ruling classes. If this were to happen, things would suddenly shift around the contestation that emerges.

Chantal Mouffe: I see. Another example would be Brasilia, which was a new seat of government in Brazil designed in the middle of the country, away from either São Paulo or Rio de Janeiro. How that city was designed, in this new beginning was also politically significant. But again, the building alone does not construct the ruling hegemonic order; it is the parliament itself as a political body, or Brazil itself as a larger political project. Architecture is always going to be inscribed within the larger political and hegemonic project. A building only acquires its political meaning by its inscription within that wider discourse.

I have to say though, such cases where architects are asked to build completely new parliaments or new capital cities are very small in number and rare. Is it not that architects typically deal with an existing context? If architects want to be radical, I would suggest that an approach that accepts the existing order but struggles to reform it radically is more useful.

This relates to my argument for what I call 'radical reformism' in my book *For a Left Populism*. In this book I outlined three ways of understanding left politics today.[3] The first approach is the pure reformist mode of left-wing politics. This includes the third-way socialist democrats, like François Hollande and Tony Blair. The reformist mode of left-wing politics accepts both the existing hegemony of neoliberalism that emerged from Margaret Thatcher's government in Britain, as well as the principle of the Western democratic regime. Their stance is to accept the hegemonic neoliberal order, but to make a few transformations *inside* its parameters. So, for instance, they advocate for a little more redistribution, but they maintain the basic parameters. The second approach I outline is the revolutionary strategy. This can be considered as the equally pure symmetrical case to pure reformism. The proponents of this second approach break with both neoliberalism and capitalism, *and* with pluralist democracy. It is a revolutionary break with the whole idea of reform as a possibility. The third approach, to which I subscribe, is something that I call 'radical reformism'. This approach abandons the hegemony of neoliberalism. It intends to establish a profound transformation of the new configuration of relations of power which would constitute a different form of hegemony, without breaking with pluralist democracy.

We might relate these three approaches – pure reform, pure revolution and radical reform – to architecture and say that the Austromarxism that was the political system behind the housing projects in Vienna in the 1930s, which Pier Vittorio Aureli discussed in his contribution, is a good model of what I have in mind by radical reformism. The example of Red Vienna could be quite an important example for architecture. It suggests that you can transform the city without having to start from scratch with a clean slate. My reading of Red Vienna would be similar to that of Aureli and it would stand in contrast to that of Manfredo Tafuri who criticized Red Vienna because he saw its reformism as being inherently compromised. Tafuri argued that the architects of Red Vienna should have made a completely new plan of the city. That would have been the second revolutionary approach, in terms of architecture. The fact that the architects of Red Vienna wanted to transform the city within the context of what existed makes it a good example of what radical reformism might mean for architecture.

◀ **Aureli:** *Tafuri criticized Red Vienna also because its politics were focused on a Municipal scale and thus disconnected with national policy.*

Joseph Bedford: There does seem to be a strong relation between these three political approaches and three corollary architectural approaches that we might articulate. In the first instance, pure reform might correspond to architectural approaches that accept the existing context as fixed and unchangeable. In the second instance, pure revolution would correspond to approaches that seek to erase the existing context, beginning again with a *tabula rasa*. The third approach which you outline might correspond most clearly to that of Pier Vittorio Aureli. This is unsurprising as the two of you draw heavily from similar sources in Italian political theory perhaps going back to concepts like 'war of positions' in the work of Antonio Gramsci.

Aureli's work is also a self-conscious recuperation of correspondences that existed between architecture and politics in Italy in the 1960s and 1970s. We can take a group like Superstudio as representing, even if ironically, what was then referred to as 'Italian Radical' architecture, which aimed to be radical in your second approach of revolution. Superstudio made collages, for example, that depicted free-loving individuals picnicking in the desert as ways to imagine how we should all live in the future. They eliminated the city, or proposed continuous monuments that even if they did not erase the city, ignored its existing order and superimposed themselves upon it. In contrast to Super Studio stands the work of Aldo Rossi, whose book *Architecture of the City* argued that the city was an existing artefact that had a deep temporal order and structure.[4] Architecture for Rossi would stand out against the city as a monument, but its monumental quality was only legible in relation to the city. Aureli has specifically repurposed Rossi's approach rather than that of Superstudio, and claimed that large-scale building forms can stand out against the city, marking clear boundaries. One could say such buildings mark a position quite literally in a 'war of positions' that unfolds over centuries upon the city as a field of battle. They become permanent sites of conflict and confrontation. So, they do not erase the city, nor treat it as untouchable, they accept its existence and attempt to radically transform it from within.

◀ **Aureli:** *Superstudio's Continuous Monument was not conceived as a revolutionary project, but as a critical narrative in the form of a negative utopia. We should not forget that both Archizoom's No-stop City and Superstudio's Continuous Monument were greatly inspired by Manfredo Tafuri's revisitation of the work of Giovanni Battista Piranesi, especially the latter's narrative methodology in his 'Carceri di Invenzione' and 'Campo Marzio'. For this reason, I do not think we can speak of this approach as 'revolutionary', but as a negative exaggeration of what is already happening.*

Where you would disagree with Aureli though is in the way that his own design projects do seem to work primarily at the level of architectural form, and not – or not yet at least – at the level of the body politic or larger political hegemonic project within which architecture is always inscribed. Aureli's work has mostly operated as what architects call 'paper architecture' which inevitably places a lot of weight upon the agency of design and its form, rather than the larger political context. Aureli did present Red Vienna in such a way as to highlight the larger political context. Yet for him the form of the project – such as the monumental courtyards and stairwell circulation – plays their own political role insofar as they both help the working-class inhabitants feel equal to the bourgeois occupants of surrounding apartments as well as feeling solidarity with one another as working-class.

This prompts me to ask another question; one about class consciousness, given that this is how Aureli rationalizes the agency of form and design. And I would like to shift a little and prompt you to reflect upon Martin's position which stands in contrast to Aureli's on this point. *Hegemony and Socialist Strategy* argued that the prevailing idea of class-consciousness needed to be revised because of the subjectivities that were emerging in society and in order to include struggles around gender, race and sexuality. In this sense you have attempted to hold on to the notion of consciousness as a part of political struggle, but to expand the conception of what constitutes consciousness so that it is not simply rooted in economic determinations of class. A key part of your argument has been that it is possible to link up diverse struggles in what you call 'chains'. Reinhold Martin, however, has argued that globalization has had the effect of producing new forms of spatial distance and separation between different class and subject positions. He claims that it is increasingly difficult to link up the subjectivities of Western consumers and workers in other parts of the world to form a common struggle. Globalization thus poses a fundamental challenge to forming such chains. How would one then build chains of equivalence and form shared struggles and new hegemonic blocs in the face of the challenge of globalization?

Chantal Mouffe: I would agree with Martin that organizing at the international level is important, though I defend the idea that it is important to *begin* at the national level and from there establish links with other movements in other parts of the world. It should not be from the top down, but from below, upwards to the international.

About ten years ago, a lot of people who were working on globalization argued that we should look past the nation state, since we can only have a real impact at the international level. Many non-governmental organizations in particular believed that organization should transcend national boundaries. Many attempts were made to develop an international social movement beginning in 2001 with the World Social Forum, and the debate on the Left at the time was precisely a debate about whether organization should take place nationally or internationally.

Another element in this is Antonio Negri and Michael Hardt's book *Empire*, which was highly influential and which basically said that organizing nationally – indeed, for him everything that is local – is fascist. At that moment I was involved with Doreen Massey in creating the London Social Forum. The Trotskyites there in London were highly critical of what we were doing, saying 'You should never organize at the local or the national level. Only international social forums are viable'. They tried to impede its development and ended up derailing the whole discussion, causing people to leave. The mood in the first decade of the millennium was thus very strongly in favour of the international, as opposed to the national scale of organization.

Yet, the energies that came together during the initial meetings of the World Social Forum did not last. While many people remarked about the fantastic discussions that took place there, there was an increasing awareness about how those discussions and energies dissipated when everyone went back home to their respective countries. The organic link to people in different countries that was brought together in the World Social Forum was eventually lost. We are beginning to see the importance of the nation state after all.

Martin appears to take a stance that is very anti-local, anti-national, and says that we need to think of problems at the international level. My position is we have to start by thinking the problem in terms of national democracies. If there is still an opportunity to practice democracy and to exercise our democratic rights, it is at the national level. We cannot just abandon that level of organization. The only effective strategies will be those that create a synergy between a strongly established movement in the country and also internationally. Things are changing now, and the Left is beginning to acknowledge the importance of the national level, though not completely.

◄ **Martin:** *I fear that this impression is exaggerated by our host Joseph Bedford's understandable efforts to draw out apparent differences among interlocutors(!), perhaps in the spirit of the agon. In my experience over the past decade, the most democracy-enhancing work on the US left has taken place at a very local level – in work, for example, by political activists associated with the Democratic Socialists of America (DSA) in New York City and elsewhere. Some of these figures are now famous; others are not.*

Joseph Bedford: I think that it is correct to say that Martin was influenced by those events and debates in the Left during the first decade of the millennium. I recall him showing slides of Hardt and Negri's *Empire* in a lecture at Columbia University in 2005 or 2006, and speaking about it in very positive terms, so I am sure it was influential on his thought at that time. His other reference for thinking about globalization has been the post-colonial and subaltern studies and work he did in practice with Martin/Baxi on what they called the 'Multi-National City' in which Gurgaon in India was linked through the 'feedback loops of globalization' with New York and Silicon Valley. The other half of Martin/Baxi, Kadambari Baxi has also led an advocacy group called 'Who Builds Your Architecture?' that investigates the global relationship between Western architecture and exploited forms of migrant or child labour in other developing countries. But I think the focus of all this work is specifically around raising awareness, and we might say political 'consciousness' that spans between different parts of the world. And so, I wonder how this relates to the predicament of raising consciousness today, and your arguments against consciousness based on class?

Chantal Mouffe: The salient issue today is not articulating class consciousness in the traditional Marxist construction of class struggle between the bourgeois and the proletariat. That is not because we have overcome class struggle, but because we need to formulate the conflict in different terms. This is why left populism reframes the confrontation not in terms of capital versus labour or bourgeois versus worker, but in terms of the people against the oligarchy. That makes it more inclusive, because the concept 'people' includes all workers, as well as the feminists and the antiracists. It is a much wider conception of the common will. That is another central point in my approach to politics, because it has to do with antagonism in a divided society. You cannot have an 'us' if you do not determine a 'them'. In Marxism, the 'us' is the proletariat and the 'them' is the bourgeoisie, but we cannot think in those terms anymore. Today, we must view class struggle as a populist confrontation between the people and the oligarchy.

Joseph Bedford: The difference between your view and that of Martin, then, it seems to me, is that Martin is still committed to the idea of class consciousness in the sense of a conflict between capital and labour and through his work on globalization, thinking through that capital/labour conflict as it occurs around the world. He has written histories, for example, of the relationship between Kevin Roche's Union Carbide's Former Headquarters in Danbury, Connecticut, and the Bhopal disaster in Madhya Pradesh, India, that seek to expose the links between the subjective experiences of workers in an office somewhere in the United States, and equivalent (though poorer) workers elsewhere in the world to whom they are related.[5] At least in the consciousness of his readers, he seeks to place these different workers in proximity to one another, perhaps under the guiding idea that greater awareness of and empathy with people on the other side of the planet would form the basis for political action.

◄ **Martin:** *Not empathy, solidarity. Anecdotally, the essay mentioned here began as a contribution to a conference in which art historians were asked to engage with the work of Jacques Rancière, with Rancière in attendance. I offered the* *cognitive divide between Union Carbide employees in Danbury, Connecticut and Bhopal as evidence of what Rancière has called the 'partition of the sensible', mediated aesthetically in this case by architecture. Both groups arguably represent class formations not reducible to proletariat-versus-bourgeoisie: In Danbury, a professional-managerial class, and in Bhopal, a pre-proletariat of surplus lives, uncounted even in death by the neoliberal calculus.*

By contrast, you argue in your book *On the Political* that we are better able to empathize with our friends and family than we are with larger abstractions like humanity, and that action is more likely to be aroused by passions for things local and familiar. Truths, such as our dependent relationships with global labour conditions around the world, will not produce that effect.

Chantal Mouffe: A common cause can have a similar effect. I am arguing that one cannot dismiss one's national history. Usually, the people who take the internationalist stance dismiss the strong affects that are mobilized by the signification of the nation. For instance, they regard patriotism as nationalism, which is fascistic and bad. They find the very idea of patriotism repugnant.

To the contrary, I defend what I call a left patriotism, that is, to feel pride, and identification with the positive aspects of your country's history. That is less problematic for some nationalities than others. For instance, it is easier for the French than for the Germans, because the French Revolution is a strong, progressive signifier. On the other hand, the left in Austria readily condemns patriotism. My Austrian friends corroborate this. They say that their way of being patriotic is being anti-patriotic. Of course, the Nazi episode is a trauma, but you cannot reduce the whole history of Austria to that episode. They also have very progressive movements. We have discussed the example of Red Vienna and Austro-Marxism. Left patriotism is defined by the progressive elements of a nation's history.

Joseph Bedford: Would you go so far as to say that the Left should advance causes that are related to place because of the power of such spatial, geographic, localized affects?

Chantal Mouffe: Yes, you can put it that way. Psychoanalysis is relevant here. Freud makes the important point that we should not underestimate the strong libidinal investment that people have in national signifiers. Habermas claims that people should accept a post-national identity in order to associate themselves with European citizenship. I do not believe it works like that, unfortunately. To take a historical example, the First World War was a big shock for the left. At the time, the socialist parties believed that the workers of France and Germany were going to unite, but that did not happen. In fact, the workers in Germany followed their national bourgeoisie, and it was the same in France.

So my idea is that rather than trying to eliminate nationalism, I propose that we redirect it towards left patriotism. For me, the mobilization of affect is very important. The right-wing uses populism towards exclusion, for example, against immigrants. The way to fight against that is to engage with that move and to reorient those affects in a progressive direction. That is possible precisely because nationalism is malleable. There are ways to mobilize those affects to create solidarity with people in other countries. The potentials of affects are not only local. The first step may be to mobilize them locally, in a progressive way. That should then develop into solidarity with people in other countries and on other continents. Mobilizing affects, first locally and then globally, should be a gradual process.

Joseph Bedford: It strikes me that architecture has a particularly privileged relationship to the local level rather than the international level, for the simple reason that unlike other media, it is not easy to move buildings around. Digital media and the internet are a much better means towards internationalizing or globalizing our consciousness, but such strategies would diminish the role of architecture, which is local and stuck in one place. I think therefore that your emphasis on specificity, the local and bottom-up organizing would be appealing to architects. Compared with books, films or tweets, architecture cannot flow around the world, it is about particular organizations of people and communities. It forms those identities on a slower scale of time.

Chantal Mouffe: That is interesting. You are right that this conception affords an important role to architecture because architecture is necessarily local. Generally, my interest in artistic practices – theatre, visual arts, but also architecture – is on the abstract level. This is Antonio Gramsci's insight: culture contributes to the construction of a common sense. Gramsci referenced architecture and urbanism in general. For instance, he insisted on the importance of street names. Street names change according to the government and political currents. The physical environment plays an important part in constructing common sense. At that level, architecture is important in the way it creates a framework for the way we see society.

I would say that specific forms of identity or subjectivity are constructed by the books that you read, the plays you see; but also, by your physical environment and the design of a city. My work might be useful to people in this way by showing the importance of the multiplicity of practices involved in the construction of a hegemony. Not all of them are artistic or cultural. Some of them are constructed through the law, through the press, and so on, and so some of them are constructed through the physical environment. But artistic and cultural practices are especially significant because that is where forms of subjectivity are established.

In *Hegemony and Socialist Strategy*, we call this a 'non-essentialist' conception. In an essentialist conception, identities are already given by people's place in relation to production, not as a result of a discursive construction. Here, the hegemonic approach is particularly useful to help us understand how those forms of subjectivity are created. But that also opens opportunities for counter-hegemonic practices. It is easier to understand the creation of common sense through theatre than through architecture, but this is simply because architecture is slower.

In my work, I am not keen on speaking of 'political art', as if there were art that is not political. Any form of art has a political dimension because art practices necessarily contribute either to reproducing hegemony or to challenging it. So instead of speaking of political art, let us speak of *critical* art. I am interested in what forms critical art can take. But I find it more difficult to conceive of critical architecture.

Notes

1. Wolfgang Streeck, *Buying Time: The Delayed Crisis of Democratic Capitalism* (New York: Verso, 2017).
2. Nancy Fraser and Axel Honneth, *Redistribution or Recognition? A Political-Philosophical Exchange* (New York: Verso, 2003).
3. Chantal Mouffe, *For a Left Politics* (New York: Verso, 2019).
4. Aldo Rossi, *The Architecture of the City* (Cambridge, MA: MIT Press, 1984).
5. Reinhold Martin, 'Subjects: Mass Customization', in *Utopia's Ghost: Architecture and Postmodernism, Again* (Minneapolis, MN: University of Minnesota Press, 2010), 123–46.

3

Can Architecture Be Political?

Pier Vittorio Aureli

I would like to answer this question with two antithetical answers. While my two answers may seem to contradict one another, both are necessary.

On the one hand, if political means the possibility of conflict – and especially the conflict between who dominates and who is dominated – architecture *cannot* be political. As a profession, architecture has always depended on what I would call the ideology of consensus. It is interesting to note, for example, that early personifications of the 'architect' in ancient Greek theatre were agents who, amid situations of danger, dared to initiate schemes whose goal was to restore social harmony.[1] This ideology of consensus in architecture has been institutionalized by our disciplinary knowledge to the extent that architecture not only depends on consensus in order to be realized, but it must presume consensus in the way it is conceived, designed and built. Even if building architecture has always been the outcome of specific interests (and especially the interests of the ruling classes), its public appearance is often understood as a civic good, as something potentially beneficial to all.

> ◄ **Whiting:** *You're correct, in that every aspect of a building has to be resolved in order for the building to be realized, but* resolution *implies the working out of complications, whereas* consensus *(for me – admittedly, consensus and resolution are pretty much synonymous) implies unanimity or solidarity. Note – consensus was a term we all discussed at the conference.*

> ◄ **Aureli:** *This is an interesting observation and in fact I was hesitant to use the word* consensus. *Yet to build up consensus implies a great deal of 'working out complications'. Moreover, many attempts to achieve consensus implies the elimination of conflict, and seldom on unanimity and solidarity. Of course, consensus achieved through unanimity and solidarity is the ideal situation, and it can happen in certain communities that at least share some political direction. In my opinion, however, it is seldom the case when large interests are at stake.*

On the other hand, architecture is always political for two reasons, one banal and one more subtle. On the banal register, architects themselves have to be political all the time because their way of working is entrepreneurial, which means that they are constantly dealing with unstable situations of confrontation and conflict. Architects are well aware (though seldom admit it in public) that they must be enterprising enough to navigate a hostile territory of clients, patronage, commissions, public hearings, and last but not least competing colleagues in order to procure work and realize their projects. Moreover, as either buyers or sellers of labour power, architects are entangled within asymmetrical power relationships which are determined by the organization of capitalist society. Architecture is thus political because its professional and disciplinary status is not the outcome of its use value as the 'art of building', but, rather, it is conditioned by the mode of production that serves the interests of the ruling class – and not always in obvious ways.

On a more subtle register, architecture is always political. Every aspect of architecture, whether it be typology, construction, use or details, and whether it be on a large project or even in the most modest of jobs is not just the outcome of efficiency or use, but presumes a subject and responds to the ways in which subjects are being governed. This is evident, for example, in the architecture of domestic space, where house typologies are often the outcome of political, economic and even ideological apparatuses through which subjects are governed. Feminist thinkers, for example, have taught us how familiar tropes such as bedrooms or kitchens are not innate aspects of dwelling, but have been invented in order to reinforce patriarchal values in our everyday life. In this sense, then, architecture is always political in that it contributes to the spatialization of the governance of subjects, and it does so down to the most familiar aspects of the space that we inhabit.

In short, we can say that any idea of space implies an idea of the political, and any idea of the political implies an idea of space.

These two answers to the question whether architecture can be political appear to contradict each other. In trying to reconcile this paradox, I posit that if architecture itself as a *form*, and part of the general mode of production, is always political, architecture as a discipline and as a profession is forced to be apolitical. Architecture is political insofar as it embodies power relationships in the way it is built and inhabited. Yet, architecture is apolitical in the way its production is organized and geared towards the ideology of consensus.

The Question of 'Architecture or Revolution' and the Rise of Urbanization

Until the recent development of 'critical theory', the entire body of architectural theory since Vitruvius can be interpreted as an attempt to formalize architecture under the ideology of consensus. In *Ten Books on Architecture*, the oldest extant Western treatise of architecture, Vitruvius composed a veritable encyclopaedia that is not just about architecture but also about the spatialization of power, from city making to infrastructure, to the measurement of time, to the fabrication of war machines.

Within this perspective, Vitruvius presented architecture and its expanded domain of knowledge as a coherent 'body' (corpus), a word he obsessively repeated throughout the whole book.[2] Vitruvius dedicated his *Ten Books* to the first Roman emperor, Augustus, and this makes clear that the book was meant to support and celebrate the emperor's effort to heal the rifts of the civil wars by means of cultural patronage and a building programme. Vitruvius's descriptions of calendars and sundials are not incidental. These are devices intended to support the managerial and administrative power of the newly reformed empire. The focus of Vitruvius' theory is not so much on architecture as an object, but rather on architecture as an institutional apparatus, as a *plan*, capable of endowing coherence to the built world in opposition to the reality of conflict. In his *Ten Books*, the practice of design is presented as a substitute for politics. With a similar underlying argument, theorists like Alberti and Le Corbusier also presented architecture as an all-encompassing design of the world, so that politics – in the sense of conflict – could be avoided.

Such an ideology of consensus endures to this day as architects often present their designs as part of a peaceful 'social contract' that claims to solve the conflictual nature of the urban world. Therefore, we can say that architecture's capacity to be political lies in its attempt to embody the ideology of consensus and the fact that such attempts suppress persistent tensions and conflicts.

The best representation of this situation is Le Corbusier's statement 'architecture or revolution', which appears at the end of his book *Vers une Architecture*. As is well known, Le Corbusier wanted to publish his book under the title *Architecture or Revolution* – a more specific and provocative title; one that encapsulates the dialectic between consensus and conflict. This position is even more apparent in Le Corbusier's ideas about urban planning. The influential French magazine *Plans* devoted an issue in 1931 to the idea of war, and Le Corbusier titled his contribution to that issue with another explicit title that took the form of another statement: 'War? Better to Build'.[3] For Le Corbusier, then, architecture was legitimized by being the antithesis of the eruption of conflict. We can read Le Corbusier as a very conservative thinker, but one who nonetheless had an uncanny ability to expose the problems of architecture's engagements with politics in its most brutal terms. More generally, one might even interpret the golden age of the involvement of architects in city planning, from the 1920s to the post-war period, as being a response to *class* conflict in particular, and as an attempt to prevent class tensions from erupting into violent conflicts. In those years, the working class found itself at breaking point, and planning became crucial as an alternative to revolution.

What Le Corbusier exposed in his writing summarizes the theoretical framework under which architecture and urban design have been practised since the birth of the modern world from around 1400 on. Against the intensification of class conflict that arose in Europe in the Middle Ages, governing elites gradually transformed politics into *police,* i.e. government not through coercion, but through control. The words *politics* and *police* share the same etymology. Both terms refer to the polis as their common origin point, and the word polis meant both the city and its organization. With the rise of mercantilism, colonial conquest and the expansion of urbanization as a political and economic apparatus at the scale of the entire planet, policing became the *deus-ex-machina* of social life. The link between policing and urbanization is apparent in two important treatises: Nicolas Delamare's *Traité de La Police* (published between 1705 and 1738) and Ildefons Cerdà's *General Theory of Urbanization* (published in 1867).

The art of policing according to Delamare did not just involve coercing people and punishing criminals. It involved making the city function like a rational machine, allowing urban flows and transactions to happen in the smoothest way possible. To a certain extent, Delamare's treatise is the harbinger of the contemporary concept of the 'smart city'. Yet, while the latter is a rather vague and ideological smokescreen for the way corporations extract surplus value out of the lives of individuals, Delamare's treatise exposed in very precise technical details all the urban operations that were needed in order to make the urban domain as peaceful as possible for the benefit of economic development. The architectural historian Cesare Birignani has shown how Delamare's treatise on policing influenced the work of architects and planners as it is evident in Pierre Patte's *Mémoire sur les objets les plus importants de l'architecture* published in 1770.[4] In this book, which is a landmark of architectural theory during the Enlightenment, we see a shift of focus from architecture as a means of representation to architecture understood as design process whose primary concerns are those of engineering issues like circulation, water drainage, waste disposal and ventilation. Inspired by Delamare's art of policing, design becomes an all-encompassing activity that regulates every aspect of social relationships.

Ildefons Cerdà's *General Theory of Urbanization* (published in 1867) went even further than Delamare in conceptualizing spatial governance. In this treatise Cerdà introduced for the first time the neologism 'urbanization' in order to replace the more politically charged term 'city'. For Cerdà, urbanization was nothing less than a theory of human cohabitation based on the frictionless space of circulation of people and goods.[5] His text made clear that his faith in the 'inherent' rationality of technology was equal to his scepticism towards the agonistic nature of politics. We could say that Cerdà's theory of urbanism was prompted by the rising conflicts between workers and capital. Yet class conflict was obscured in his text by his faith in the inherent rationality of planning and science. Of course, both Delamare's and Cerdà's treatises can be interpreted as political projects of the bourgeoisie. Both projects represent technical responses to mounting pressures of class struggle from the mid-eighteenth to the late nineteenth century. Their politics remain *implicit*, however; hidden behind a thick layer of solutionism and managerial control. They both demonstrate that even if urbanization is the outcome of political intentions its way of working, which mobilizes a vast apparatus of bureaucracy and technical expertise, is necessarily premised on the neutralization and de-politicization of people. In this view, the theory of urbanization, the concept of government, the idea of the city as a machine and architecture as the ideology of consensus all align.

Urbanization is thus a paradoxical state of things: it is a political project whose main goal is the elimination of the political. Yet the history of the city offers plenty of exceptions where architecture makes its underlining politics not simply implicit, but deliberately legible in its very appearance. I would like to offer two examples of such politically explicit architecture, one conservative and one reformist, respectively. The first, and more conservative example, is the reclamation of the Venetian countryside put forward by the Republic of Venice in the sixteenth century, of which Andrea Palladio's reinvention of the villa is one of the most emblematic cases. The second, and more reformist example, is the housing programme advanced in Vienna by the Social democratic municipality from 1919 to 1934.

◄ **Whiting:** *Are architecture and urbanization (the city) interchangeable? Perhaps they were historically, but today's urban administration is different from its design (and its architecture).*

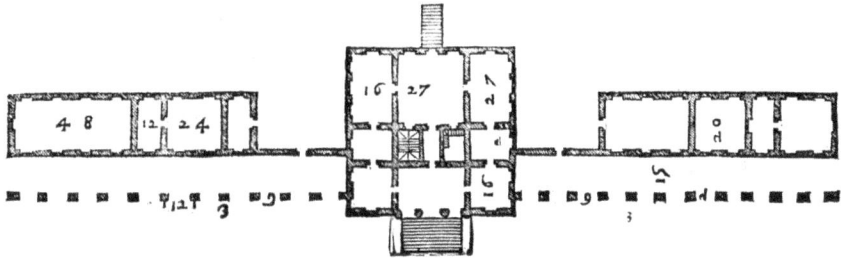

Figure 1 Andrea Palladio, Plan of Villa Emo in Fanzolo (1555–61), Original Woodcut from I quattro libri dell'architettura di Andrea Palladio. Public Domain.

◄ **Aureli:** *In my view 'urbanization' as managerial apparatus dominates everything, including architecture, in the way architecture is commissioned, built, inhabited and administered. So yes, architecture is part and parcel of urbanization. Only when architecture makes explicitly legible its political preconditions – and this happens very rarely – does it, for better or worse, exceed the mandate of urbanization.*

Two Cases of Politically Explicit Architecture: Palladio and Red Vienna

From the eleventh to the fifteenth century, the Republic of Venice rose to become the richest city in Europe as a result of its colonial conquests within the Adriatic and Aegean seas and its extremely lucrative trade with the Near East and Asia. Starting with the Ottomans' conquest of Constantinople, Venice underwent a sequence of catastrophic events such as the Ottoman blockade of trade to the East; the defeat by the League of Cambrai that ended Venice's influence on the Italian peninsula; and the 'discovery' of the Americas, which empowered Portugal, Spain and later England as new and more powerful maritime Empires. By the mid-sixteenth century Venice reached a dramatic economic crisis, which prompted its ruling elite of rich merchants to gradually shift from maritime trade to agriculture by reclaiming the *beni inculti*, the marshes, through large-scale public works. These marsh reclamation projects were developed on two registers: on the one hand, they were developed through the building of canals, dams and advanced systems of irrigation and, on the other hand, they were developed through the building of aristocratic residences in the form of villas. With their appearance in the desolate and scarcely populated Venetian countryside, these villas were meant to symbolize the entrepreneurial effort of the Veneto nobility in reforming the economy. It was in the context of this political reappropriation of the rural territory that the architect Andrea Palladio perfected the villa type as a composition of the landowner's house flanked by the more vernacular 'barchesse', the rural barns whose architecture belonged to the peasant tradition. The best example is perhaps Villa Emo in Fanzolo (1555–61) (Figure 1).

Starting in the early fifteenth century, the re-evaluation of rural life by the wealthier classes in Italy provided the ideological and cultural grounds that prepared the way for this shift towards a more agricultural economy. An example of this was the Medici family of Florence, the richest bankers of Europe at that time, who invested part of their revenue in the building of villas outside the city. It was the Medici who resurrected this type and made it the de facto residence for wealthy families.[6] Here we have to understand the meaning of the villa in both antiquity and modernity. The villa has been the quintessential symbol of patriarchal authority since the time of ancient Rome, where it anchored authority not only in wealth, but in the possession of land. In times of economic crises and political instability, when more mobile forms of wealth fluctuated, the possession of land was both the best financial collateral and a symbolic reassurance of stability. It is not by chance that the architects of the Renaissance Villa, from Giuliano da Sangallo to Palladio, reinvented the villa by adopting a number of tropes from religious architecture such as columns, pediments, domes and axial symmetry. As is most clear in Palladio's work, such tropes were used in villas in order to present the house as a secular temple that celebrated the cultivation of land as the very core of political power. Here we see the essence of colonialism clearly expressed in architectural terms. The word *colonialism*, in fact, comes from the Latin word *colere*, meaning 'to cultivate' and it refers to the use of agriculture as a means of political control. It is not by chance, then, that the Palladian villa became influential within the tradition of European colonial architecture around the world in the eighteenth and nineteenth centuries, because it served to symbolically reinforce the authority of the landowner as patriarchal ruler. As in Roman times, such a celebratory image of patriarchal power was not meant only as the representation of the individual owner, but also as an image of the state itself as the ultimate patriarch. This is why Palladio conceived all his villas as iterations of the same recognizable archetype, the temple flanked by barns. In this way, all the villas designed for different clients would be recognizable as a *whole*, as one project. They all represented the interests of the landowning classes united by an overarching economic plan; that of the state.

As the historian Angelo Ventura has noted,[7] the patrician colonization of the Veneto countryside cannot be interpreted as a process of primitive accumulation of capital, but rather as the conversion of profit from trade into landed property. Rather than dispossessing peasants from their land, in many cases the new estates were meant to attract sharecroppers to previously uninhabited land. The Palladian villa was meant to represent a paternalistic 'new deal', an asymmetrical alliance between 'capital' and 'labour' that would lead to the transformation of the countryside into a new productive territory. In this context, the Palladian villa was the direct translation of the political project of the Venetian state. And it serves us here as an example of the way that architecture is explicitly political both by enabling the wealthy classes to consolidate their power, and by making legible in explicitly symbolic terms the architectural premises of that power.

Something similar is at stake in the case of 'Red Vienna', whose political premises lie in the radical reformism of the Austrian Social Democratic Party (the SDAP). The story of Red Vienna begins with the foundation of the SDAP in 1874. At the time, the party was allowed neither to enter parliament, nor to unionize workers, and because of these restrictions, its members chose to use cultural activities in order to organize. It is within this context that the SDAP addressed the housing question and social reproduction in general as a fundamental means of creating and consolidating class consciousness. With the end of the Augsburg Empire after the First World War and its partition into smaller nation states, Vienna was no longer the capital of a vast Empire, but only of Austria, which was then a small, rural and conservative nation. After being permitted to enter the national parliament in 1907, the SDAP became a leading party and after losing majority in the parliament, the SDAP concentrated its political efforts on the city of Vienna and it was in this context that the programme of building a huge quantity of social housing was advanced. When thinking of Red Vienna, we immediately think of the heroic forms of the Karl Marx Hof designed by Karl Ehn (Figure 2), but seldom do we consider that the case of Red Vienna contains, to this day, an example of the most radical urban policy advanced in the capitalist world. The figures are impressive: between 1920 and 1934 the programme produced 400 housing blocks which included 64,000 units for circa 300,000 inhabitants.[8] The radicality of the policy consisted in financing the building of new housing through taxation rather than debt, and by forgoing a return on invested capital. Moreover, by introducing rent control, and heavily taxing unused land, the municipality pushed land value down, facilitating the public purchase of land not far away from the

Figure 2 Photographs of Karl Marx Hof by Martin Gerlach Jr. (1879–1944). Images courtesy of Wien Museum Online Sammlung. CCO Public Domain.

centre. The maintenance of the social programmes such as libraries, collective kitchens, laundry rooms and kindergartens that were included within each housing project was paid by taxes levied on capital investments, properties and luxury goods like the notorious taxes on Champagne and Sacher Torte. The case of social housing in Red Vienna should not be viewed as a concession of capital to labour or as a paternalistic concession of the state, but rather as the initiative of a socialist municipality that took advantage of its position of power. In this way, Red Vienna reinvented social housing as an antagonistic project whose goal was to combine the pragmatic solution to the urgent problem of housing the working class with and the ideological and cultural celebration of the working class against the subaltern position to which it had been assigned by the capitalist metropolis.

Like their Venetian predecessors, the Viennese reformers also utilized a particular building type that could translate and make legible in concrete terms the political premises of their reform. But whereas for the Venetians that type had been the Villa, for the Viennese it was the courtyard building or Hof. Even though the housing blocks were designed by private architects hired by the municipality, the municipality imposed upon them strict guidelines regarding how they should be designed. For example, all designers were expected to work with the courtyard type and to rely on traditional building techniques in order to make construction a labour-intensive process that would increase demand for labour force while limiting its deskilling. Projects thus avoided reinforced concrete, and used prefabrication only for fittings such as windows and door frames. Even the most salient formal and typological aspects of Red Vienna including the siting and the architectural language of the blocks were not decided by architects but were determined directly by the Municipality in its guidelines. Rather than building housing in the form of garden cities far away from the city centre, as was the case with many housing estates built in England or Germany at the time, the Viennese reformers built their housing as large-scale courtyard blocks in the city. The exceptional scale of these blocks was monumental and it sharply contrasted with the typical speculative bourgeois housing around the city whose architectural form merely reflected the maximization of land use. Contrary to the ventilation shafts typical of speculative blocks, the spacious courtyard was meant to host a plethora of communal services supported by the municipality in order to emphasize the role of reproduction as a fundamental site of political intervention.

◄ **Whiting:** *Interesting. This example points to a critical distinction of whether architecture is (or architects are) political or whether it is (or they are) rendering visible the politics of a system that employs them.*

◄ **Weizman:** *This is such an interesting analysis and example for social housing as an antagonist project, also because you describe how it involves architectural detail, materiality and modes of construction. Red Vienna, and also similar initiatives of the Neues Bauen, or Neue Sachlichkeit movement in Austria and Germany, were invested in modelling and experimenting with new modes of design and public involvement on a municipal scale. I guess, when*

> *in the mid-1930s the construction industry, with cement and steel corporations working nationally and internationally, began to impact the housing market, the intricate scale of negotiations of municipal interests and conflicts were lost to economic calculation.*

In short, if the Palladian villa made legible the hegemony of landed property and the hierarchical relationship between property and labour in the image of the residence of the land owner flanked by the working barns, the Viennese Hof, with its generous courtyard and monumental architecture made legible working-class solidarity within and against the speculative logic of the capitalist city. In both cases, a political policy was directly manifested through the scale of architecture, and by means of a specific architectural form that staged in an almost theatrical manner the power relationships at stake. In both cases, conflict is not eliminated but is given a form. Both examples should thus be seen as instances of what Antonio Gramsci called a 'war of position' through which one class seeks hegemony over society at large.

◄ **Whiting:** *Exactly.*

Close Reading and the Organization of Labour

Although the current regime of late capitalism is driven by class interests, its architecture is more often a mystification of these interests rather than their explicit manifestation. This is because, ideologically speaking, late capitalism is informed by values such as diversity and inclusion. Any project of architecture, even the most controversial, is always promoted on the behalf of a generic 'public good'.

◄ **Whiting:** *I would not say that late capitalism is* informed *by diversity and inclusion as much as it* exploits *the appearance thereof (what has been termed 'racial capitalism').*

Confronted with this situation there may be two ways in which architecture can be politicized. The first way is to meticulously close-read every aspect of architecture as an instance of the ways in which subjects are governed. This includes even the most mundane, familiar and apparently non-ideological aspects of architecture, such as rooms, window openings and landscapes. This kind of forensically precise close-reading of architecture has been on the decline in architecture schools for some time now. The surge in interdisciplinary studies and cultural theory now discourages students and teachers alike from studying in depth architecture *as building*. Paradoxically, it is these kinds of discourses in cultural studies that seek to locate the political 'beyond architecture' which obfuscate the ways in which the political also operates concretely *through* architecture.

◂ **Whiting:** *Though one should take care not to attribute this governance solely to the architect.*

◂ **Whiting:** *I could not agree more with this point; the repercussions of not learning how to look closely at buildings will outlast all of us.*

The second way in which architecture can be politicized consists in questioning the way in which architecture is organized as labour. Architecture is both labour-intensive and capital-intensive and its production happens through an extensive division of labour, which not only separates designers from builders, but also fragments both design and building into a myriad of competences and skills. With the rise of architecture as a recognizable profession in the Middle Ages, the architect acquired a preeminent position over the builder, whose role was professionally downgraded. But in recent times architects themselves have also been professionally downgraded. As argued by construction historian Andrew Rabeneck, neoliberalism and the globalized trade and investment that this economic regime engenders have deeply marginalized architecture culture: unlike the past, today architectural *ideas* are of only incidental interest of capital.[9] As a consequence of the division of labour within the process of design itself, architects are increasingly illiterate about the 'technical' aspects of architecture, such as engineering and construction.

Paradoxically, in many European countries the deskilling of architects as technical experts has its roots in their employment in large-scale projects during the welfare state. A very good example of this situation is post-war England where the majority of architects were employed by the state. In a time like ours, when most of the architecture that is produced is by private investment and when most architects work in precarious economic terms, we tend to be nostalgic of a time when architects were hired by the public sector to design for the benefit of society. And yet, as argued by Rabeneck, it was precisely when architects were elevated to positions of power as influential public servants, that they understood their role as social reformers while they were more than happy to delegate all the technical aspects of implementation to a vast army of 'experts'. Rabeneck writes about how, at this time, architecture's technical aspects were enthusiastically picked up by quantity surveyors, emergent 'project managers' and contractors through design-build arrangements. All of these professional domains that challenged the traditional professional role of the architect in the name of cost certainty and technical know-how.

With the opening up of the profession to market competition, the division of labour between the 'artistic' and the 'technical' further diminished the architect's capacity. It did not only change the way architecture was produced, but also changed the understanding of how architectural production works. It was this process of 'knowledge deskilling' that – like stonemasons before them – has downgraded architecture as a profession. Like other 'liberal' professions, architects are subject to the intense process of proletarianization that is typical of capitalist development. The rise of 'critical theory' and 'cultural studies' which have otherwise been of great importance in raising the awareness of architecture's complicit relationship with capital, has nonetheless unwittingly contributed to this knowledge deskilling, since the absence of technical competence looms large in many critical interpretations of architecture.

If we want to rigorously politicize architecture, we must first map the way architecture is produced in more concrete terms. We must analyse all of its technical aspects and understand how we can reform them with a view towards a more emancipatory condition – a task which inevitably questions the way that architecture is produced as a commodity. Yet such a goal should not be pursued as an exercise only within the architectural discipline. We should also seek to position the production of architecture within a larger landscape of social movements and reforms.

A good example of this is the work of Sao Paulo's collective of architects and engineers USINA, whose goal is to provide technical advisory services to empower social movements to plan, design and build. USINA helps local communities find access to public funding in order to finance projects like social housing. They also offer assistance in the self-management of design, construction and maintenance of buildings. Against the romantic activism that has for decades preached the virtues of 'informal' urbanism, USINA support communities to formalize their right to the city *through* architecture. USINA's projects are thus not just gear to the ideology of consensus. Rather they position themselves in an antagonistic way towards the city ruled by capitalist accumulation. Often this political position is reflected by the formal resolution of the building themselves. For example, while social housing built by private developers with the support of the Brazilian state is delivered in the form of small single-family houses, the housing built by USINA is often organized as a block with collective spaces such as galleries and courtyards which reinforce and celebrate the collective ethos of shared housing. USINA is thus a positive example of how the formal, the technical and the political aspects of architecture are being addressed simultaneously within a project that does not aim at consensus, but takes a side within the political struggle.

I would like to conclude my intervention by looking at a photograph that my teachers at school used to show to us in order to explain what political commitment in architecture consists of. This photograph is a portrait of the 'May Brigade', the group of architects who worked on the ambitious housing plan for Frankfurt under the direction of the architect Ernst May between 1925 and 1930 (Figure 3). In 1930, on the strength of their experience in Frankfurt, they decided to move to the Soviet Union to help the Bolshevik state to plan and build cities. In doing so, the 'May Brigade' deliberately betrayed their class, the bourgeoisie of which the liberal profession of the architects was a most emblematic symbol, and proletarianized themselves as anonymous technicians. Today architects are being proletarianized, not by choice, but by the latest cycle of capitalist development within which the once-celebrated liberal professions such as that of the architect are increasingly deprived of their professional privileges. Perhaps it is precisely this situation that can push us to reconsider our professional mandate, by shifting our understanding of the role of the architect from 'authors' of buildings to workers among other workers, that is, as producers within a general mode of production.[10] In order to

Figure 3 Photograph of the 'May Brigade' (1931). Image Source: Wikimedia Commons. Creative Commons Public Domain. CC-PD-Mark.

do so we need to link disciplinary knowledge to social conflict and consider them not as opposites but as two parts of the same body.

◄ **Weizman:** *Yes, only that they were not received as anonymous technicians under Stalin's Bolshevik state. Rather they were forced to take sides under Stalin's regime of paranoia that escalated in the Great Terro. While Ernst May and Margarete Schütte-Lihotzky took consequence in leaving the Soviet Union in 1937, other members of the brigade stayed and collaborated with the regime. Some of its members like Heinrich Eggestedt took on leading roles as architects in Nazi Germany. Also, a similar 'brigade' following Hannes Meyer to the Soviet Union in 1930 dispersed. Tragically, many of its members were murdered for their political views.*

Notes

1   See: Lisa Landrum, 'Before Architecture: Archai, Architects and Architectonics in Plato and Aristotle', *Montreal Architectural Review* 2 (2015): 6.

2   Indra Kagis McEwen, *Vitruvius: Writing the Body of Architecture* (Cambridge, MA: MIT Press, 2003).
3   Le Corbusier, 'La Guerre? Mieux vaut Costruire', *Plans* 6 (June 1931): 65–7.
4   Cesare Birignani, *The Police and the City: Paris, 1660–1750* (PhD. diss., Columbia University, 2013).
5   Andrea Cavelletti, *La Città biopolitica. Mitologie della sicurezza* (Milan: Bruno Mondadori, 2005); See also: Ross Exo Adams, *Circulation & Urbanization* (London: Sage, 2019).
6   See: Raffaella Fabiani Giannetto, *Medici Gardens. From Making to Design* (Philadelphia: Pennsylvania University Press, 2008), 10–87.
7   Angelo Ventura, 'Considerazioni sull'agricoltura veneta e sull'accumulazione originaria del capitale nei secoli XVI e XVII', *Studi Storici* 3–4 (July-December, 1969): 674–722.
8   Eve Blau, *The Architecture of Red Vienna 1919–1934* (Cambridge, MA: MIT Press, 1999), 2.
9   Andrew Rabeneck, 'The Place of Knowledge in Construction' (2016) https://www.academia.edu/30231811/The_Place_of_Knowledge_in_Construction
10 In this sense is important to note the rise of architect's unions in the last decade, spearheaded by the pioneering work of the Architecture Lobby.

Interview

Joseph Bedford: I find it a fascinating paradox that architecture is both never and always political. For that to be the case, though, 'architecture' must mean several things at once. On the one hand, people use it as a metaphor for something associated with power and structure, in the way that people speak about the architecture of government. That may include buildings, but it refers to phenomena broader than architecture in the narrow sense. On the other hand, there is architecture as a local practice. If, as you argue, the major tendency in architecture since Vitruvius has been an ideology of consensus, then architecture occupies a place of bad faith in regard to politics, simply from its default position of complicity. Since architecture is not defined by its politics, however, it always has the capacity to be otherwise, even if we rarely acknowledge or realize that potential.

Pier Vittorio Aureli: Yes, that paradox is fundamental. The relation between architecture and politics means little without it. Historically, architecture has always evoked stability, organization and putting things together. It has always implied political consensus, not just literally, in terms of peoples' agreement, but also constructing institutions, political bodies and spaces that forge stability. As such, architecture has inherent political dimensions, but it also suppresses the political – if, as Chantal Mouffe has argued, the political is the possibility of agonism, or conflict. In that sense, architecture really is the opposite; architecture denies that possibility. In its most radical forms, architecture becomes political, paradoxically, because it attempts to create an explicit unity or consensus. It thus exposes its stability as a façade. In the face of danger and conflict, the image of architecture as a forceful, political vector is liable to collapse. This is one of the characteristics of all great architecture, from the architecture of the time of Augustus to Bramante, to the early sixteenth-century Renaissance. It claims universality and unity, but it becomes so forceful and explicit in its intentions that it reveals its political identity. This architecture is always rooted in the possibility of conflict.

Joseph Bedford: The word *political* has the same kind of tension. Mouffe posits that it makes no sense to regard some art as political and some not because all art is political. Some people use the word to mean radical and disruptive, but even when people comply with a consensus position and not rupturing, they are acting politically. For you, 'politics' was moving back and forth between those two positions either of active rupture or deliberate inaction.

Pier Vittorio Aureli: I agree that architecture is always political in all its aspects, from practicing to searching for clients. But those politics are not always manifested in explicit or intentional terms. Most of the time we are not conscious political agents. As architects we can also address politics by orienting our practice towards specific ends. This requires a lot of effort on the part of practicing architects, because we are constantly under pressure to find clients or institutional support. These are all political acts, but it is a kind of politics that as architects is difficult to control. On a self-critical register, architects – including myself – are very good at talking about politics when we can determine the arena. But we grow uneasy when we have to reveal our place within the larger political apparatus. For example, in competitions we are compelled to accept a prescribed brief. There is little room to manoeuvre or propose something entirely different that questions the premise unless you accept that your project will have zero chances to win. Institutions like schools or universities support our research. But they are not innocent or neutral. They are inherently political. We, as architects, often refrain from engaging that level of political struggle, and grappling with how those politics interact with our own production of books, writings or projects.

> ◄ **Martin:** *Just a caveat: In my experience, too, most architects are politically committed. But we should not assume that their politics lean left. Most architects I know fit comfortably in the socially progressive neoliberal camp.*

> ◄ **Aureli** *I agree, and indeed in my presentation I hope I have made clear that being political does not mean being leftist.*

Joseph Bedford: That must be why your work leans heavily on form. If, for you, facile design is often naively complicit, then form has the potential for resistance. Is form political because it can offer alternative patterns for making space that imply a 'mode of life'?

Pier Vittorio Aureli: For me, form is legible. The term suggests something that has a specific orientation, which implies a political position. When form is legible, it has the potential to be disruptive. This offers a way out of the quandary of architecture that aims for consensus but, in its formal explicitness, actually impedes the possibility of consensus. This is why the discourse on form has become so contentious in the last thirty to fifty years: because discourse defines boundaries or thresholds with flows of words, concepts and ideas. Form disrupts those conventions, so it has become taboo. People generally discuss form today as though it is circumscribed within aesthetics, or purely a matter of style or language and thus disconnected from political resonances. We often hear that discourse on form is a withdrawal from the political and social dimensions of architecture. On the other side, those who are interested in political and social capacities tend to dismiss discourse about form. Of course, when talking about form we need to agree what we mean by form. For me form is not just the physical shape of a building, but also the way that shape has been produced and what and who take part in that process of production.

> ◄ **Whiting:** *Would you agree that form can also create positive relationships (that might not be 'consensus' but that connect populations or programmes)? Or is form for you always a disruptive agent provocateur?*
>
> ◄ **Aureli:** *Perhaps disruptive was not the best term here, considering also the way it is used today.... Yes, of course form can create positive relationships, (depending how we define what is 'positive'). Yet, for me, political legibility goes beyond positive or negative values, because I believe that, differently from ethics, politics is not about what is positive or negative, but, rather, about power relationships.*

Joseph Bedford: The phrase 'mode of life', in relation to form, is provocative. It suggests deeply ingrained behaviours and habits. In that case, the interpretation of form does not depend on a grammarian, academic architect uniquely capable of reading syntax and structures at a distance. Rather, form has developed agency over a long period of time, over generations. The difference between the typical structure of a terrace house versus an apartment block versus a suburban house is not about the form's legibility in an academic discourse. It is about the modes of practice that it constitutes.

Pier Vittorio Aureli: Yes. I am really interested in the close reading of form, and I push students to be extremely forensic in the way that they look at plans, sections, construction details and the way architecture is concretely produced. This is because it is in this dimension of architecture that one can make interesting and subtle assessments about the political in a more original way than the way in which many theorists put forward an idea of the political that is totally disembodied from space. The detachment of politics from its spatial and physical implications is the thing I am most uneasy about in political theory. In many cases we discuss politics in mere linguistic terms, like for example a lot of people talk about class or gender without a very precise idea of what these terms imply in the way spatial relationships are constructed. At the same time, I am a big fan of a book like *Georgian London* by John Summerson.[1] This is one of the best books you can read about the architecture of the city, especially London. Summerson is precise and wide-ranging in analysing the phenomena of Georgian London, but he fails to grasp the political project that was behind the speculative projects that took place in London after the Great Fire. So, you see that there are these two aspects: on the one hand, there is political theory that sees politics as completely removed from the space in which the political takes place and, on the other, there is a great deal of architectural and art history that looks to form in a way that is removed from the political. In all of my work I try to open up a crack between these two positions, which I find problematic.

◄ **Whiting:** *This effort to find this space is exactly why I love reading your writing!*

Joseph Bedford: If you will allow me to still assume that there is an attachment to typology, even if you do not want it to be tied to the way that the typological discourse unfolded in the past, let us take the structure of terrace houses as an example. Reflecting on the power of these types of structures in architecture, there seems to be a question of whether it is actual or exemplary and paradigmatic. One can argue that the Georgian London terrace house is powerful because it was actual, and the whole structure of the city and bourgeois life unfolded according to it. But, at the same time, we can return to the phrase you offered in your talk that: 'any idea of space implies an idea of the political, and any idea of the political implies an idea of space'. There is a level at which form implies an idea even if it is not actualized. You can have typological understandings of form that suggest a mode of life, even if it has not necessarily had any actual manifestations in the world. In this sense, there is an idealist side to speculation on form.

Pier Vittorio Aureli: Yes. I do not see such a big gap in the history of architecture between the built and unbuilt. The way that space, architecture or architectural knowledge is produced transcends this dichotomy. There is always a possibility for the agency of form. I do not see form as being only a register or index of certain conditions, which is why the discourse on typology is a bit difficult. I use typological analysis a lot; it is a very important way to understand certain kinds of conditions that we just spoke about. The problem is that, at that level of architecture, these analyses seem to operate as simply an index or a register, something we deploy to understand the milieu or the condition in which the city has been produced. But as an architect, I am interested in how we can produce a specific form that can (or cannot) influence the way we think and later on, how we actually build or use the city. I find the category of the archetype fruitful, and have tried to elaborate on it in my writings. Architecture can sometimes be reduced to fundamental operations that do not pretend to project an overall logic for space or for the city, but try to insert exemplary forms. The logic of the paradigm is very important for me, which is why I have recently been interested in monastic architecture, for example.

◄ **Whiting:** *Yes, although the built has often had to deal with extra exigencies and compromises, which should be acknowledged.*

◄ **Aureli:** *Yes, you are absolutely right, my remark here is not entirely correct. I was referring to how, in the production of architecture which involves not just building but also resources of all kinds from manual to intellectual labour, the distinction between built and unbuilt architecture is relative, considering how unbuild ideas can influence the general understanding of what is architecture.*

In the history of monastic architecture, the elaboration of specific archetypes was there to produce exemplarity, and I think that this presents a possibility for form to be not just a register of the existing. Typology, in a way, is always trying to resist the possibility of proposing a specific, singular object. Typology, in the way it has been theorized from Quatremère de Quincy to Aldo Rossi, is more like an intelligence or an overall framework out of which you can extrapolate singular objects or motifs, but you can never grasp the entire type. As such, it exists only in a kind of endless multiplicity, and that is why typology works better as a register or index. For me, the concept of an archetype is almost the opposite of type – it is always the outcome of a general understanding of space, or space in a certain kind of condition, but it always manifests itself in the singularity of a specific object. One example would be the courtyard, in the case of Red Vienna. In the case of Red Vienna, all the buildings are different. In this case, the archetype does not pretend to develop a general logic. It only creates singular examples. Such a reading of form opens up a possibility for something more active than just a passive reading of what is being produced.

Joseph Bedford: I would like to shift to the topic of the city. In your writings, you have discussed the city as an archipelago of discrete parts and have used the term *agonistic* and referred to Mouffe's work. There are clear parallels between your ideas and those of Mouffe who also sees democratic institutions as an archipelago of discrete parts. What do you think of the relation between the way you use the spatial model of the archipelago and Mouffe's idea of agonism?

Pier Vittorio Aureli: I see a lot of connections. However, I wanted to avoid viewing the city of parts as a democratic project because this would imply consensus to too great a degree. In my book, *The Possibility of an Absolute Architecture*, I place more emphasis on the agonism and antagonism that exists between the parts of the city.[2] That condition becomes explicit and visible in the way the city is organized. I feel very sympathetic to Chantal Mouffe's framing of democracy because she too avoids presenting democracy in terms of consensus. For her, democracy is precisely a constant tension between parts. It is in the very enmity of the parts that they share some kind of common ground. It is a common ground that can never be stabilized or taken for granted and which should always be contested.

Joseph Bedford: What do you think architecture brings to the table that political theory does not? Is architectural discourse in a better position to understand the role of cities and their spaces as part of democracy?

Pier Vittorio Aureli: Democracy has become a veneer to keep us from understanding that we live in conditions that prevent any democratic action or institution from surviving. That is why I remain, in my writing, critical of democracy. When we use the concept of democracy in relation to the city, we should remain critical. When O.M. Ungers, for example, theorized Berlin as a green archipelago, he presented the project as *the only* democratic project. The problem with such readings of the city – and we might include that of Colin Rowe also – is that they limit democracy to a very formal, almost linguistic category. They conflate democracy with value-free pluralism. Ungers and Rowe do not take into account that democracy is a very specific form of power; one which is not innocent.

◄ **Whiting:** *Although one might ask if there are any forms of power that are innocent?*

There are some interesting critics of democracy such as Mario Tronti. I would follow these critics to some degree and resist presenting democracy as an entirely innocent concept. The way that architects and theorists try to translate democracy into a specific idea of the city is often very problematic.

Joseph Bedford: Do you think that the affinity that you share with Mouffe has anything to do with your common interest in figures like Gramsci and Massimo Cacciari? That is, is Italian political theory the common source of your mutual interest in notions like the archipelago, a city of parts or multipolarity?

Pier Vittorio Aureli: Yes, I think there is a common background. In different ways there are connections to a certain idea that has been very important for both of us, which can be simplified through the concept of the archipelago, a theme which Cacciari has written about in a very important book.[3] It is the idea of not giving up on a certain legibility of the political, but, at the same time, not making the legibility too obvious – taking for granted that a constant, unresolved tension is one of the fundamental characteristics of Italian political theory, from Machiavelli to Tronti.

Joseph Bedford: There is something about Italy's unique history and geography that has fostered a partisan mindset illustrated by concepts such as 'campanilismo'.

Pier Vittorio Aureli: Yes, it is very much reflected in the history of Italy as an extremely weak nation-state, with a constellation of strong cities. Italy has always been in deep conflict and I think conflict characterizes Italian political theory. Roberto Esposito, a very interesting political theorist, has recently published a book called *Living Thought: The Origins and Actuality of Italian Philosophy*, which is a history of Italian political theory.[4] He chose one specific image to represent this legacy, a famous and, I think, very

Figure 4 Peter Paul Rubens's copy of The Battle of Anghiari (1603) (Louvre, Paris). Image Source: Wikimedia Common. CC-BY-SA-4.0.

topical representation of what we are discussing. It is the preparatory drawing of the Battle of Anghiari by Leonardo.

In the Republic of Florence, in the early sixteenth century, they decided to celebrate two very important battles that shaped the history of Florence in the fourteenth and fifteenth centuries: one is the Battle of Anghiari and the other one is the Battle of Cascina (Figure 4). They gave these two commissions to Leonardo and Michelangelo, who made these two frescoes next to each other for a few months. The battle is this very rhetorical channel, in which you have two clearly opposing parties and everything is very legible, friend and enemy. Yet Leonardo composed the scene as an incredibly convoluted assemblage of people and horses. It expresses a lack of any balance and resolution. It shows conflict as a kind of permanent vortex in which the parts cannot be stabilized into a single position. I would choose this image also to represent my own idea of the political as a tension that can never be settled and never reduced to a single form or order. Attempting to give form to things is necessary, yet one should understand the synthesis of things in a final form as impossible.

Joseph Bedford: Let us turn to the theme of architecture as a form of political representation. In our debate with Mouffe, she suggested that Red Vienna might be a suitable model for an agonistic architecture. Red Vienna in the way that you presented it could represent a powerful image of class struggle and class consciousness. Yet, we should acknowledge that Red Vienna was built in a time before post-Marxist theorizations of the fragmentation of class consciousness into multiple identities and multiple subjectivities, each with their own atomized consciousness. Given this fragmentation of class consciousness in recent decades, how does one go about representing class struggle within the city through discrete projects with monumental form today?

◄ **Whiting:** *Excellent question.*

Pier Vittorio Aureli: First of all, when we look to Red Vienna, we should really get rid of the Red Vienna myth. What is really problematic in looking to that project today is not the politics that it produced, which were rather pragmatic and realistic politics, but more the myth that has made that project like an impossible dream for the class struggle. That is actually the first thing we have to remove when we look at that project – the overly monumental reading of these buildings. What is really remarkable about the project is that it was born of a condition of emergency in which there was a housing crisis. It was not an ideological project of designing a monument to the proletariat. These people had to win the elections – they were in power in Vienna, but they had no power at the national level. The only way they could politicize the city was through housing, because that was dependent on the municipality. They could not change the economy, but they could act through housing. Secondly, they had to solve the housing crisis. A lot of people after the war were coming to Vienna; something we are very familiar with today. Housing crises are one of our fundamental problems now. Vienna has a very long history as a city built by speculators, since the seventeenth or eighteenth century, which is why it is a very high-density city. It was a city built entirely to make money; the main business of the city was, in fact, building speculation. The social democrats were not communists. They had a very pragmatic approach to politics which actually made them despised by communists. They said: 'if we allow this speculation to continue, we can tax it and use the revenue to build social housing projects, and give those social housing projects a recognizable presence in the city.'

Joseph Bedford: Did the social democrats specify this recognizable presence through monumental architectural form?

Pier Vittorio Aureli: I do not think it was monumentality. It was the idea that whoever would live in these buildings would feel part of a strong community. The inhabitants of these projects would become the voters who would then support the social democratic party. The social democrats could be said to be using housing to build their political base. For me, the symbolic surplus of this project does not come from it being monumental, but from the way that it was positioned vis-à-vis modes of capitalist real estate speculation in the city, creating a tension with that dominant mode. The social democrats did not pretend to destroy capitalist development. Instead, they used the *contradictions* of the capitalist city in order to insert their presence.

Joseph Bedford: Do you think class consciousness today can still transcend the other forms of identity and subjectivity constructed around gender, race and sexuality that have become more prominent in recent decades?

Pier Vittorio Aureli: Gender and race are very important issues. They help us to reconstruct and to understand that there are fault lines between subjects that, in the end, suffer the same problem: exploitation. We should not ignore the fact that gender and race issues are often profoundly intertwined with class and this should help us to rethink the concept of class conflict based on what we have learned from gender and race struggles.

Joseph Bedford: If we cannot necessarily raise class consciousness around the proletarian figure modelled on the factory worker, could the city provide a focus? Could it be the right to have a place in the city, rather than workers' rights – something like the Just City movement?

Pier Vittorio Aureli: I think workers' rights remain a sacrosanct issue to be valorized and defended at all costs, but we also need to expand the bill of workers' rights. Today, there are movements that are emerging which are trying to go beyond the idea of ownership and private property. There are a lot of people who want to live together in ways that are not determined by the market. However, these emerging movements do not yet have a clear idea of architecture or of the organization of space.

Joseph Bedford: I would like to attempt to draw a connection between yourself and Reinhold Martin, around the theme of the public and its relationship to visibility and representation. Martin spoke specifically about the history of the idea of the public of its relation to the spatial and urban forms of the ancient Greek city, suggesting that we have too often romanticized the idea of the public, in the manner of Hannah Arendt, seeing it in as a privileged political realm in contrast to the private which is less visible and in architectural terms less representational. In contrast to Martin, you have suggested that the very visibility of public architecture as a form of representation can still be a key to politics and felt it beneficial to preserve the idea of the public rather than shifting entirely to the concept of *the common*. Perhaps I am putting words into your mouth here, but I felt that you were implicitly connecting architectural representation and the idea of the public.

Pier Vittorio Aureli: Yes, it is a very important point. I am not talking about the public in the way that the idea of the public has been appropriated by the state, what we call 'public space', a category I find problematic. I understand the public in terms of the public dimension of society, not in terms of any fetish for 'public space' or 'public buildings'. In this sense, I agree with Martin that we should not overstress the idea of the public and see the concept of the public as synonymous with that of politics. But I also find the rejection of the public problematic.

The concept of *the common* in political theory was introduced in order to go beyond the public-private dichotomy. In this tradition such a dichotomy is something advanced by the State in order to capture society. Yet one of the mistakes that I now see among many political theorists like Hardt and Negri is this idea that the concept of *the common* replaces that of the public and that we can get rid of the idea of the public altogether. This is a mistake because it is giving up a fundamental sphere in which the political is produced. I do not disagree with Martin's critique of the public. It is a very important critique to make. It helps us not fall into the cliché of thinking that politics lays only in the politics of the agora. Yet, at the same time, the questions of the public and of representation remains important. It would be a pity if architecture gives up on this sphere. One of the biggest issues with the idea of *the common* is that it is not something that you can easily represent. The common is a ubiquitous condition which is why it is often not recognized. Many people who are not political theorists would, I think, struggle to distinguish the common from the public, and for this reason, the representation of the public remains important.

◄ **Martin:** *Yes. When it comes to housing, over the past decade in the United States, left-progressive politicians in cities like New York have begun to affirmatively use the word 'public' in public again. Many of these figures are affiliated with the Democratic Socialists of America (DSA). In my experience, architectural design faculty and their students, imprisoned as they are in the neoliberal academy, have found it difficult to follow suit.*

◄ **Aureli:** *Today I would slightly disagree with my own comments here because the common, in the form of 'commons', or the very process of commoning implies a specific spatial structure made of customary practices. So, the common is not as formless as my comments suggest.*

Joseph Bedford: So, in your view, there is still something to be learned from the tradition of architecture as a form of political representation in the ancient city?

Pier Vittorio Aureli: We cannot be naïve and expect the political to manifest itself in the kind of way in which it once manifested itself in the ancient Greek agora. Martin pointed out the hidden side or shortcomings of the model of the Greek *polis* today. While we have to be careful about these simplifications, the question of how the form of city is politically legible and how it supports political life still remains. There are cities that by virtue of their form allow a certain kind of politicization of life to happen, and there are other cities that completely prevent it from happening. For example, we know that suburbia is a fundamentally political project. It was a form of city intended to eradicate politics, though one which became an extremely politicized space. The consequences are evident in the most notorious manifestations like racial segregation.

Joseph Bedford: You just used the term legibility. That is a word that Sarah Whiting has also found useful. It seems to me that the blank white walls in the collages of DOGMA are both a refusal of legibility in the sense of signs, meanings and images as a kind of bourgeois apparatus. They are a kind of expression of architectural form as purely formal, purely a boundary between friend and enemy. They mark a binary distinction more clearly. Whiting, by contrast, argued that architects should recognize that it is not enough to leave the wall as a mere blank white cut. Her engagement with the legibility of surfaces and signs in the tradition of Jenksian or Venturian pluralism – or more recently the work of Sam Jacobs, and the cartoon work at the school of architecture at the University of Illinois at Chicago under Robert Somol, or the work of BIG at the Superkilen in Copenhagen – is connected to her political insistence that as much as the wall is inevitably a mark of exclusion, it also has to be an invitation to understanding between the two parties separated on either side.

Pier Vittorio Aureli: I agree with what she said, that the wall or the cut is not always a simple line. Even in its simplicity it has a lot of ambivalences, and therefore requires a much more sophisticated understanding. There is something excluded and something included. The history of architecture is made of walls that are very ambivalent in the way they structure the city, even when they pretend to make clear gestures of separation. I find it problematic to try to create this kind of ambiguity and richness through architecture, because I do not think architecture in itself can produce that. I think it is the interaction between architectural structure and the way that they are used, accepted or opposed by people which creates a richness of meaning. It would be arrogant to assume that architecture could produce that. This is why I am sometimes very unsympathetic to Robert Venturi's effort to try to make architecture ambiguous and contradictory. For me, how architecture is appropriated by people is not something that architects themselves can design. Architects can create some kind of stage, or background, but to think that architecture can produce everything is something that I try to refuse.

◄ **Whiting:** *Absolutely – 'producing everything' is equal to an aspiration to consensus – something for everyone. Both are impossible.*

Joseph Bedford: Martin commented during the round table debate that what we need is to historicize these issues and speak about the history of the enclosure movement, of English country houses and of socialism and how it became impossible to speak of socialist architecture today. For Martin, it is the patient work of the historian that opens up the space of discursive possibilities again, to speak again about things that we could not speak of a few decades ago. What do you think about the agency of the historian in contrast to the agency of the architect, or the choice that many architects face in their career as to whether to continue to pursue design as a channel for their political concerns, or, like Tafuri, to follow the path of the historian, as an alternative channel? I am partly asking you this because you ended your talk by giving two scenarios or two possibilities that you saw for how to operate politically as an architect: one of them was that you need to write a history of architecture as a question of politics which recuperate practices of close reading the concrete technicalities of building.

Pier Vittorio Aureli: For me, the role of history is crucial; if we do not have awareness of the discussion that we are having, we will have no background from which to begin. The problem is in the way that architects relate to history, as a domain from which you can plunder things by which to design. From Leon Battista Alberti to Fischer von Erlach, it is a domain where you make a catalogue of possible forms to use. This is the way that postmodern architecture treated history. In the 1990s there was a strong backlash against this kind of approach to history. I too am critical of such an approach. Recently, there has been a return of interest in history and we should be cautious about returning to history in this way in which it is seen simply as an archive of materials. For me, history is a way to build our own consciousness of the present, and in a manner that helps us to re-examine the past again. In order to build this consciousness of the present there needs to be a constant work of historical inquiry, but the mistake would be to let history become an authority *over* the present. This is where I see some historians failing to transform history into a fallible domain, something that can be discussed not only in philological terms, but also in political terms by realizing what kind of narrative historical studies – however rigorous – support. Rather than describe myself as a scholar, I prefer to describe myself as an architect. My unruly approach to history is part of my effort to prevent it from becoming an authority over the present.

◀ **Weizman:** *I completely agree with your points here. However, a slight difference appears in postmodern architecture in the context of late Soviet state socialism, where this archive of materials and architectural references was not fully accessible, or even forbidden to access. In the 1980s, in the East and West alike, national and local histories started to regain new appreciation in architectural culture, and modern architecture's pretensions to technological utopianism, universality and rationality were critiqued to advocate a return to the values of urbanity, history and site-specificity. But in the East, this same critique, aimed at a modernist architecture thoroughly embedded in state ideology, was seen as a form of dissent. The very idea of utopia was seen as totalitarian, while the archive of architectural history was understood as a site of endless possibilities and liberation.*

◀ **Whiting:** *What you call an 'unruly approach to history' is such a wonderful understanding of how history, close reading, specificity and architectural knowledge (technical, material, etc.) all work together. This synthetic approach is a much more powerful way to teach, rather than segregating history from practice.*

Joseph Bedford: It appears to me that over the past couple of decades there has been something of a divorce between architectural design and architectural history. From the 1960s to the 1980s it was quite common to find figures who both taught history and design studio in school, think of Frampton, Vidler, Rowe, Vesely, Evans, etc. In the process of the development of PhD programmes in architecture there has been a process of professionalization and specialization of architectural history as distinct from architectural design within the context of architectural schools. As a result, it is rare to find figures today who still span both practices. And as a result, there is an underlying tension or rift within schools and within the discourse between design and history.

Pier Vittorio Aureli: Without constant inquiry into the past, architecture becomes design service, pure managerial problem solving or default optimism, and without a constant tension with the present, history becomes an authority that often serves to justify questionable identities and ways in which contemporary institutions are built.

Notes

1 John Summerson, *Georgian London* (London: Pleiades books, 1945).
2 Pier Vittorio Aureli, *The Possibility of an Absolute Architecture* (Cambridge, MA: MIT Press, 2011).
3 Massimo Cacciari, *L'arcipelago* (Milan: Adelphi Edizioni, 1997).
4 Roberto Esposito, *Living Thought: The Origins and Actuality of Italian Philosophy* (Stanford, CA: Stanford University Press, 2012).

4

Polis-Oikos

Reinhold Martin

Can political life be described in properly spatial terms? The question has been asked many times, often enough with the classical *polis* as a principal referent. Not necessarily coincident with the city or the city-state per se, the *polis* is, as Hannah Arendt would have it, a 'space of appearance' before others for the purposes of 'acting and speaking together' in a political fashion.[1] Although Arendt uses the term in a general sense, she locates its origins in Periclean Athens, where citizens frequently gathered in the urban space of the agora, or marketplace. Although she notes that 'tyrants' had persistently sought to transform the Greek agora into 'an assemblage of shops like the bazaars of oriental despotism', Arendt does not mention the most visible monument to the *polis* as a site of political speech.[2] That would have been the *bouleuterion*, or council chamber, located in the Athenian agora's central precinct, where five hundred or so propertied male citizens, serving as representatives of the people (or *demos*), assembled regularly to debate and vote on day-to-day political matters and attend to the daily business of the city-state.

Stretched to its widest scope, this scene constitutes an imaginary ground on which the figure of democracy has been erected over the past three centuries or so in Euro-American political discourse. It does not, however, account for the topologies that underlie that figure. Reconstructed archaeologically, the *bouleuterion* exhibits several distinct, although hardly unique, topological characteristics: separation from dwelling houses, inward orientation and enclosure. Another space, however, more decisively locates the *polis* as topos. During the city-state's periods of democratic rule, once a month, six thousand or so Athenian citizens would gather in a popular assembly on the Pnyx. In contrast to the representative nature of assembly in the *bouleuterion*, and taking into account the differentiation of the Athenian populace by socioeconomic status and by gender, which limited citizenship and participation in formal political life to male property holders and excluded women and slaves, the Pnyx was nevertheless much closer to being a site of what is now called 'direct' democracy.

The Pnyx is located on a small hill adjacent to the agora and opposite the ancient Acropolis of Athens. Today it resembles a large earthwork in which a slightly sloped, semicircular, open-air auditorium has been cut into the side of the hill, facing inward towards an orator's podium, or *bema*. Archaeologists tell us that the Pnyx was constructed in three stages, from the sixth century through the fourth century BCE, although it is unclear whether the third stage was ever completed. Some accounts point out the orientation of the auditorium away from the Acropolis, on the slopes of which earlier assemblies had been held. This seems to indicate a turning away from divine authority in a gesture of what our era might call secularization. Archaeologists do not all agree on how many citizens typically occupied the Pnyx during meetings, although consensus tends towards six thousand, which was the number required for a quorum. All sorts of inducements were tried to encourage or coerce citizens to climb the hill at dawn to attend the meetings, including a stipend for political service not unlike that offered for modern jury service. Relatively little is known about how the assemblies were conducted, including such details as whether participants sat or stood during the deliberations.[3] Regardless of these unknowns, it is fair to suggest that the popular assemblies held at the Pnyx offer the most accurate paradigm of Arendt's 'space of appearance' in the ancient *polis*.

The popular assemblies also help us to grasp the *polis* as a set of topological relations – topological rather than topographical because, by virtue of its location on a hilltop, the Pnyx, like the *bouleuterion* and like most modern parliaments, though by different means, lies outside the everyday space of the city. It thus helps constitute the *polis* by way of a primary topological distinction. In Arendt's schema, as in ancient Athens, the *polis* stands conceptually differentiated from the household, or *oikos*, just as the political is differentiated from the social and as outside is differentiated from inside. The household is a site of production and reproduction that, by virtue of being sharply distinguished from the *polis* while also supporting it, remains subject to despotic rule by the same male citizens who – in principle, if not in fact – engaged in monthly democratic deliberations on the Pnyx.

In her idealization of the Athenian model, which endorses this division of political life from economic life, or public from private, Arendt tacitly accepts this contradiction. She and many of her interpreters also generalize the underlying topology into an imaginary map or diagram by which any city might be partitioned, in which the 'public' space of the *polis* is opposed to but dependent upon the 'private' space of the *oikos*. To be sure, the opposition of public to private is easily deconstructed, and has been many times. But we might dwell on it for a moment to explore its implications for a political topology adequate to the contemporary city.

In a short essay in the exhibition catalog *Making Things Public,* edited by Bruno Latour and Peter Weibel, the political theorist Chantal Mouffe summarizes several key aspects of her thought: the irreducible antagonism that defines the political; the differentiation of the political from the social, or the realm of sedimented practices; the role of hegemony in temporarily stabilizing foundational contingencies; and the 'taming' of the Schmittian friend–enemy relation into an agonistic set of we–they contests where the adversarial component remains irreducible but is based on mutual recognition rather than annihilation.[4] In a publication for which, in Latour's introduction, the assembly (and, more surreptitiously, the parliament) acts as a master signifier for political activity, it is not surprising that Mouffe speculates, in the final section of her essay, on what she calls 'the consequences for envisaging the public space of the agonistic model of democratic politics'.[5] Her answer elaborates the radically democratic pluralism that she and Ernesto Laclau developed as an alternative to the twentieth century's univocal socialisms, as well as in opposition to a liberal pluralism that equates democracy with an enforced consensus shaped by market-oriented individualism rather than genuinely adversarial political debate. For an agonistic politics that presupposes irreconcilable positions and interests, Mouffe argues, 'public spaces are always plural; the agonistic confrontation takes place on a multiplicity of discursive surfaces'. In acknowledging the evident affinities, she distances herself from Arendt's agonism, which, notwithstanding its emphasis on plurality and contestation, Mouffe calls an 'agonism without antagonism'.[6] The problem for Mouffe is that Arendt, like Jürgen Habermas, considers consensus to be the defining feature of political life, albeit via persuasive argumentation rather than rational proof. Hence Mouffe's concluding exhortation: 'What a democratic politics requires is the fostering of a multiplicity of public spaces of agonistic confrontation.'[7]

This essay succinctly connects the main theses of Mouffe's work, from the collaboration with Laclau in *Hegemony and Socialist Strategy* onward, with a spatial imagination by locating the political in a 'multiplicity of public spaces'. In taking issue with Arendtian agonism, Mouffe does not explicitly reject the division of public and private on which it is based. On the contrary, she tacitly accepts Arendt's argument, in *The Human Condition*, that this distinction, which modernity has gradually obliterated, ontologically grounds the differentiation of the political from the social, however unstable and fugitive that differentiation may be. She and Laclau certainly suggest that 'the distinctions public/private, civil society/political society are only the result of a certain type of hegemonic articulation'.[8] And they define the social as a 'non-sutured space', crosscut with antagonistic fissures and hence politically constituted.[9] Still, it is difficult not to conclude that the 'space of appearance' remains paradigmatic of political space as such, for which the Athenian Pnyx stands now as just one among any number of public arenas, large and small, in which the agon, or struggle, might be waged.

In some contrast to this notion of the political as lodged in the res publica, which, as Latour reminds us, could just as well be a public 'thing' as a public space, a more classically Marxist critique of capitalist modernity would focus on specific sites of production, such as the factory, as topoi of political organization and contestation. During the late 1960s, for example, the Italian workerists responded to the failure of organized labour and the Communist Party to decisively challenge industrial capitalism from the factory floor, by emphasizing historical changes whereby the whole of society had effectively become a site of production. Alternatively formulated as the 'social factory' (by Mario Tronti) or the 'factory without walls' (by Antonio Negri), this diffusion became central to accounts of informal post-Fordist or postindustrial production, in which the older division between workplace and home, or between work and leisure, had, for all practical purposes, been abolished.[10] Although most visibly associated with newer forms of intellectual work gathered under the somewhat misleading category of 'immaterial labour', this account of the dispersion or deterritorialization of factory work, and of both exploitation and organized political resistance, is the strict obverse of Arendt's public sphere. Particularly in its post-Fordist iterations, the 'factory without walls' is nothing other than Arendt's 'household', or *oikos*, the realm of the social but also of production and reproduction, generalized. The workerist model, especially as updated by Negri in his recent collaborations with Michael Hardt, thereby matches up with Arendt's claim that the modern period has seen the replacement of the properly political agon with household administration under the sign of the social.[11]

That Hardt and Negri analyse the consequent regime more frequently through the lens of Foucauldian biopolitics than through Arendt's categories is of lesser importance for us, because, despite their significant differences, the two models converge on this crucial point: Arendt's *animal laborans* is the reanimated *homo oeconomicus* of Foucault's late reflections on neoliberalism. The economic, in the form of household management, enters into Arendt's scheme as what Mouffe would call hegemony, as *animal laborans* overtakes *homo faber*, the social overtakes the political, and managerial capitalism is consolidated around a human subject reconceived as what Foucault called an entrepreneurial 'abilities-machine' (i.e. human capital) in need of biopolitical care.[12]

Which returns us to Athens. Among the fragmentary evidence that archaeologists have adduced to reconstruct the workings of the Pnyx is a passage from Aristophanes, in his comedy *The Assemblywomen*, which was most likely written and performed in the fourth century BCE.[13] In the play, a group of Athenian women disguised as men leave their respective households at dawn, enter the Pnyx, and join the popular assembly. There, they propose that women rather than men govern the *polis*, and, because the disguised women are in the majority, they win the vote and assume power.

In the play's opening scene, as the women gather on a city street and don their disguises, they conduct a mock assembly to practice their speeches and decide who among them should address the people. After some unconvincing attempts, the play's protagonist, Praxagora, emerges as the group's lead orator. Her practice speech is a blend of accusation ('[Y]ou, the sovereign people, are responsible for this mess!'), logic ('I propose that we turn our governance of the *polis* to the women, since they are so competent as stewards and treasurers of our households') and morality ('[T]heir [women's] character is superior to ours').[14] Aristophanes thus parodies the arts of persuasion around which a properly agonistic *polis* might form. But what is most interesting for our purposes is that we never see the women at the Pnyx; indeed, we never see the Pnyx at all. Having chosen their representative, the women depart for the assembly, and, after a choral interlude and an encounter with the men of Athens dressed in their wives' clothes (for the women took theirs), the action resumes with Praxagora presiding over a reformed *polis*. The *polis* that emerges is essentially communist in that it renders all property common (though slaves remain excluded) and establishes social equality and sexual freedoms. But our question is less *how* it does so than *where* it does so. Gradually, the symbolic and practical role of the popular assembly gathered on the Pnyx, by which the new regime was voted in, gives way to sedimented, everyday activities that revolve around food and sex. Whatever political consensus was achieved remains illusory, as it was obtained by deceit. Underlying antagonisms persist. Praxagora makes good on her proposal to 'remodel the city ... into one big household', but the Pnyx itself remains offstage.[15] We can interpret its occult position in three ways: it stands awaiting further political deliberation; it is obsolete, as the postpolitical utopia has been achieved; or it is redundant, as politics has moved into the household.

Although the titular characters of Aristophanes's play are the 'assemblywomen' of Athens, their politics are enacted not so much in the assembly, or even in the street where they first rehearse their speeches, as in the day-to-day work of governing, where household administration has become paradigmatic. In Mouffe and Laclau's sense, this is the work of hegemony: the institutionalizing of a dominant regime that brings temporary order to the contingencies around which the agon, or political struggle, plays out. That the rule of women reverses that of men does not fundamentally alter the terms of struggle; it is always possible for the legitimacy of the new government to be debated anew in a popular assembly. The status of the Pnyx as the archetypal space of politics seems thereby preserved, *except* insofar as women, in the classical *polis*, are representatives of the social rather than the political. Yes, their actions can most certainly be said to have laid claim on the 'space of appearance', and thereby to have changed valence; but those same actions could equally – and quite undecidably – be said to have annulled that space.

◀ **Weizman:** *Thank you for this reference to the Assemblywomen and this sharp revisiting of the agora in Arendt's text. With his comedy Aristophanes probably did not truly think about a society in which there would be a reversal of gender roles, or equality between them. Rather than considering the empowerment of women, his mockery of contemporary politicians critiqued a certain weakness of governing that would fail 'as if led by women'. I wonder whether, in her own script, Praxagora and her friends would have ruled successfully and whether she would have made use of the Pnyx.*

That is where the constitutive asymmetry lies: in the precedence of public over private in the determination of the *polis*, and therefore of the political. Remember that one of Praxagora's arguments to the assembly is that women ought to govern because they are 'so competent as stewards and treasurers of our households'. That the assemblywomen achieve their aims in Aristophanes's play does not simply mean that the historically male *polis* has been feminized; it also means that the political order as *such* has been overturned.

Already at the alleged point of origin, then, in classical Athens, the *polis* was capable of being reconceived as a household, an *oikos* to be governed like a domestic space. That this domestic space writ large could take the place of the 'space of appearance' (rather than simply become that space) and still democratically refound the *polis* is the antiessentialist wager with which we, as moderns, must play. Incomplete and ambiguous though it may be, the possibility announced by Aristophanes is also an answer from within the classical tradition to Mouffe and Laclau's call to invent new, contingent hegemonies capable of displacing the liberal-capitalist one that currently presides over the playing fields of the political; not because it puts women in charge but because it designates 'housekeeping', as Arendt derisively called the managerial disposition, as the locus of the political *within* which – rather than outside of which – the agon might occur, in a kind of internalization of the Pnyx made possible by its initial constitution as radically outside: the Pnyx as a paradoxical 'space of (dis)appearance'. The wager is also that the social, which, according to Arendt, has neutralized contestation among a plurality of voices, can inaugurate a political topology adequate to Mouffe's exhortation that we take plurality as foundational rather than circumstantial.

This type of political topology, wherein the *polis* is potentially reconstituted everywhere *except* in the formal assembly, which remains outside the frame, is related to but also different from that imagined by theorists of a 'factory without walls', in which the social field and the means of production coincide. It shares with these theorists an emphasis on the economic sphere, in which the social factory – which Negri would later designate as the 'metropolis' – and the household are one and the same thing. But rather than conceiving the metropolis as a factory writ large, or reverting to the older, Renaissance notion of the city as a large house, it takes seriously the reversal of the political order established by the new hegemony of the social.

However much we justly desire and agitate for a more robust public realm, then, such a thing – a reconstituted res publica – will remain condemned to repeat its past unless we attend to the more basic repetitions on which it is founded. These are the repetitions of the social: the small, technical rituals by which we are governed and the 'abilities' that define human capital, including administrative ones. For hegemony is also repetition; and if we would be wise not to ignore the current order, we would also be wise to consider any hegemony capable of replacing it to be one for which repetition underpins not only political institutions, like the once-a-month meetings on the Pnyx, but also social practice, including the day-to-day activities of caring for oneself, for others and for the collective household.

Housing is one such repetition. It remains a commonplace among architects and urbanists that housing is a privileged site of political articulation within the city. It would be more accurate to describe it as a site for reproducing the 'social', in Arendt's sense but also in that of Gilles Deleuze, who, commenting on Jacques Donzelot's *The Policing of Families*, described the 'rise of the social' as the emergence of a 'hybrid form of the public and the private ... a novel interlacing of interventions and withdrawals of the state'.[16] For about a hundred years, the construction and maintenance of housing was a key arena in which socialist and welfare states attempted not only to mitigate the predatory effects of speculative capital but also to 'police' (Donzelot's term) or regulate collective life through the reproduction of social norms, including sexual and gender norms, mainly through the apparatus of the family. Housing has also been a site where these two historical agents – states and markets – have brazenly joined forces to secure the reproduction of capital, predominantly as real estate development. None of this, however, exhausts the real political makeup of what Friedrich Engels called the 'housing question'.[17]

In Engels's original formulation, that question extended well beyond the proletarianization of workers newly migrated to the great modern metropolis, though this was a motivating concern; it opened onto the inherently political character of the house itself. That, in our own era of informal labour and immaterial production, factory and house seem to have merged only argues further for a thought that is capable of considering the house – and, with it, housing – as a site in which the agon repeats, daily. Housing, then, serves not only as a recurrent site of bourgeois reform (as Engels would have it) but also as one among many linked sites in a new political topology.

Since the nineteenth century, housing has been most commonly studied typologically, whether in reference to building types or in reference to the social types that inhabit those buildings.[18] These types have been naturalized in the halls of culture, including architecture. If Engels regarded both radical and bourgeois responses to the periodic housing shortages afflicting European cities as ideological distractions that obscured capital's artifice, he nevertheless accepted and deployed the spatial and social typologies with which his discourse equipped him, including that of the worker. Shortly after Engels wrote, around the turn of the twentieth century, iterative spatial techniques for the production of housing became increasingly common. These techniques included standardized unit and building types, construction modules, Taylorized furniture arrangements, factory-made fixtures, design standards calibrated to the measurements of statistically 'average' or 'normal' bodies, and, eventually, prefabricated modular building components. These are the elements through which the social was and still is produced and re-produced with respect to housing. The household, a descendent of the ancient *oikos*, is the governmental and financial unit of the social. This unit was repeated differently through the course of the twentieth century in modernizing regimes around the world. With each repetition of each household, each housing unit, and each standard, the social has been assembled, disassembled, and reassembled.

Understood this way, housing is a topological rather than a *typological* question – as is the city itself. For we are not speaking of archetypal figures stored in the memory palaces of culture; we are speaking of scaled measurements, statistically derived norms, and regulatory parameters stored in charts, databases, filing cabinets, and hard drives. In these, the apparatuses that formerly distinguished inside from outside, house from city, *oikos* from *polis*, 'housekeeping' from politics, have been abolished. A universal urbanization, with no absolute inside or outside, has taken their place as the governing hegemony. As Arendt feared, this is the hegemony of the 'social', managed today less by states than by capital. Grasping its topology means tracing the nestings, linkages, networks, inversions, erasures, inclusions and exclusions through which the new, thoroughly urbanized household, or *oikos*, is being assembled. Then, and only then, will we have grasped the changing topology of the *polis*.

> ◄ **Weizman:** *This is a fascinating analysis. I also think here of the 'ideological state apparatus' that Louis Althusser describes as when a hegemony creeps into the everyday, unnoticeably. The subject for him is 'always-already' interpellated.*

Notes

1. Hannah Arendt, *The Human Condition*, 2nd ed. (Chicago: University of Chicago Press, 1998), 198.
2. Ibid., 160.
3. On the archaeology of the Pnyx, see the papers collected in Björn Forsén and Greg Stanton, eds., *The Pnyx in the History of Athens: Proceedings of an International Colloquium Organized by the Finnish Insti-tute at Athens*, 7–9 October 1994 (Helsinki: Foundation of the Finnish Institute at Athens, 1996).
4. Chantal Mouffe, 'Some Reflections on an Agonistic Approach to the Public', in *Making Things Public: Atmospheres of Democracy*, ed. Bruno Latour and Peter Weibel (Cambridge, MA: MIT Press, 2005), 804–7.
5. Ibid., 806.
6. Ibid.
7. Ibid., 807.
8. Ernesto Laclau and Chantal Mouffe, *Hegemony and Socialist Strategy: Towards a Radical Democratic Politics*, 2nd ed. (New York: Verso, 2001), 185.
9. Ibid., 126.
10. For a useful summary, see Alberto Toscano, 'Factory, Territory, Metropolis, Empire', *Angelaki* 9, no. 2 (August 2004): 197–216.
11. See especially Michael Hardt and Antonio Negri, *Commonwealth* (Cambridge, MA: Belknap Press of Harvard University Press, 2009), as well as the companion volumes, *Empire* (Cambridge, MA: Harvard University Press, 2000) and *Multitude: War and Democracy in the Age of Empire* (New York: Penguin, 2004).
12. On *animal laborans*, see Arendt, *Human Condition*, 320–5; on the transformation of *homo oeconomicus* from a 'partner in an exchange' to an 'entrepreneur of himself', see Michel Foucault, *The Birth of Biopolitics: Lectures at the Collège de France, 1978–1979*, trans. Graham Burchell (New York: Palgrave Macmillan, 2008), 225–6; and on *homo oeconomicus* as an 'abilities-machine', see Foucault, *The Birth of Biopolitics*, 229.
13. For a summary, see P. G. Calligas, 'Archaeological Research on the Athenian Pnyx', and Mogens Herman Hansen, 'Reflections on the Number of Citizens Accommodated in the Assembly Place on the Pnyx', in Forsén and Stanton, *Pnyx in the History of Athens*, 1–5 and 24–33, respectively.
14. Aristophanes, 'The Assemblywomen', in *Three Plays by Aristophanes: Staging Women*, ed. and trans. Jeffrey Henderson (New York: Routledge, 1996), 162.
15. Ibid., 178.
16. Gilles Deleuze, 'The Rise of the Social', foreword to Jacques Donzelot, in *The Policing of Families*, trans. Robert Hurley (1872–3; repr. New York: Pantheon, 1979), x.
17. Friedrich Engels, *The Housing Question* (New York: International Publishers, n.d.).
18. On spatial types and social or 'human' types and their relation to normalization, see Georges Teyssot, *A Topology of Everyday Constellations* (Cambridge, MA: MIT Press, 2013), chap. 2, 'Figuring the Invisible', 31–82.

Interview

Joseph Bedford: You began your paper by asking how politics is spatial, and then why we regard the public as political, but not the private. You identify the space of the *Pnyx* as emblematic to Hannah Arendt and her reflections on the public. Do you interpret Arendt to say that the difference between private and public corresponds to a sharp spatial distinction between interior and exterior?

Reinhold Martin: Yes, that's basically what she says. The household, or *oikos*, is the site of the social and of production. It is a despotic space over which the male property owner presides, where women are either subordinate or enslaved. In Arendt's somewhat idealized view of classical Athens, the agora is a site of agonistic political encounter between propertied, male citizens. Appearance in public space depends, in this case, on the sovereign character of the male citizen. My purpose in this particular text was not to engage in agonistic struggle with the work of either Hannah Arendt or Chantal Mouffe.

Rather, it was to explain the spatial *a priori* of this tradition in political theory. In one way or another, this tradition requires a spatial correlate to its concept of the public, whether we call this the space of appearance, or the space of struggle. Broadly speaking, this tradition opposes that space to the private sphere, which it does not restrict to private property. This private sphere can also refer to certain types of social behaviour that stress individual autonomy. But rather than simply adopting or contesting that framework, I am reminding us of its architecture.

In the essay, I point out that the actual space of assembly in the ancient agora, the *Bouleuterion*, was not the most democratic place in the world. The *Bouleuterion* was more like a modern senate, in which the *demos* was represented by a limited number of elite male citizens. Meanwhile, the more popular and inclusive assemblies (still all male) took place in the *Pnyx*, up on the hill. The *Pnyx* is almost always overlooked in architectural or para-architectural discussions of Athenian democracy. Such discussions tend to fetishize the agora – the marketplace – as the foundation of political life in the *polis*. I want first to modify that, by reminding us that historically this was not the case. Secondly, I want to understand the topology of these ideas.

When I refer to the architecture of Arendt's argument, then, I am talking about this underlying topology of public and private, or the relations between inside and outside that structure these concepts.

Arendt is very clear about this. She argues that, in what we call modernity, the *polis*, the purest version of political life, has been superseded by administration, or what she calls the *social*, which originates in the household, or the managerial sphere. Arendt associates this with state bureaucracy, and with capitalism. There is in her work a sense of an original, primary division between public and private, the *polis* and the *oikos,* such that political life can come into being as such. That is where I propose that we begin our inquiry, though we should not end there.

Joseph Bedford: The distinction between necessity and freedom is important. You discuss it explicitly towards the end of your text, with regard to essentialism and anti-essentialism. I would draw an analogy between the place of Martin Heidegger in the background of Arendt's thinking, and Carl Schmitt in the background of Mouffe's thinking. If Arendt seeks a space in which, as she puts it, 'men gather and have a world in common', it is that conscious commonality which spurs people to act freely and virtuously.

Mouffe's morality is based on Schmitt's observation, that since everything is contingent one must make decisions in a vacuum, so everything depends on recognition of a fundamental freedom.

If you would accept this parallel between Arendt and Mouffe, you read Mouffe as saying that everything is contingent, despite Mouffe's denial of anti-essentialism. You are holding her to account for implicit elements of essentialism, insofar as she speaks of a space – even if it is symbolic – in which one gains a conscience of contingency and therefore freedom.

Reinhold Martin: Again, I don't intend to take issue with the claims of either Arendt or Mouffe. Instead, I am trying to show that this public-private opposition is itself contingent. The appearance in public of male, propertied citizens is contingent upon a whole set of power relations and economic structures that are concentrated in the household. This historical fact is too easily seen as an unfortunate archaism that modern political thought can overcome. I disagree with that.

I see the topology of public and private as structural, figured in the households at the bottom of the hill and the *Pnyx* up at the top. This above-below, inside-outside topology structures the political thought to which we are referring, at least in part. Philosophically speaking, no one is essentializing anything here, although as I have said, Arendt does tend to idealize classical Athens. This is the loosely Heideggerian strain in her thought, reaching back to classical times in search of fundamentals.

From an epistemological point of view, one of the purposes of approaching the discussion from this perspective is to ask what critical spatial thinking can add to – rather than derive from – political theory.

We are all familiar with influential approaches in urban studies and architecture that attempt to interpret lived space by way of theoretical abstractions. I propose inverting this approach, to consider the abstractions of public-private and inside-outside as overdetermined by historically contingent spatial arrangements. What if the space precedes the theory?

Joseph Bedford: So in some sense, Athens left its spatial imprint on political space?

Reinhold Martin: Yes, as a historical space. Not a mythical space like Mount Olympus, where classical metaphysics begins and ends, but the actual city of Athens, which is why I refer to archaeological evidence and to actual urban spaces.

Joseph Bedford: What slippages might you be allowing to take place in the debate over the word *space*? You draw our attention to a passage from Mouffe in which she defines the agonist public sphere as a multiplicity of discursive surfaces. Is that a false convergence between the fields of architecture and political theory? In the tradition of discourse theory, Mouffe uses the word space symbolically. When you refer to the *Pnyx*, and the space of Athens, you are talking about a literal space. Is that a moment of one term having two different meanings in two different disciplines?

Reinhold Martin: Maybe, but this is why it is not a contest. We may disagree in other areas, but this is not one of them. Whether it was Mouffe's intention or not, speaking of a multiplicity of discursive surfaces sounds very much like Michel Foucault. In Foucauldian terms, discourse entails an encounter between regimes of language and regimes of knowledge and knowledge-making.

I would, however, ask: What is different when we conceive of space literally rather than figuratively? What is the difference if we begin by observing that there were certain spaces in which a certain type of politics was enacted? Formal or parliamentary politics does not exhaust the notion of the political that authors like Mouffe and Laclau, or Schmitt and Arendt theorize. But it does give us some sense of what is historical about political theory. By historical, I do not mean the origins of these ideas, but rather their purchase in empirical life.

In that regard, I really do want to ask 'What it is to do politics with space?' rather than presuppose an abstraction that is *a posteriori* grounded in some historical situation. To do theory with history is different.

Joseph Bedford: Are you arguing here that history is the process by which the social replaces the political? You refer to Aristophanes's *The Assemblywomen* as the demonstration of that process. But you also suggest that the spaces of ancient Athens hang over the social in some sense. Aristophanes illustrates that ghost of the political spaces of Athens, you suggest, by always setting events that happen at the Pnyx off stage.

You then seem to argue for an 'anti-essentialist wager', however, and for us to finally and fully cast off that ghostly trace of the political spatial encoding of the public sites of ancient Athens. What would it mean to not be nostalgic, that is, to not yearn for the space of the *Pnyx* to come back to centre stage, but rather to do politics solely within the space of the social?

Reinhold Martin: What I am referring to with the phrase 'anti-essentialist wager' is Aristophanes's simple reversal of the social order, in which women rise up from the household and govern. Of course, this in itself easily leads to a gendered essentialism, if we say, 'The men are not good at leadership, maybe the women will be better', and leave it at that.

Instead, the anti-essentialist wager is that a politics of gender registers in this reversal, which, in itself, is historically contingent. We must play within that contingency, since that is what history has given to us. The wager is that politics is not founded on any *a priori* principle of men belonging out in public and women in the household; but nor will simply reversing the topology somehow turn the tables on history.

Nevertheless, in this literary example, the reversal does unsettle the situation to a sufficient extent for us to examine the political infrastructure. Again, I am suggesting that theorists have most commonly described that infrastructure in terms of public-private topologies. These have persisted whether one is differentiating between the public institutions of the state and the private interests of capital or of civil society, or celebrating the street as a space of spontaneous political expression and struggle – somehow outside those institutions – to this day.

This cognitive infrastructure is historically produced; it is not essential, it is contingent. In that respect, the infrastructure has strategic value that we cannot overlook. Elsewhere, I have defended received topologies of public and private against, for example, an understandable enthusiasm to replace these with something like a 'commons', free of such distinctions.[1]

Joseph Bedford: Do you oppose the idea of the commons?

Reinhold Martin: I do not oppose it, but I want to distinguish between these ideas, and to insist that they interact with one another. The commons, too, is historically contingent. It is not a metaphysical concept or ideal that descends from above. Actual spaces, in England and elsewhere, were referred to as such.

With political models, it is important to beware of inadvertent idealizations, as distinct from strategic ones. We all know how quickly the public-private dichotomy deconstructs itself. We barely have to do any theoretical work to show the fragility, at best, of that opposition, whether in the contemporary city or in classical Athens. Yet it remains useful under particular circumstances.

For instance, in the piece on the commons to which I am referring, I argue that Michael Hardt and Antonio Negri among others give up on socialism too quickly. They see it as belonging to the same spatio-political system of biopower as liberal capitalism. But those of us who work with cities have to acknowledge and remember that the public-private division that structured Keynesianism and the welfare state in Europe and the UK left behind a set of juridical, economic, political, institutional and physical structures – contradictory and ruined as they may be – on which we can still build.

Over the last forty or fifty years, those institutions have been systematically eroded, but the tide sweeping them away is not inexorable. The battle over the ruins of the welfare state is constant and ongoing. Even history's failures and incomplete projects leave ruins behind. Architects are dealing with this right now, with what remains of social housing in the UK and elsewhere.

We need to learn to live with those ruins rather than throwing out the entire socialist project, or even the reformist social democratic project. We cannot, in some millenarian fashion, try to start from scratch by returning to the fifteenth or sixteenth century to idealize the agrarian commons.

The contemporary *polis* is a heterogeneous space. It is not reducible to these figures. In a sense, that is its strength. In emphasizing this obdurate historicity, I am also attributing a certain priority to material configurations. These infrastructures do not have causal agency per se – that can easily be misconstrued. Rather, they are mediators. They set out a range of conceptual possibilities and delimit a horizon within which these possibilities may be considered, without fully determining the outcome.

To return to Athens – real or imagined – what is intriguing is how often the *Pnyx* just falls right out of the picture. Whether in Aristophanes's play or in Arendt's figurations of the classical past, the actual space of popular assembly seems to cause trouble. That may be due to the troubling enigma of what is historically real. But here I'm speaking as a historian. The argument I presented during the exchange was mostly theoretical. It does gesture towards historical actuality, however, and in the case of my reference to Aristophanes, towards an imaginary that is structured by the actuality of the *Pnyx*. Reshaping that imaginary entails restructuring or at least loosening the bonds imposed by history.

Joseph Bedford: I would like now, to ask you about the idea of hegemony and its relation to symbolism and representation, and to do so particularly in terms of the problem of housing and Red Vienna.

Where Mouffe has argued that hegemony involves articulating links and overlaps between struggles to form a 'we', a bloc and a frontier, that can win in the game of parliamentary democracy, and thus where she sees hegemony as a fight over those structures of representative democracy, you have argued that we should understand agonism as being located within the repeated small technical rituals by which we are governed and therefore that we should think of hegemony as a fight within the now-ubiquitous realm of the social and of biopolitical governance, and not within representational sites of parliament.

> ◄ **Martin:** *Here again, think of kaleidoscopic scale shifts. It is not a matter of choosing between micropolitics and monumentality. As with many other parliament buildings before it, the assault on the US Capitol in January 2021 showed that monuments matter, especially when it comes to the biopolitics of white supremacy.*

I would like to pose this as a question about housing and the case of Red Vienna that Pier Vittorio Aureli has put on the table in this exchange.

Housing *is* as you insisted, a matter of repetitions of small rituals, and practices, in which spaces are delineated from one another based on social norms – children should sleep separately from parents, the bathroom is inside but enclosed, and so on. And these repetitions and rituals are also technical and regulated by regimes of knowledge and discourse. As you put it, evoking a Foucauldian language, they are 'scaled measurements, statistically derived norms, and regulatory parameters stored in charts, databases, filing cabinets, and hard drives'.

But another reason why Red Vienna seemed to matter in this debate as an example of housing was not only because of this element of the repetitions of social and technical rituals, but also because of the question of symbolism, representation and consciousness. I might guess that these aspects were also why Mouffe showed excitement about its potential to exemplify an agonistic conception of architecture. Red Vienna, as Aureli argued, was both part of local level community struggles in its creation and it left a lasting trace upon the city of the meaning of those struggles. For Aureli, it was the very fact that the large courtyard blocks differed in scale from the usual site and scale of bourgeois property development that enabled Red Vienna's housing to stand visibly and symbolically against that bourgeois urban logic. It seems to me that this symbolic dimension of housing also has significance in terms of the way such symbolism relates to what we might call class consciousness, or at least, in Mouffe's terms, group identification.

◄ **Martin:** *I appreciate Aureli's realism in describing social housing in Red Vienna as a matter of political expediency. Still, what looks reformist in one setting can have revolutionary implications in another. Most important is not the architectural legibility of Karl Marx Hof – admirable though it is – but the stark discrepancy between the world to which that housing complex belonged and the one that it's in now. This is a structural discrepancy, running from the macroeconomic to the micropolitical. In this way, historical examples like Red Vienna continue to represent possible ruptures in today's neoliberal fabric.*

◄ **Aureli:** *I agree, and this is exactly why I argue that, in the Red Vienna example, what matters is not the heroic gesture of the building per se as a symbol of socialism, but the tight relationship between policy and typology in which the use of the 'Hof' type becomes emblematic. In cases such as the Karl Marx Hof, the idea of a legible architecture was not limited to mere monumentality. It shaped a plethora of details and spaces, from ornamentation to the provision of social facilities, whose purpose was to make reproduction politically visible as part and parcel of the socialist democratic organization of life.*

So, I want to ask, perhaps in relation to housing or perhaps just in general, what place do you give to the symbolic dimension in your thought? Are you proposing that the symbolic has no place in relation to politics?

Reinhold Martin: In making a literary reference to Aristophanes's play, I hoped that I was clear that we are working in the realm of imagination and of explicit symbolism!

But we can start with the housing question. You are citing a section of my text in which I am indeed indirectly referring to Foucault and to scholarship on modern housing that emphasizes the technical characteristics of architecture and urbanism. That includes zoning, the positions and configurations of bedrooms and the type of construction, including techniques like fireproofing.

In the Arendtian schema, all of these belong to the sphere of the social. Foucault reminds us in his work that the social – not so much in Arendt's sense, but in the sense of the social sciences or social work – arises at a certain point in history. Arendt is less historically or geographically precise. The version of the social that she describes emerges over about two thousand years, during which time the division of labour changes, and other factors that concern her arise.

But already by the nineteenth century, with the rise of industrial capitalism, the managerial and technical sphere of 'the social' did not necessarily rely on the public-private schema. Arendt, I think, somewhat idealized the public-private distinction and hence overstated its collapse into this generalized social sphere. But either way, that subsumption was expressed in the modern, bureaucratic state and, for example, in company towns, or in Haussmann's Paris.

For Foucault, each of those examples entails specific forms of power-knowledge or, in his later work, governmentality.

What happens when we compare these two ways of understanding housing? Following Arendt, one cannot entirely separate housing from the *oikos* – the metaphysical home. That is different from modern housing, whether in Red Vienna or elsewhere. We would therefore have to accept that there is nothing more inherently political, in Arendt's sense, about those housing projects in contrast to other spheres of administration or social arrangement in Europe in the early twentieth century.

In terms of Aureli's argument, then, I agree that such projects are exemplary in a variety of ways, but I disagree that they are fundamentally different. This is where Arendt is helpful. Architecturally, there are certain characteristics that can and should be celebrated. The courtyard is not one of them. The turning inwards, the monumentalizing of the working class in the name of its now-distant historical agency if not autonomy, is not necessarily symbolically redemptive.

◄ **Martin:** *My position here is overstated. Celebrate the courtyard!*

It is true that architecture played a role in that situation that might otherwise have been reduced to some political-economic reality to which the architecture would be secondary. In that case, architecture did do the symbolic, spatial, urban or even typological work that we can expect of the political in its different forms.

The question, however, is whether both the spatial structure and the symbolic structure were essentially fighting the last war: that is, seeking to represent the working class in civic space. In Vienna in the 1920s this was possible. But one hundred years later it is almost inconceivable, not because the historical agency of working class has diminished, but because the international division of labour has resulted in the spatial diffusion of that class. This division is a significant barrier to class solidarity. Where is the working class in New York City? Of course, a centre-periphery geography remains, in which we can still call certain areas working-class neighbourhoods, but that geography does not explain New York's political economy, let alone its imaginative life. We would find it difficult to assimilate the Senegalese community in Harlem, for example, to this structure. The reduction necessary to make Red Vienna a model is anachronistic at best. What is not anachronistic, however, is the need to build class solidarity.

> ◀ **Martin:** *To clarify: Fighting for working-class solidarity does not amount to fighting the 'last war' under global neoliberalism. I only want to emphasize the international character of class conflict. Again, think across kaleidoscopic scales: not merely solidarity among an urban proletariat within a given locale, or among subjects of a nation-state, but also among a truly international class of workers. Still, I would temper my comments slightly: Red Vienna is a fine model.*

Joseph Bedford: Your point here about the problem of class identification today relates to a central point in Mouffe's theoretical project. She asks how to produce consciousness after the working class. How can we produce chains of equivalence around plural struggles, based on plural identities that link local phenomena to a collective consciousness that does not have a uniform force?

Reinhold Martin: That is possible in a pragmatic sense, but not theoretically. The only way that pluralism would hold up philosophically would be to presuppose some spatial limit within which political agency or political organization occurs.

What are the conditions for plurality? My sphere of interest and that of someone else may not coincide. We ought to respect the boundaries of each, as the basis of a robust and authentic *agon*, to use Mouffe's term. But the international division of labour does not respect those boundaries. In dividing a particular task into many tasks distributed around the world, it also connects one worker to another. Our job, our responsibility, is to make the connections.

I do not see any reason, for example, why we cannot think in terms of the specificity of political activity and local interest – and with it, a correspondingly planetary solidarity – not as a chain of equivalences, but as a chain of differences. For better or worse, the clothes we wear link us intimately to someone sweating in a factory on the other side of the world, while simultaneously opening up a nearly unbridgeable gulf.

Joseph Bedford: Hypothetically, one might say that the local working classes of a nation should identify with the immigrant population who have arrived there from other parts of the world on the basis of a shared economic situation; but as Mouffe argues, and as she claims is shown by the capture of working class votes by a right wing populism that pits the traditional working classes against the figure of the foreigner, these articulations are not at all necessarily given by economic conditions alone but must be constructed politically at an ideological register also.

> ◀ **Martin:** *Yes. We should do absolutely everything we can to reject the wedge driven by the far right between native-born workers and immigrants. But it is*

not only the right. See the early, 'neotraditional' aesthetic programme of the Congress for the New Urbanism, mentioned above, for a highly politicized, liberal version of architectural nativism.

So, when you talk about the clothes we wear, are you saying we should identify ourselves with the people that made the clothes across the globe because of their economic condition and because we too ultimately share that economic condition?

Reinhold Martin: It is not that we identify with them. We are not the same. But the intimacy of that relationship is something that we have to acknowledge. It is proximate and bodily, not an ideological abstraction.

Joseph Bedford: But right-wing populism, even in English politics, is precisely, for Mouffe, an example of the fact that people do not currently acknowledge that connection.

It does seem to me then that the argument here is still about class and class consciousness, which goes to the very heart of Mouffe's work.

Can we pivot back to talking about the question of the symbolic dimension of housing though? Even though you say that we would find it difficult to assimilate the Senegalese community in Harlem to the structure offered to us by the case of Red Vienna, is it not the case that still, even the New York housing projects, function as a symbol, offering some kind of visibility in the city to those who cannot afford a home otherwise? Do the housing projects of New York not give symbolic visibility to a particular situation on the economic spectrum?

Reinhold Martin: I agree, but we need to think about this issue dialectically. In a sense, the housing projects in Harlem help to produce a working class, but one that is also specifically racialized, in the American imaginary and demographically, as African-American, or non-white. Those kinds of projects have been attacked from the left and the right as 'ghettos', for their isolation and abstraction, and rightly so.

Yet, when the New York City Housing Authority, under the pressure of austerity from Washington, tries to sell off land on those sites – the park areas and the playgrounds – to make up for budgetary shortfalls, it is the resident groups, the people living in these buildings, who protest. Selling off that land for someone to build on it would integrate the complex more seamlessly into the immediate context, so it may seem counterintuitive for the residents to object. Why would they not want more shops on their site, for example?

The answer reflects a mix of two factors. The first is that the residents recognize this as gentrification, and that the next step will be their own eviction. The second is that they feel a sense of belonging, and selling off land violates the space of solidarity. In that sense, public housing projects in New York *do* function like those in Red Vienna, as sites of solidarity.

So, I am not arguing contrarily for assimilation, at all. What I am arguing is that we cannot turn this into an essentialism, in which all forms of withdrawal and fortification –

architectonic, symbolic and economic – are justifiable. What in one context is ghettoization, is solidarity in another context. Those contexts coexist, so looking for working-class space per se, in a housing project or elsewhere, may not be fruitful. I sympathize with the motives, but I do not see that as a compelling strategy.

Instead, we need to be conscious of our own nostalgia, and clear about what is actually happening. When we identify a particular class with certain forms of production, what does that mean? How does that work spatially, economically, technologically and socially? That identification, too, is available for symbolic expression. But it will not be expressed in the same way as in Red Vienna, because too much has changed.

Even then, the idea of the Viennese working class or the European working class was only possible, as Rosa Luxemburg pointed out a century ago, against the backdrop of European imperialism. That is what I mean in referring to the international division of labour. The old empires, with their class structures, broke up and reshuffled into something else. We cannot just assume that their monuments will remain prototypical in the prescriptive or normative sense. Analytically, even Manfredo Tafuri writing about Red Vienna – to say nothing of other, less dialectically sophisticated architectural historians – remains quite blind to the extra-European conditions of possibility for the European working class.

Today, the problem has become even more vexing, the imperative of class solidarity is even more important and pronounced, and yet the sands have shifted under our collective feet. I only insist on historical specificity.

Joseph Bedford: Since you mention your role as a historian, I would like to ask you to reflect on the distinction between historians and designers in architecture today. Given that readers of this interview will include both architects and historians, would you regard analysis as being more the work of a historian than a designer? When architects are given a problem of designing housing, are the symbolic dimensions larger? In that moment, the architect would have more of a grasp on the symbolic than as analysts of large, complex systems.

Reinhold Martin: Let me give an example that connects to your previous question about the working class, and speaks to the politics of social space. This is a local example, but it is not limited to New York City.

In 2011, when Occupy Wall Street took over Zuccotti Park, the protesters addressed their action towards the physical Wall Street, which is southeast of the park. Immediately to the northwest is Ground Zero. It was quite striking that they made no gesture towards that space, though the memorial and the new office buildings were under construction at the time.

Theoretically, there could have been an Occupy Ground Zero. For that to have happened, all the group would have needed to do would have been to turn around and face in the other direction: northwest. But they did not. My impression is that they did not because their internal solidarity was very fragile. That solidarity was based on an alliance between the middle-class students and members of the intelligentsia who were the protagonists of the occupation, and the labour unions and other more classically proletarian forms of political organization, some of whose constituents – though by no means all – supported the US invasions of Afghanistan and Iraq. If there had been an Occupy Ground Zero, as an anti-imperialist symbolic gesture, it would most likely have split this fragile coalition along very real lines.

Joseph Bedford: Along the lines of Nationalism versus Cosmopolitanism?

Reinhold Martin: Yes. Architecture figures right in the middle of that because we are talking about Ground Zero. Architectural designers and architecture students participated in Occupy Wall Street, and I would assume that they had the acumen and the specialized knowledge to consider the symbolic meanings and repercussions of that type of action. Some artists tried to address the World Financial Center, but Ground Zero was off limits.

This example also demonstrates that what we call design does not simply follow from a politics external to it. Design circumscribes politics. This is not the only level on which politics works, but it certainly is one that remains under-articulated. Design students often ask: 'What do I do? How do I resolve this impossible situation? I have to go out and work in an office', or 'What do I do, even if I have my own practice?'

Joseph Bedford: What do you say to them?

Reinhold Martin: Well, there are always moments of truth. There will be moments when you really have no choice but to say yes or no, and that yes or no will be consequential. In everyday life you are always doing that, always assenting. We all submit to forces we oppose. Professionals, including architects, find themselves in this bind because they are authorized, accredited and employed by powers beyond their control.

◄ **Martin:** *But if you have the right, vote!*

Joseph Bedford: An anecdote from my experience that illustrates that comes to mind. I worked for Architecture Research Office (ARO) on the design of the Goldman Sachs headquarters. It was the mirror image of Zuccotti Park and Ground Zero because ARO's employees had refused to work on the project that they did in Times Square for the United States. I think some of the employees in the office, just before I arrived there, had actually gone to Time Square and protested at the Armed Forces Recruiting Station there that ARO had designed. When I arrived in that office I was put to work on the health and fitness floor of the new Goldman Sachs headquarters at Ground Zero. I was in effect, as to work on the design of what was a finely tuned machine of high finance. I recall the number of defibrillators we had to install everywhere and the private elevator direct from the executive's office to the surgeon's operating theatre on the eleventh floor. That, plus the massive provisions for fitness was precisely the local biopolitical aspect of global high finance.

I found myself similarly unable to work on that kind of a project and I left the office a few months later, ultimately never returning to practice after that.

Reinhold Martin: There is no formula. Your example sounds like one of countless instances in which politics as a perpetual struggle with one's own conscience becomes quite real. Architects certainly do not need to divide themselves in two, as citizens who vote, exercise their rights or speak politically, on the one hand, and as professionals who serve, on the other. The whole ideology of professionalization exists to divide critical consciousness, by distinguishing a citizen or a voter from an employee. It is crucial to refuse that division to whatever extent is feasible. Whether that means pointing out what it means to work for Goldman Sachs or something else is a matter of context.

Joseph Bedford: I would like, now, if I may, to ask you to reflect on a topic central to Sarah Whiting's paper that concerned the possibility of acting 'protectively'. Whiting's projective discourse has challenged us to approach our technical expertise and professional engagement in a cunning way, without relying on creating a critical image.

I agree with your assessment of the importance of concrete material and technical dimensions of architecture. But in her discussion of the legibility of Bjarke Ingels's Superkilen Park project, Whiting proposed a counterpoint to that focus upon the material and technical, which involves rearticulating a new order *through the semiotic aspects of architecture*. That tension speaks to this topic in terms of the choices one faces as an architect. Architects have technical expertise and can engage in background processes without anyone realizing, but architects can also engage by working with super-graphics, colour, ornamentation and other affective and semiotic aspects of architecture.

Reinhold Martin: On the topic of the 'projective' discourse, Whiting and I have been on opposite sides of this for years, and to some extent we still are, in a friendly but real way. I do not presuppose that everybody wants to change the world. Rather, I take as hegemonic the attitude that it would be too inconvenient to work towards major change.

I therefore read such strategies as the one you describe as expressions of a prevailing hegemony. This is also how capital often confronts dissent. Rather than saying 'No', capital – or hegemonic power – says, 'Well, that's okay, but don't go too far'. But in the end, the question is, simply 'Do you dissent?' To which the real answer is usually: 'No'. Which is fine. When someone takes responsibility for such a position, it's clear.

But if you make a pretence of dissenting under the guise of a clever, coy strategy that feigns complicity, then you are in fact complicit with what you supposedly oppose! In any case, I have always thought of the projective debate as basically a fake debate, which covers for the actual neutralization of dissent. It is not a debate about strategies. This debate was never really about whether to confront capital full-on, frontally, or to work within the cracks.

Rather, the debate has been about the necessity of structural change. That is why I have continued to defend something like public housing, as a non-negotiable alternative – potentially – to the dominant order. Even while clearly confronting the spectre of ghettoization and of racism.

The effects of state intervention in housing have certainly been problematic, especially in the United States, where public housing has been entangled with structural racism. Nevertheless, at some point, you either have to be willing to defend that project or not. That is an example of a moment of truth. In the end, the people living in these housing projects have been willing to defend them against privatization despite the contradictions. Why? Because as I said, they know that playing along does not just mean making a deal with the devil, it means eviction.

The notion that 'we can beat the house' is cover for saying that everything is fine, that we are all managing in our own little, technical ways, and that the system just needs a few adjustments. Maybe one person will adjust with a cynical wink, and someone else will do it more earnestly, but the result will be the same: the foreclosure of dissent. I am not saying that this is intentional. But the ruse of foreclosing dissent by feigning agreement says, 'Yes, you are right, but you are being impatient'. Or, it threatens, 'Do you understand that you are going to lose?' Or, 'Do you understand that this is not how we work anymore?' None of which is true.

That is why I reject the premise of the debate to which you are referring, and why we have to change the name of the game: public or private? In other words, rather than asking, 'Who pays for housing?' ask the reverse: 'Why should housing be a commodified privilege and not a political right?' I have been outlining some of the ways in which the underlying public-private distinction deconstructs itself. But deconstruction does not mean collapsing all distinctions into one another. Politically and economically, whatever remains of the social democratic welfare state is under assault from all sides, and right now we must defend what remains, contradictions and all.

Joseph Bedford: Would you call that strategic idealism?

Reinhold Martin: I would call it historical consciousness. In Western Europe, Eastern Europe or the United States, public housing is in ruins. Preventing privatization – selling it all to the developers – is a continuous struggle.

Antonio Gramsci makes a distinction between a war of manoeuvre and a war of position. A war of position can entail a multiplicity of agonist struggles like this. Chantal Mouffe's and Ernesto Laclau's work reflects this. They do not insist upon a single revolutionary programme. But there will be moments when the multiplicity must crystallize into something more like a war of manoeuvre, a movement of direct opposition.

Joseph Bedford: Finally, can I also ask for your comment about Ines Weizman's paper, and particularly the strategy of dissidence she discussed, and particularly its relevance to us today in a context which she originally described in the first version of her paper as 'neoliberal authoritarianism'?

Reinhold Martin: We are in the machine; for those of us who benefit, this is a comfortable place to be. Western capitalism is not East Germany, but it is still a machine, and it is killing people every day. So, what does dissidence, when enacted by professional practitioners, look like from within this machine? There are many possible answers, but one can certainly imagine dissidence.

Standing up for public housing, social housing, is one answer. I can also imagine refusing to participate in a competition, like the one for the new Guggenheim [in Helsinki], because of what is happening in the Middle East with workers on construction sites in Abu Dhabi, including the new Guggenheim there.

Examples tend to be transnational these days, but they can be very local, too. Either way, the opposition to critical work must be understood as ultimately anti-socialist or anti-communist. That is what *projective* really means. It is based on the fear that all modern utopias tended towards totalitarianism, usually either communist or socialist rather than fascist. That is the coded message.

Another type of anti-communism, which Weizman described, appears when someone says, 'We need to stop criticizing and just make projects'. Regardless of the political convictions of the people making these projects, the projects themselves – what gets built – typically end up reproducing the status quo. Even if they are not built, designs must comply with the status quo in order to be legible as 'real'. Everything else, including socialist dissidence from within, is dismissed as mere critique.

In the discussion with Mouffe, we started to talk about what socialist strategy is today, or what it should be. I suggested that it should include housing. For architecture, housing is the sphere most available for testing and experimentation. But what is masked by all of this is shaped by the burdens of our own times. We are close enough to the socialist experiments of the twentieth century to be aware of the dangers, and yet we are not far enough away to be willing to take the necessary risks. We are in an intermediate moment where there is not enough critical distance. But that is starting to change.

For example, the new historiography of modern architecture in Eastern Europe is very interesting because its tone is distinct from that of the Washington consensus, or from Francis Fukuyama's *End of History*, after the Berlin Wall has fallen and we celebrate our liberal capitalist future.[2] The work that many scholars are doing today on Eastern European socialism in architecture and urbanism tells quite a different story. Red Vienna looks different when we see it from this perspective, as do some of the examples explained by Weizman. This is neither to idealize nor to demonize the socialist project, the nuances and complexities of which we ought to be able to discuss. We must be able to speak about these phenomena together.

Joseph Bedford: Do you think there is such a thing then, today, of an architecture that could be against capitalism?

Reinhold Martin: I am not sure that, when it really comes down to it, we can find any real anti-capitalism in most modern architecture. After all, every good capitalist is in some ways already an anti-capitalist. That's the whole idea. Anti-capitalism begins on Wall Street itself, with resigned objection to the immorality of it all, and with an emotional, moralistic and almost theological rejection of the premises with which one operates nonetheless. That is: moralizing anti-capitalism as capitalist ideology.

We could try to formulate alternatives for architecture. But these would probably be ineffectual. The proof is what happens in architecture schools every day. Almost every jury I have ever been on has been somehow critical of the 'system', in one way or another. And yet most of the projects discussed beautifully reproduce that system. No one is giving instructions. The reproduction happens from within.

Joseph Bedford: If you are doubtful about the possibilities of architecture today being positioned against capitalism, I wonder whether your position is ultimately similar to that of Manfredo Tafuri, who seemed to think that there could not really be an anti-capitalist architecture. For Tafuri, this pessimism about the possibilities of architecture led him ultimately to choose the path of the historian in place of that of the designer.

Reinhold Martin: I find Tafuri to be one of the few modernist architectural historians worth arguing with, if not the only one. Tafuri is a mature thinker; by comparison the rest can at times seem infantile. He poses the most difficult questions.

Most historians are academics, and we might presume academia to be a privileged site of dissidence, or at least of comparatively unconstrained political speech, especially in the United States. But it is not that. Yes, it may be a little easier to have the discussion we were just having, about rolling up our sleeves to design a socialist future, in the academy rather than in a more commercial environment. Still, we might have to do so quietly, because someone might get suspicious.

In any case, design is not discourse. What I look for from designers is a surprise or a challenge. As a historian or a theorist, I am not looking to give anyone instructions. This repeats my opening point that the way that the world is made shapes our thoughts just as much as our thoughts shape that world. If the traffic is one way, where theory gives instructions and practice follows, it is both uninteresting and theoretically problematic. My earlier example of turning around at Ground Zero was a metaphor for many other things.

The imagination of many designers is so profoundly constrained that, even in their dissidence, and in their reflexive and sometimes even angry reaction to the world that is given to them, they are unable to recognize alternatives.

Again: The fact remains that in capitalist countries, even old-fashioned, public sector, social housing is not understood by most architects, critics, theorists and historians, as an available historical alternative. In US architecture schools, for example, designing real social housing remains almost inconceivable. It does not even occur to most housing designers. That is why we have to start there, contradictions and all. Designers need to understand that the real moment of truth arrives when they say it would be unrealistic to do something different. That is when reality becomes real – not under the so-called real-world constraints imposed by a client, but in the imagination of the designer. That the imagination of students or that of their teachers is so constrained that they cannot even imagine another set of constraints is shocking.

Joseph Bedford: So, it has less to do with practical limits than with imaginative limits then?

Reinhold Martin: For me, as a teacher, those are the front lines of the battle, for which it is not a matter of imposing a dogma, but of opening students' minds to possibilities, by encouraging them to understand that, for those who do object to what is given, the implications of their dissent may not be fully evident. I try to explain how one step implies another, and another, and so on. And so why not cross the first line, and at least reopen the housing question? After that, what about this other line? And so on. This pedagogical work, which is also the work of exercising the political imagination, has to be done very concretely and patiently. It is not done with slogans, formulas, paradigms or archetypes. That is another reason that, while I sympathize with what Aureli wants to do with Red Vienna, I find it to be a shortcut.

> ◄ **Aureli:** *But why is the Red Vienna example a shortcut? Are not its policy, its land use strategies, its debt-free financial tactics, its architectural legibility and consistency what make this example still relevant today? Moreover, it is precisely its municipal scale that makes it feasible, given that municipal politics have been in the last two decades the only favourable ground for socialist politics such as in cities like the Barcelona of Ada Colau.*

Joseph Bedford: And, like you said, it is a form of battle. To come full circle, the polemic about taking more seriously the small techniques of daily life is a way to prompt the imagination of designers differently because they so often get hung up on solidarity or the symbolic.

Reinhold Martin: Yes, that would be one strategy. There are many possible moves in this game. It is a strategic game, and like all games, it takes a while to play out. I do not know what the end game is, but I do know that I am not going to settle for the status quo. Simply accepting the rules as given is a ruse. Students need to learn that human societies – human, social beings – have collectively produced those rules over time, historically. This does not mean that I, as an individual, can change those rules. But collectively, we can act.

I know it can be exasperating, but remember too that we are most often not seeing the whole picture. Remember the classically Foucauldian axiom, that power generates the order of things, or the rules of the game. If you want to oppose that power, you have to contest its rules; and if you want to change those rules, you have to oppose the power that makes them.

Notes

1. Reinhold Martin, 'Public and Common(s)', *Places Journal* (January 2013) https://doi.org/10.22269/130124
2. Francis Fukuyama, *The End of History and the Last Man* (New York: Free Press, 1992).

5

Mobilizing Dissent: The Possible Architecture of the Governed

Ines Weizman

Chantal Mouffe and Ernesto Laclau's book *Hegemony and Socialist Strategy* was formative reading for me, as it was for many of my colleagues, while we were writing our doctoral dissertations in the social sciences in the UK in the early 2000s.[1] My dissertation was in architecture, and was concerned with the transformation of East German cities during the meltdown of the Cold War and the dismantling of the Iron Curtain.[2] Small tears were visible everywhere throughout the 1980s but the speed and power of the collapse were shocking. My work attempted to examine architecture as a symptom of this transformation – looking at it was like a seismograph showing the terms in which the reunification of Germany in 1990 had radically transformed East German cities like Leipzig, where I grew up. My dissertation was written in a cultural environment that had no interest in the final years of the communist regimes. Mouffe's and Laclau's theoretical writing offered a lifeline in that they promised to reconnect me, us, to a political world torn apart all too abruptly, deservedly, but some of its values were dismissed with it, and thus *Hegemony and Socialist Strategy* allowed me to reconnect – from another entry point – to a project I did not want to abandon: of reinvigorating the struggle of the Left in my new home in the West.

In the early 1990s, a mere couple of years after reunification, I began studying architecture in Weimar, in the same building of the Staatliches Bauhaus founded there in 1919. None of my architecture professors had been there during the GDR days. We were taught by new appointees from the West. Like political commissars they were there to make sure no continuity with state socialism existed. Where had the old professors gone? They must have been deemed ideologically unsuited to educating a generation of former East Germans in democratic values. Yet, with the loss of the system I also felt the loss of political spirit almost immediately.[3]

The political matrix I had grown up in was riddled with contradictions. The meltdown years of the Cold War were a time of increased dissident activity and a growing opposition movement unfolding against the massive backdrop of 'real existing socialism', a defunct, ideologically and financially corrupt state apparatus that admitted its failures in achieving the aim of communism. The term had been used by ruling parties since the 1960s to describe the so-called realistic limitations of the socialist project. Strands of Left ideology remained, though: support of pan-Africanism, the Non-Aligned Movement and the international anti-colonial struggle was kept alive in major intellectual debates and in much of my schooling. And, of course, there were the dissidents, the subject of my essay here.

Despite restrictions on travel and communication, there was also an awareness and a shared experience of struggles by intellectuals on both sides of the Wall. I am not sure how large of a readership *Hegemony and Socialist Strategy* had in the East, but readership it had. It must have been one of several books traded under the counter by adherents of reform movements. Mouffe's and Laclau's call to recharge critical thinking on the Left was inspiring and encouraging for a group of intellectuals, even if their struggle was then directed elsewhere, and even if it had not yet been forced to deal with the challenge of neoliberal political economics.

Written in 1985, four years before the fall of the Wall, *Hegemony and Socialist Strategy* captures well the sense of disappointment and disillusionment: 'From Budapest to Prague and the Polish coup d'état, from Kabul to the sequels of Communist victory in Vietnam and Cambodia, a question mark has fallen more and more heavily over a whole way of conceiving both socialism and the roads that should lead to it.'[4] Indeed, by that time, 'real existing socialism' became, as Slavoj Žižek later put it, 'a proof of socialism's utter failure'.[5]

There was an unlikely corollary in my field. Architecture is perhaps the least likely of practices to articulate a dissident position. Producing buildings requires political powers that are largely conservative and institutional – land and capital. But situated at the confluence of political, commercial, financial, military, ideological and cultural forces, architecture has the potential to serve as a medium in which ideas of resistance, critique, reform or evasion can be articulated through different forms of subversion and evasion. Architectural dissidence was a form of political action. Through withdrawal from state-sponsored production, or insistence upon design features that would interfere with the attempted efficiency of the planning system, it transformed the conceptual matrix of urban production from dim solutions to statistical problems of housing (which is what the Soviet Bloc was reduced to in its later years) to a realm of fantasy and subversive critique. The questions I wanted to ask were: What happened to them? and How could their practice inform the activist architect of today?

In our exchange, where I presented the work of some architect dissidents in Eastern Bloc societies, Chantal Mouffe seems to have doubted such practices existed, or if they were, that they had any value. Yet I still think that the political topics of democratic politics that Mouffe and Laclau were advocating share a discursive space, strategies and history with those subjects and political activists who had struggled against the past regime. Those dissidents were not operating within democratic or democratically elected institutions, nor could they risk discussions in the open, nor could they be efficient in isolated action. Agonism would have landed them in jail or worst. Rather, they had to combine a difficult mix of strategies of 'engagement' with and 'exodus' from the regime in order to be efficient in the long term. The fact that their actions were often intended to be hidden, ephemeral and disguised – techniques of withdrawal – makes the work of the historian looking for traces quite challenging.

'A spectre haunts Europe: the dissident', wrote psychoanalytical scholar Julia Kristeva in 1977, the year when the first conference to monitor the Helsinki Accords was held in Belgrade.[6] Replacing Marx's revolutionary communist with the 1977 Soviet Bloc dissident – a figure who was operating against precisely those states that claimed to be Marxist – Kristeva hailed an independent intellectual avant-garde that was the instrument of a new discursive rationality with the ability to 'break through' the closed institutions of the family, the state and the Party. She described dissidence as the politicizing of the effort of thought.[7] With a Lacanian undertone, she connected aesthetics and the political in the dissident's attempt to continuously break cultural hegemonies: 'There is a new synthesis between sense, sound, gesture and colour, the master discourses begin to drift and the simple rational coherence of cultural and institutional codes breaks down.'[8] Taking the 'master discourse' to its revolutionary conclusion demands an ongoing dissent that is never satisfied. Even if stated goals have been met, it remains oppositional and contrarian in nature.

Few people these days remember that Human Rights Watch, an organization that reports on human rights violations and abusive governments across the world, started as a private American NGO in 1978 under the name of Helsinki Watch. The organization tasked itself with observing the compliance of former Soviet Bloc countries with the Helsinki Accords of 1975, which sought to guarantee individual freedom. This group, along with many others, reported on and supported Eastern European dissidents. On the eastern side of the Iron Curtain, the Moscow Helsinki Group was formed, as was Charter 77 in Czechoslovakia and in 1979 the Helsinki Watch Group in Poland, amongst others. The spectre of the dissident haunted the final decade of the Communist Bloc and contributed to its meltdown.

While Western human rights activists could use the media for 'naming and shaming', Soviet Bloc dissidents had to operate largely underground, using painstakingly prepared *samizdat* publications, declarations, exhibitions, performances, gatherings, open letters and communiqués under the omnipresent risk of state persecution, physical violence, imprisonment, forced exile, social discrimination and abuse. To be a little diagrammatic, we could say that on the one side of the Wall was the Western *activist*, while on the other was the Eastern *dissident*. The former is the prominent model for political engagement in the world, while the latter – now seemingly extinct – is a model of retreat from it.

The main reason for the disappearance of 'dissidentism' is obviously the collapse of the Soviet Bloc states that gave it a target and meaning. But the dissidents of Eastern Europe wanted mostly to reform their regimes rather than upturn them. 'Dissidence' is used here to mean a political practice that does not seek to overthrow and replace a government, to take over the power to govern, but one determined to radically and fundamentally contest the way in which people are governed. It is a fundamental questioning of professional, cultural and political conventions.

During the Cold War, architectural dissent was articulated mostly by *refusal* – a refusal to participate in state projects that seemed stale, grey, bureaucratic and lacking in spirit and beauty. It was also articulated by *subversion* – not in the physical world, but conceptually – of the norms and language of dominant or dominating architecture, or by a *retreat* into the private domain of paper architecture or hidden pedagogy, where a space was found.

The violent suppression of protest movements, from East Germany in June 1953, to Hungary in 1956 to Prague in 1968, foreclosed for many of this generation the possibility that communism would be reformed from within. In those years, and in the lead up to the violent clashes with the military forces of the government, a vivid, although secret, underground cultural scene had formed in many cities of the Soviet Bloc. Starting in 1968, Eastern European dissidents increasingly questioned the foundations of the communist system altogether, rather than aiming to reform it.[9]

In May 2008, along with my former supervisor at Cambridge University, I conducted an interview with Dalibor Vesely, an architect from Czechoslovakia who had emigrated during the Prague Spring and who later became a professor of architectural history at Cambridge University. Vesely described to me the way groups of critical architects and artists devoted their personal lives to organizing secret lectures, seminars and even exhibitions that often had to appear and disappear within a few hours: 'It was [in rebelling] against the Soviet-style technocratic and dehumanised architecture that many of us aimed to escape the boundaries of architecture as they were then defined, collaborating with and taking on other engagements such as in stage design, painting and sculpture.'

In order to critique the state or distance itself from it, this quasi-movement of dissident architects had to opt for a form of inner migration. They hoped such withdrawal would allow them to find a community of what the philosopher and co-founder of Charter 77 Jan Patočka called 'spiritual people'. The spirit was pitted against socialist historical materialism. Patočka's embrace of critique – of the 'negative experience of life' – called for replacing utopia with a general acceptance of life's 'problematicity'. Vesely and Patočka thought that the most effective practice of critique was to wonder.[10] Again, this is a form of political withdrawal that is not in the world, although it is intensely political. Influenced by readings of humanist philosophy and phenomenology (partly discussed in the Chartists' 'underground university') and by the works of the Surrealist movement, architects and artists engaged in collective dreaming and other exercises in enhanced subjectivity, a retreat into a private realm as the last bastion of freedom, where they could more easily avoid political conformity and artistic instrumentalization.

For young architects, an important impulse manifested itself in the late 1970s, when the Central Glass International Architectural Design Competition in Japan and the architectural journals *The Japan Architect* and *a+u* started to call for overseas entries to international competitions of ideas without requiring an entrance fee. It was these platforms that enabled architects and students from all of the communist countries to present their work internationally. The submissions were in many ways indicative of the art of imagination. Every corner of the draft or submission papers was filled with architectural details, perspectival views, façades and spatial narratives. Most indicative was the use of traditional drawing techniques combined with watercolours and even elaborate etchings. The project for a 'Columbarium Habitabile', which Alexander Brodsky and Ilya Utkin submitted to a competition of the Union of Architects of the Soviet Union in 1984 and again to the Shinkenchiku Competition of *The Japan Architect* in 1986, proposed a colossal archive in which plans, models and other documents drawn from Moscow's historical architecture would be filed. It presented a surreal setting that commented ironically on the dilapidation and neglect of the historical city. These drawings conveyed fossilized time: firstly, through the time necessary for the labour of completing their drawings. This time was an inefficient investment in the functionalist environment of socialism. Secondly, the images depicted the layers of historical time that are inherent in architecture. But the etchings also created the temporal illusion of having been created in the past. Moreover, the antiquated and operose gesture of the needle cutting into the plate (which also allows for the reproduction and further circulation of the work) and the melancholic romanticism of their motives created a sense of despair that in its sheer 'inefficiency', absurd lethargy and bizarre search for beauty amounted to a political statement.

A different strategy of subversion can be seen in the work of the architects Vladislav and Ludmila Kirpichev in Moscow. In the late 1970s and 1980s, they founded the Experimentalnaya Detskaya Arkhitekturnaya Studia (EDAS), exercising a form of dissidence in workshops that encouraged children and young adults to express their fantasies through drawings and architectural design. Today, this practice can be regarded as being situated between pedagogy and therapy – a 'repairing' of the suppressed imagination of youth living under communism. Teaching made it conceivable to liberate private imaginations and collective fantasy. Children's drawings were effective by virtue of conveying an uncontrollable and irresistible message that called for independent thought.

The work of Mikhail Filippov and Nadezhda Bronzova referenced the Baroque period of the eighteenth century. Here it was the reinvigoration of history, represented in classicist architecture but perfected in antiquated watercolour paintings, that emphasized minute architectural and scenic details, essentially highlighting the blind spots of the 'technocratic regime'. In their work, dissent was articulated by stylistic irony and the use of pencils and watercolours rather than the modernist hard line. Imagination, even the imagination of a historical period, was conceived of as a locus of liberation. The very idea of utopia was seen as totalitarian, obsessed with efficiency and bureaucratic control, while imagination combined nostalgia and fantasy.

In none of the Soviet Bloc countries was it imaginable to simply mail the submissions to the competition organizers in Japan. Rather, participation was feasible only through an intermediate architects' association that managed, censored and decided which submissions could be forwarded to Western magazines. Helen Stratford, an architect and theorist who researched Soviet-era architecture, described how in Romania entries were first collected and discussed by the Romanian Union of Architects, and that participating architects needed additional certification to have their works sent off.[11] The Romanian secret service, the notorious Securitate, was well-informed and even held copies of the individual architectural entries – so much for the non-political nature of the work. One day there should be an exhibition of architectural drawings from the collections of the KGB, the Securitate and the Stasi.

But this perhaps frustrating necessity of collecting works also had the effect of bringing together architects who later formed groups in informal shows. In Romania, students from architecture schools in Bucharest and Timişoara, after some exposure in the Japanese competitions, formed groups and initiated exhibitions. The group Form-Trans-Inform, under Constantin Petcu, also developed alternative teaching programmes that included conceptual research in collaboration with philosophers, artists and scientists, as well as performances and events.[12]

In 1978, architects in Tallinn (later grouped together as the Tallinn School) organized an architectural exhibition in which they showed evocative collages, photographs and conceptual drawings that effectively functioned as an unambiguous comment on the degradation of a profession that had had to subsume itself to the planning economy and the simplifications of standardized constructions.[13]

In 1984, a group of architects from the MArchI Institute in Moscow collected work for an exhibition titled 'Paper Architects'. This led to the best-known of all Soviet-era movements at the time. The group included architects Yuri Avvakumov, Michael Belov, Alexander Brodsky and Ilya Utkin, Iskander Galimov, Mikhail Filippov and Nadia Bronzova. They became well known for presenting their work in various international exhibitions. Their most visible exhibition was at the Venice Architecture Biennale of 1991. Their invitation to present at the Russian Pavilion was a sign that political transformation had already occurred. But the exhibition coincided with the August coup and with the almost daily announcements of former Soviet republics breaking away. Iskander Galimov, whose drawing 'City Cathedral' depicted a dreamy version of St. Basil's Cathedral on Red Square and was used for the exhibition poster, decided not to return to Moscow and settled permanently in Austria (Figure 5). Since the mid-1980s, when control over artistic expression in the Eastern Bloc somewhat eased, Galimov experimented with the use of architectural allegories, assembling an eclectic archive of the icons of architectural history into imaginary structures. Using the finest ink lines and seeking freedom in the endlessness of perspectival depth and minute detailing, he understood his work as a simultaneous call to expand the limited choice of available references in Soviet architecture and to rebel against its ideological underpinnings (Figure 6). The ship of fools was a common trope in the Soviet art of the Glasnost years. It also acquired several architectural articulations. In 1989, Iskander Galimov and his collaborator Michael Fadeyev submitted a red-toned gouache painting on this theme together with a set of detailed architectural plans, sections and structural calculations as their entry to an ideas competition for a Russian Centre in Bologna

How Is Architecture Political?

Figure 5 City Cathedral. Iskander Galimov, 1989. Image courtesy of Iskander Galimov.

Figure 6 St. Peters. Iskander Galimov, 1988. Image courtesy of Iskander Galimov.

(Figure 7). A gigantic ship loaded with Russian monasteries, church spires and Kremlin-like fortresses is 'beached' at the edge of a generic block-city. The oarsmen who propel the ship are unaware that their vessel is no longer mobile. In this architectural proposal, they aim critical barbs both forwards and backwards in time, at the old Soviet system and its all-too-rapid adoption of the safe refuge of myopic nationalism.

In the early 1990s, the historicist architecture of Filippov and Utkin began to inform an emergent post-Soviet architecture. Filippov's drawings of neoclassicist architecture had previously conveyed a form of critique, but were now understood in the context of the creeping and strange post-Soviet melancholy. They began to resemble what the Moscow skyline would gradually become. The towers he depicted hanging over the grey city began to be rebuilt as churches (constructed or reconstructed). Belov became increasingly known for his designs for residences in the form of ancient settlements and amphitheatres, built with massive stone walls and columns in classical orders. The historicist gestures of some of the now post-Soviet paper architects aligned them with what the West called postmodernism. And, as in the West, this architecture

Figure 7 Russian Centre in Bologna, Italy. Iskander Galimov in collaboration with Michail Fadeyev, 1989.

suited the new corporate, neo-liberal culture that began to prevail in the privatizing East of the 1990s.

An example from East Germany presents a rather extreme case within the possible spectrum of architectural dissidence. In the work of the architects Christian Enzmann and Bernd Ettel, imagination and fantasy did not remain in the domain of the private, but rather burst the elastic boundary between private dissidence and its public expression with dramatic effects and grave personal consequences. The two architects, who were research fellows at the architecture school in Weimar, smuggled competition briefs from West Berlin into the GDR and smuggled out their submissions with the help of a network of Austrian monks. Their drawings were formatted to letter-sized sheets in order to deal with the constraints of their perilous journey from East to West Berlin. The unlucky moment occurred in 1983, when one of the jury members reviewing Enzmann and Ettel's submissions in West Berlin was most likely a Stasi informer and alerted the East German authorities.

The competition was the first in a series of competitions for a new building in Berlin now known as the 'Topography of Terror'. The drawing was headed by four lines in large type that read, '*Diktatur*' (dictatorship) (Figure 8). Rather than making reference

Figure 8 Competition for Prince-Albrecht-Areal. West Berlin. Christian Enzmann and Bernd Ettel, 1983–4. Image courtesy of Christian Enzmann and Bernd Ettel.

to the dictatorship of the Third Reich, they drew part of the Wall, watchtowers and tree-lined pathways in an apparently idyllic landscape design, making an obvious but ironic connection to the architecture of surveillance under the GDR regime. They operated by seeking to produce architectural narratives that were legible in built-form.

Astoundingly, while this smuggling operation was underway, the young architects participated in two more competitions in East Berlin, proposing even more radical designs that explicitly confronted the regime. The project description for the competition for Bersarinplatz in Berlin presented a laconically overstated urban allegory, both drawn in ink-rendered axonometrics and clearly presented in a model that they also submitted to the competition (Figure 9 and Figure 10). It proposed that a cannon-like machine be placed at the centre of the square and which would 'shoot' citizens into freedom. Yet a net positioned nearby would make sure that the escape would fail, and that citizens would instead be captured and imprisoned in small allotments. The architects chose to confront the regime, expressing their dissent in drawing and fully aware of the consequences.

They aimed to push the system in order to expose the limits of its intolerance, which were still very real during the gradual meltdown of the Eastern Bloc. Or perhaps

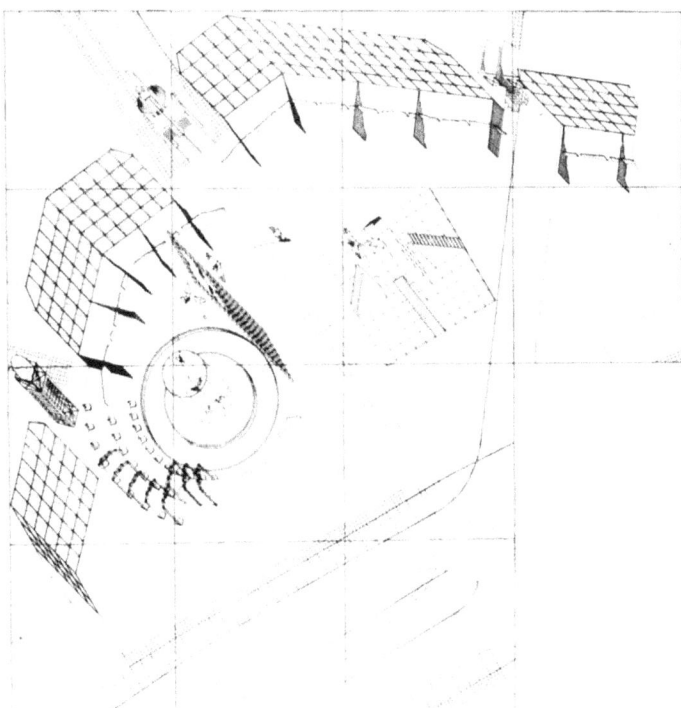

Figure 9 Axonometry submitted to urban design competition for Bersarin Platz, Christian Enzmann and Bernd Ettel, 1984. Image courtesy of Christian Enzmann and Bernd Ettel.

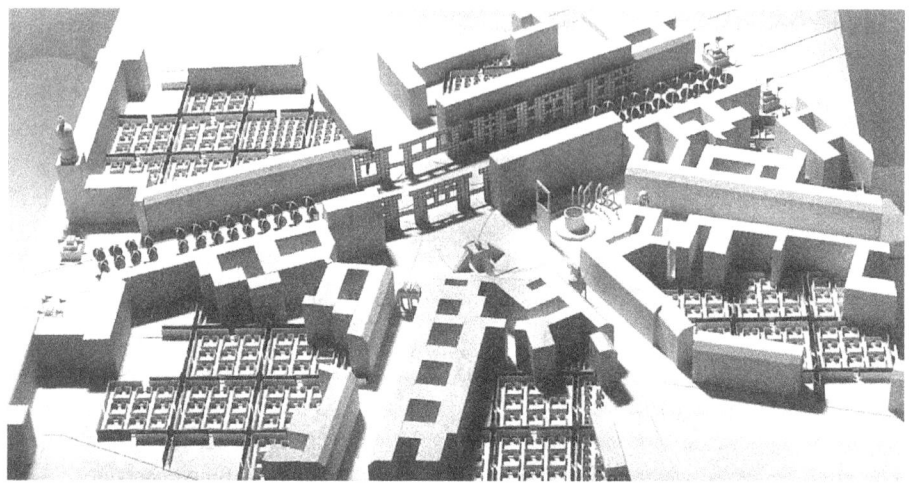

Figure 10 Photograph of model submitted to urban design competition for Bersarin Platz, Christian Enzmann and Bernd Ettel, 1984. Image courtesy of Christian Enzmann and Bernd Ettel.

they were eager to be deported to the West. Either way, they preferred to go to prison on their way out of the country.[14] If we think of dissident practices as a rather delicate interplay between the private and the public domain, between subtle gestures of refusal, subversion and outspoken critique, the work of Enzmann and Ettel pushed this boundary. In its radicalism, it perhaps marks the limit in the possible range of dissident architecture. Here the rules were broken, rather than observed differently. By seeking to provoke a 'crisis', the two self-declared enemies of communism practised the utmost tactic of revolutionary socialism. The two architects were captured and charged with offending the GDR and were imprisoned for twenty months. In the anonymous competition for the site of 'Topography of Terror', their entry had been not recognized and had not even made it to the second stage. After their release in 1986, they were left unemployed until they managed to exit to West Berlin at the end of 1988, merely a year before the fall of the Wall.

The imagery of flight and escape was very popular in Soviet-era art. Ilja Kabakov's 1986 installation 'The Man Who Flew into Space from His Apartment' illustrated quite fittingly the urge of the individual who was trying to break free of the state's tired claims of communist utopia (this time by slingshot). The room, decorated in communist paraphernalia and housing a makeshift slingshot from which the 'hero' had apparently catapulted himself into space, had to be installed in and removed from private apartments in order to be shown only to an underground scene of artists, architects and intellectuals. Numerous such exhibitions and installations were held throughout the Soviet Bloc without any record or testimony.

Most architects I have interviewed have claimed that their forms of protest had nothing to do with dissidence – a designation they reserve for the heroic sacrifice of 'political dissidents', many of whom were imprisoned, killed or tortured. I agree to an extent, but I argue that there are dissident practices, dissident moves and dissident gestures that were camouflaged in the technical language of architecture, in drawn and built forms. I also would dare to say that as my research progressed, their understanding of the term 'dissidence' also shifted, and the architects interviewed began to feel more comfortable with the designation.

The activities of dissident architects were not primarily directed at the removal or even reform of a regime, but rather at the expansion of a sphere of autonomous action. Gestures of refusal, disagreement with professional conventions and the creation of an autonomous realm of creativity and freedom are essential when understanding what dissident agency could mean in the field of architecture. Dissidence might just be a different name for the complex practice that continually questions the relationship between architect and political power, between client and service provider, between ideology and built form. It might be the name for the practice that continually engages, measures and challenges this variable distance.

What these activities share is an essential component of real politics – discontent – transformed into aesthetic practice. Finding a balance between its limiting concepts is the challenge presented when practising dissidence. It aims to take the civic passion for conflict, confrontation, struggle and resistance and to mobilize these things in support of a radical reorganization of the existing structure of power. And it does so without assuming a horizon of ultimate satisfaction and a moment of absolute liberation. As such, dissidence could never be a purely ideological practice; it merely inserts itself as a negative political practice. Dissidents would find themselves at odds with any political or ideological hegemony.

This form of practice blurs the often too-clearly drawn distinction between activism and dissidence. Although both activists and dissidents are perceived as critical, largely progressive forces, their motivation is different. Whereas activists take action in the real world, constantly and overtly pushing the boundaries of what's possible in the political realm, dissident aesthetics quite often represent a retreat into the imaginary, ironic, dreamlike and impossible. The sites of dissident architecture were the *kitchens* – private sites of social interaction and production behind closed doors – and the *paper* – the ultimate site of architectural fantasies that did not need to be materialized. If the dissidents' retreat and their work of fantasy and imagination were indeed a political gesture, the activists' modes of action were engagement, potential co-option, collaboration and subversion of norms.

In the present context of architectural discourse-practice, with the cloud of dust and rubble from the collapse of the titan star-architects of the '68 generation, it is essential to expand on the given options of architectural action and add dissidence to the architectural and spatial realm of the possible. Contemporary architectural and other aesthetic practices have in recent years developed a host of new strategies and techniques for articulating their distance from and critique of dominant political and financial structures. They come across problems and paradoxes and must navigate complex political force fields and possible complicities. Perhaps contemporary political action must fuse the spirit of the activist with the ghost of the dissident.

Notes

1. A version of this essay was previously published and presented in: Ines Weizman, 'Citizenship', in *The SAGE Handbook of Architectural Theory*, ed. C. Greig Crysler, Stephen Cairns and Hilde Heynen (London: Sage, 2012), 107–20; Ines Weizman, '*Dissidence through Architecture*', *in* Kurt Evans, Iben Falconer and Ian Mills, *Perspecta 45: Agency* (Cambridge, MA: MIT Press, 2012), 27–38; Ines Weizman ed., *Architecture and the Paradox of Dissidence* (Milton Park: Routledge, 2014); Ines Weizman ed., 'Dissidence through Architecture', *Architecture and Culture* 2, no. 1 (2014). Ines Weizman, *Documentary Architecture. Dissidence through Architecture, Arquitectura Documental. Disidencia a Través de la Arquitectura* (Santiago de Chile: ARQ Ediciones, 2020).
2. Ines Weizman, *Iron Curtain, Plastered Walls: The Architectural Transformation of Former East German Cities* (Dissertation: Architectural Association, 2005).
3. In 2016, I presented an exhibition as part of the International Bauhaus-Colloquium at the Bauhaus-Universität Weimar that researched the academic discourse at the Hochschule für Architektur und Bauwesen (HAB), which to some degree was also part of the reform movements and opposition to the socialist regime. In 1996, the HAB was renamed and reconstituted as Bauhaus-Universität Weimar. See also the website on the history of the International Bauhaus-Kolloquium 1976–2019: https://bauhaus-kolloquium.documentary-architecture.org (accessed 29 January 2023); see Ines Weizman, 'The International Bauhaus-Kolloquium in Weimar (1976–2019): Transcripts of Filmed Interviews', in *Dust & Data: Traces of the Bauhaus across 100 Years*, ed. Id. (Leipzig: Spector Books, 2019), 376–82.
4. Ernesto Laclau and Chantal Mouffe, *Hegemony and Socialist Strategy* (New York and London: Verso Books, 1985), 1.
5. Slavoj Žižek, *On Belief* (Milton Park: Routledge, 2001), 115.
6. Julia Kristeva, 'A New Type of Intellectual: The Dissident', in *The Kristeva Reader*, ed. Toril Moi (Oxford: Blackwell Publishers, 1986), 295.
7. As Kristeva wrote, 'For true dissidence today is perhaps simply what it has always been: thought'. Ibid., 299.
8. Ibid., 294.
9. Ines Weizman, 'Citizenship', in *The SAGE Handbook of Architectural Theory*, ed. C. Greig Crysler, Stephen Cairns and Hilde Heynen (London: Sage, 2012), 107–20.
10. Jan Patočka, 'The Spiritual Person and the Intellectual', in *Living in Problematicity*, trans. Eric Manton (Prague: OIKOYMENH, 2007).

11 Helen Stratford, 'Enclaves of Expression: Resistance by Young Architects to the Physical and Psychological Control of Expression in Romania during the 1980s', *Journal of Architectural Education* 54, no. 4 (2001): 218–28.
12 Ibid.: 221.
13 Andres Kurg, 'Architects of the Tallinn School and the Critique of Soviet Modernism in Estonia', *The Journal of Architecture* 14, no. 1 (2009): 85–108.
14 Ines Weizman, 'Als die Architekten die Revolution verließen. Regimekritiker und Dissidenz in der DDR und Osteuropa vor 1989', in *Vergessene Schulen. Architekturlehre zwischen Reform und Revolte um 1968*, ed. Nina Gribat, Philip Misselwitz, and Matthias Görlich (Leipzig: Spector Books, 2017), 291–306.

Interview

Joseph Bedford: You frame dissidence similarly and differently from the way that Mouffe structures her theory. I would like to start by talking about points of contrast, beginning with hegemony, a concept that is central for her. Based on her reading of Gramsci, she defines the agonist as somebody who tries to wrest power and struggles for hegemonic order. Conversely, for you, the dissident does not seek to overthrow and take over the power of government. Can you reflect on the difference between struggling for hegemony and not doing so?

Ines Weizman: I think the dissident and the agonist share the same struggle for hegemonic order. Both test the political arena of the possible. The dissident might not act with the overtness and perhaps anger in which Mouffe's agonist wrests power, but is instead someone who is manoeuvring against and through a political regime. Gramsci's and Mouffe's agonism describes a more idealized or theorized political agent who is able to confront the consensus for a renewed democracy, while the dissident's political critique and struggle for emancipation from oppressive forces is more embedded in the politics of the everyday as part of one's professional or social practice. I arrived at the figure of the dissident as I encountered them in the fields of art, music, architecture and intellectual discourse under the communist regime. Already telling was the fact that they were hardly known within more established architectural history narratives, neither in the East nor the West. To learn about their efforts, I had to tune into stories of professionals, family and friends' experiences and memories, or scroll through flyers, magazine cuttings or photographic collections, traces of a more intimate life. However, in a political situation in which nothing seemed possible, they exercised enormous creativity in order to become politically active. They were ready to risk their lives, at least the comfort of their lifestyle, to initiate reform. But also, they had to be careful to make their actions and refusals efficient under a regime that structured its power on surveillance and the suppression of freedom of speech. Indeed, dissidents do not necessarily seek to overthrow and take over the power of government. Dissidents would find themselves at odds with any political or ideological hegemony. When the Berlin Wall collapsed, some political activists of the reform and opposition movements felt they had fulfilled their objective and relinquished their critical position towards the regime. Others did not. I am interested in the latter, who keep struggling under whatever regime, never accepting, always alert to the politics that surround them.

Joseph Bedford: So, the true dissident, in that moment of truth when the wall comes down, will always remain a dissident because they never had the ambition to govern?

Ines Weizman: Yes, especially as the collapse of the Wall did not mean that they had achieved the society they had fought for. The moment of truth that you describe lasted only moments, and East Germans were trapped again in a new hegemonic system. The Wall might have collapsed under the internal pressure generated by the people. But the people were unprepared for the degree of power they seemed to have acquired – power which was magnified by a series of global political and economic forces. It had been too much, too quickly. With the recognition that a 'third way' could not be established at short notice came the realization that their defeat of the state now invited a takeover by the eastward expansion of the West, with its own ideologies and institutions. Overwhelmed, the public slumped into a strange mood of inarticulacy. Gradually, the idea of a reunited Germany – a prospect which had barely seemed conceivable a few weeks earlier – began to seem like a promising solution. The reunification of Germany on a legal and political level created an economic, cultural, psychological and spatial vacuum in the New Länder, the regions of the former German Democratic Republic (GDR) which had been incorporated into the Federal Republic. The harshest critics of that takeover were dissidents. Dissidents will always struggle because their goal is never politically consummated, even at that moment when they could take on a role in the hegemonic order.

> ◄ **Aureli:** *In the leftist milieu I grew up within, there was suspicion if not dismissal of political dissidence in the 'Eastern Block' as it was called at the time. Especially after the wall fell and socialism was finally defeated, there was an idea that political dissidents in the East were all in the CIA Payroll, or actively trying to dismantle socialism. What was ignored is precisely what Ines is showing here, that some of these dissidents did not settle in the new liberal democratic regime, and their political aspirations were not exactly the end of socialism. I think this is a very important issue to consider in revisiting the history of 'the end of history'.*

Shumi Bose: What happens at that moment? Does that struggle have to be reconfigured?

Ines Weizman: My field is neither political theory nor philosophy, but architecture. Even within that, it is architectural theory or history. I am interested in the opportunities to be creative which arise at the moment of toppling, but also under conditions in which freedom of expression is suppressed. The energy lies therein, both when people struggle against hegemony and when they achieve it. How may we think of design as inviting this moment of struggle and reform of the social and political order?

Joseph Bedford: In the moment when the Wall came down, was the struggle of some of those dissidents effective? Some of the weaker dissidents were simply struggling for freedom from the ruling regime, but their struggle was over, once the Wall fell. But were some other dissidents able to reconfigure the struggle even after the Wall came down? Were they still opposing something else, related to the new neoliberal market ideology of Eastern Europe, for example?

Ines Weizman: That moment when the Wall came down was a creative moment. Everyone breathed a sigh of relief and thought, 'Great! Now we can think'. Unfortunately, it did not last long. As I said before, after 9 November 1989 we continued the demonstrations that we had started in the summer. By December, calls for reform, free elections and democracy for the people, and freedom of speech were replaced by demands for reunification with the Federal Republic. There were people, including dissidents, who completely withdrew from politics because they could not see past that moment.

Of course, some reformers and opposition leaders were involved in the negotiations for reunification and remained politically active in reunified Germany, but in the field of architecture I would say the break was abrupt and hard. Dissidents began to communicate a sense of political estrangement and alienation from the worlds they had inadvertently brought into being. This was why I wanted to write the story of dissident architects. They felt they had been ignored by the new regime. Almost all who had been employed in the construction industry had lost their jobs. Some were trying to move to West Germany in search of better job opportunities; some decided to retire early; others burned their drawings and cut their ties to colleagues and friends. It is really sad.

Western planners, who seemed to have been waiting for this moment all their lives, leapt into action to 'repair' all that had gone 'wrong' in the 'other' Germany. Rather than seeking to integrate home-grown expertise, the 'cultural occupation' simply rebuilt the entire planning profession, including its historical framework and methodologies, along liberal, Western lines. I am sure Eastern planners would have been able to re-articulate orders, but they simply did not get the chance.

◄ **Martin:** *Yes. Which is also why we still need critical histories of the 'end of history' – which many western liberals associate with the fall of the Berlin Wall – written from the east.*

Joseph Bedford: Is that because dissidence is localized and diffused, since it emerges from a 'bottom-up' process in society? Dissidence comprises diverse constituencies, rather than a unified common cause with a clear identity.

Ines Weizman: Well, yes. Under the communist regime, dissent had to be diffused. Also, in response to your earlier question, I would not think of weaker or stronger dissidents. Reformers and dissidents had to invent – design, perhaps – a whole spectrum of possible ways to exercise their dissent with the regime, some more courageous and outspoken than others. Some confronted the regime directly, ready to face the consequences; others were effective through withdrawal. Often, their actions and gestures were hidden in double meaning, which makes it very difficult for us to detect and appreciate them today. This also makes it hard to understand what kind of constituencies they formed. When simple gestures could potentially betray your political manoeuvre, the blink of an eye could be dangerous and you would not risk leaving documents or evidence behind. But the dissident cannot fully withdraw from society, even not into the realm of dreams and imagination. Artists and architects also exhibited and presented their works to informal groups of friends, in short-lived pop-up apartment shows, or in happenings outside of the city. These things had to be organized, and even if they were not permitted, I think to some degree the regime also allowed them to happen.

Joseph Bedford: That suggests another point of contrast with Mouffe's theory. If dissidence is diverse and pluralistic, then what defines the dissident? Is dissidence connected to ideals of human freedom and human dignity?

Ines Weizman: Yes, of course. But what I experienced as paradoxical was that the regime would also propagate that it was connected to the ideal of human freedom and dignity. Dissidence addressed the moment when, at some point, the hollow claim of the state met the reality of everyday life and the actual possibilities of freedom and dignity. For example, resistance to join the Party was possible, but if you refused it you had to pay the consequences that you could perhaps not progress in your career, your children could not join universities, or that you were intimidated. Best was to avoid being asked to join [laughing]. In addition to being locked in geographically, people were confronted on all sides by a repressive government. What I found so interesting in the work of the dissident architects and artists I researched was that they were trying to find a space that was not subject to surveillance or ideological censorship. That space could literally have been a hiding place, but it could also have been on the drawing board or in an imaginary realm. Joseph, I know you are conducting research on Dalibor Vesely. Something Dalibor always spoke to me about, when I studied at Cambridge under his supervision in the late 1990s, was how in Prague in the 1960s he and other architects and artists engaged in collective dreaming and drawing. In fantasy they could find an alternative realm where they could avoid political conformity and artistic instrumentalization. It was of course a private fantasy, but they discussed it in artistic collectives, among groups of friends, and later in the so-called 'underground university' of Charta 77 in Prague, where they did form alliances and find a shared discourse. Also, there were the so-called 'paper architects' of the Soviet Union, who drew these fantastical worlds in the 1980s when they wanted to participate in a competition in Japan. Their drawings did not remain hidden in drawers. As the young architects wanted to send their drawings to Japan, they had to present their drawings to a party-related architectural board in Moscow. Of course, submitting to this board represented a considerable risk, as it was not clear whether their drawings would be censored and what consequences they would have to face if they were not permitted.

Shumi Bose: You are suggesting, though, that architects can engage in dissidence as a part of their creative practice.

Ines Weizman: Exactly. That is what I was trying to show. Even under a repressive regime, architects working in probably the least likely of practices to articulate a dissident – a political – position found ways to fight the limitations and clumsiness of the regime. They used architectural competitions to undermine the brief, but also to develop architectural proposals that clearly would not be possible under state socialism. Or they used drawing techniques and skills to present a different kind of care for the site and society. Instead of the standard carbon-copied blueprints, they sometimes submitted original drawings, watercolours or copperplate prints. Others stood up in public presentations and debates or refused to participate in competitions and planning projects. I think these practices and the possibility of refusal could still be considered as models for today's architectural practices.

Shumi Bose: Would you draw structural distinctions between dissidence and agonism? Agonism implies disparate groups who gather together around a specific local concern. Dissidence, on the other hand, connotes several marginal practices that strongly oppose a regime, and its practitioners are connected to one another based on much more essential ideas. You are suggesting that the essential idea is to oppose, but what actually connects these actors is not just opposition, but, in fact, creative practice.

Ines Weizman: Well, yes, I would draw a distinction, especially as I respect Chantal's hesitation to acknowledge the dissident. Architects who were ready to confront the regime had to, at some point, present their work to a certain group: either a group of friends, students and colleagues at a university, architecture boards, or even in large-scale housing collectives. I am thinking of Peter Kahane's film *The Architects* (1990), which brings across so well that sentiment and struggle of a group of young architects against the tedium of socialist planning doctrine.

I think the agonist and the dissident are not necessarily different persons, or that they belong to different groups. The agonist/dissident refers to a different methodological spectrum of political struggle through the medium of architecture. Thinking of architects, I have a different diagram in mind. I would see the possibilities of political engagement as a spectrum ranging from more articulated gestures of confronting a regime to those that have the effect of making it difficult for a regime to manifest its power and suppress freedom of speech over the long term. This work of questioning things and studying the structure that makes a problem possible is not directed towards a single moment of salvation, nor necessarily the toppling of a regime; it is necessary in any regime or hegemony as a form of learning and culture of discourse. I think such work needs both the activist and the dissident, and this could be a single figure or a collective. And indeed, what is so interesting to me is to see how the activist and the dissident can work through architecture and creative practice. This is where I would like to move away from political theory and look specifically at case studies in architectural history to see how architects and urban planners have articulated their critique in different political and cultural contexts.

Shumi Bose: That is distinct from agonism. You are suggesting finding a way of practicing that is individual to each practitioner. That mode of critique is necessarily marginal compared with the act of getting together with others.

Ines Weizman: I am not so sure. I came to speak about dissidents as I found them in architectural practices under the communist regime. I wanted to study them because I realized that their struggle, which to some degree led to the toppling of the regime, was not appreciated in the neoliberal environment of post-communism. The reason for this reticence might be the fact that Western historiography seems to assume that dissidents were wrestling with power in order to achieve something like a Western neoliberal state, rather than an alternative model to state socialism. Another reason might be what I have described as the paradox of dissidence, which makes political activism not a clear-cut and unbiased endeavour. To be politically efficient, dissidents sometimes had to take a position with the regime. Architects and planners working along this precipice had to shrewdly navigate being at times incorporated into or complicit with a state's system, normalizing and thus perpetuating its forms of injustice, while using a certain position of influence at another point for a much more efficient confrontation. Foucault said somewhere that we need to escape the dilemma of being either for or against something. Working with a government implies neither subjection nor blanket acceptance. One can work and be intransigent at the same time.

Joseph Bedford: You are returning us to the opening question of hegemony, because the state is the governing power. You are arguing that Mouffe's whole framework is based on a relationship to the power of a hegemonic state.

But the gesture of the dissident to refuse that entirely introduces an anarchist model, in the sense of scattering or individualization of the struggle into many personal practices.

Along the lines of idealism, Mouffe has also been trying to theorize at a bottom-up, local level. She has been trying to reconfigure the left to adopt the anti-essentialist philosophies of Derrida, Freud and Lacan. They argue that there are no universals, like the human, or the idea of human dignity and freedom, that are the absolute bases for struggle. Mouffe asserts that, in a pluralist society, what we can hope to achieve is 'chains of equivalents'; local connections between feminist and ecological struggles. We advocate, legitimately, for so many diverse struggles that we should not try to consolidate under a single, big idea, but rather simply find commonalities between causes.

This is similar to your figure of the dissident, in that the dissident is also quite local. But for her, one is still obliged to form local alliances for the purpose of gaining power. Dissidents, on the other hand, do not seek to expand their own individual practices beyond themselves to make alliances. They operate as anarchists, or at least, as individuals.

Ines Weizman: I do not think that they only work as individuals. Say, to work as an architect, or an artist, or a pedagogue also means to work with alliances, both personal and institutional. You need to comply to some form of professional conduct between commissioner and a user, or through an official curriculum at an architectural school. I still find it productive to look at the points where the dissident and the activist intersect. It is one thing to be in a position of struggle, but it is not enough to just be an individual, with one's own, personal ideals. I think dissidents do make alliances and also seek to expand their own individual practice. I have not encountered them as anarchists, really, but I would say that the dissidents I have in mind were not just concerned with a single political aim: they also shared connections with the feminist and ecological struggle or supported Pan-Africanism and the Non-Aligned Movement. While one struggle was in principle shared with the state and could be articulated openly, others had to be more disguised practices and articulations. As I was not looking for a theoretically abstract figure, but for architects, tracing the contours of the dissident in practice is certainly difficult. But I would strongly agree that the dissident does not struggle against a single enemy, but that the struggle is pluralistic and diverse and develops differently over time. To describe it, or to write its history tasks us to explore anew the intersections of subjectivity, emotional life and the public spheres of law, science and society, but also to acknowledge the silence and gaps in this history.

Joseph Bedford: Are you saying that her theory is incompatible with totalitarian states?

Ines Weizman: Chantal hinted at that, which surprised me. But of course, *Hegemony and Socialist Strategy* was not addressed to work in a totalitarian state. Rather, it was written in light of the disappointment of the political Left with real existing socialism. The totalitarian states had completely ruined the enthusiasm for socialism and the project of the Left. I was surprised that she rejected in some ways the struggle of dissidents of the communist regimes. I thought that the agonist fighting the neoliberal society she advocates would share the discursive space, strategies and history with those subjects and political activists who had struggled against the past regime.

Joseph Bedford: A moment ago you mentioned another difference between your ideas and hers, regarding visibility versus invisibility. She defines agonism through a contrast of adversarial struggle against the struggle of enmity. She prefers adversarial struggle because it accepts all parties to the struggle as legitimate. Rather than trying to vanquish one's opponent, one accepts them as an equal in the fight. She describes that as agonism, whereas setting out to vanquish an enemy is antagonism. You take a different stance. If the agonistic and adversarial mode legitimates the struggle, its visibility might only be possible in a democracy. In a totalitarian situation, on the other hand, struggle itself is illegitimated.

Ines Weizman: In some ways I want to resist having all too harsh distinctions. This is also not how I would write the stories of my protagonists. I rather work in the context of intersectional thinking where one never looks at a single issue alone. From the point of intersection, struggle perhaps, one begins to unpack, navigate and travel outwards along those assembled nodes of knowledge. I think the act of designing something or the analysis of architecture allows us to make visible the contours of politics. In this context it might be a bit overstated to think of 'vanquishing an opponent' or 'accepting an equal in the fight', especially as the lines of power are not running along a constant axis. There is always a certain entanglement with power.

In the late 1980s in East Germany, towards the end of the regime, I experienced the dual reality of what could be said at school and what could be said outside of it in closer circles, such as in my family, that strongly opposed the regime, or in church groups that provided us with a safe space to discuss our opinion freely. It is hard to describe this cultural environment; at the same time, I am still amazed by the complexity of discourse at the time. Even though the regime's power was melting, you still could not trust its apparent openness, as the consequences of critiquing it were harsh. I remember how I got caught up in some kind of treacherous rhetoric of double negation at school when they actually encouraged us to express our critique of socialism. Even though it might seem that under state socialism it was clear who was friend or foe, this was by no means always evident. So in that sense, I think that dissident discourse was not outside of the established political structure. It is a dynamic effort of negotiation to expose, oppose and challenge political power relations.

See, for example, the International Capital Berlin Competition in 1957/8, to which the Senate of West Berlin had invited exclusively Western architects. Architects were so keen to redesign the centre of Berlin that they had overlooked, or had decided to neglect, the fact that the capital of the Federal Republic was Bonn and that Berlin was the capital of the GDR. The general setting of the competition was to launch an affront to the GDR government. Also, the brief of the competition included most of the territory of East Berlin. So, celebrated teams of international architects like the Smithsons, Team X and Le Corbusier happily joined in this provocation. But I am not entirely sure that they were even aware of the political meaning of their visionary design proposals. In some ways, to the organizers, I guess the more visionary the proposal, the more painful it was to be for the Eastern side. I think any questioning of the significance of participation was missing entirely.

Joseph Bedford: Is such an opposition between totalitarianism and democracy viable in our present moment? The way dissidence operated in Eastern Europe under totalitarian regimes suggests that one still has to work to find the place where antagonism can be directly addressed. Your example of the projects for the 1957 Berlin competition shows architects who were oblivious to the actual antagonism in that situation. And, even in the West, one has to draw out that antagonism, to locate where opportunities for struggle or dissent lie. But that implies that even though we think that, in the United States and Europe, we live in democratic states where things are visible and open and subject to debate, we should nevertheless challenge those presumptions. Maybe that is the tension between liberalism and democracy: that in the liberal democracies of the West, we cover over those antagonisms instead of confronting them.

Ines Weizman: Yes, you are right. I think looking particularly at architecture also reveals that it is necessary to operate long-term, or more methodically within some field of critique. I like Chantal's concept of 'chains of equivalents' that might be tied along and through such a field.

When in 2007 the Chinese artist and dissident Ai Weiwei invited me as one of one hundred architects to design a luxurious neighbourhood in Ordos in Inner Mongolia, my initial impulse was not to build at all. I did not want to touch the sands of the Gobi Desert and also felt uncomfortable with the whole setup of inviting Western architects to submit their design fantasies for a context they were not familiar with. As you know, trying not to compete within the economy of the new, I proposed the construction of a building that was never realized, yet which is well known to architects and architecture students. It was the house that the famous and infamous Viennese architect Adolf Loos had designed for African American dancer and entertainer Josephine Baker in 1928 as one of the icons of architectural modernism. The displacement of this project, which could have been an architectural love letter, was intended as a withdrawal from the project, but led to a whole range of questions and findings. From copyright, to doppelgängers, to the architectural details and details of ownership in the work of the architect, his lovers, his publishers, and even his clients, to his hearing impairment and Baker's involvement in the resistance movement, I found areas within a field of operation which I could explore in more depth while still critiquing the project itself.

Critique shifted from the commission itself to questions about inconsistencies in the architect's archive, about preservation, ownership and the political entanglement of contemporary architectural practice.

Joseph Bedford: So, you were acting as a dissident?

Ines Weizman: Not quite, and I say that out of respect for the dissidents and activists who were ready to risk their careers, their livelihoods and even their lives. I was, however, trying to find my own territory. The project came from a position of refusing to play the game.

Joseph Bedford: But it does seem to be analogous, to the ways you describe dissidence in Central Europe under totalitarianism. There were many practices – theatre, art and architecture – and many different ways to orient practice in relation to antagonism.

Ines Weizman: Yes. Look at the dissidents in Prague in 1968. They started their own university, meeting in living rooms, and reading Plato and Aristotle – maybe later Ernesto Laclau and Chantal Mouffe as well. I would not be surprised if their early texts and books were smuggled through. That was, in a sense, a practice. Even if the results were not immediately visible, or being heard, filing complaints, reading poetry, indulging in dreams and theatre design, and employing different drawing techniques from Beaux-Arts traditions were operose gestures that also represented sand in the gears of a regime striving heartlessly towards rationalization and efficiency to achieve dull programmes set in five-year plans. It made politics complicated.

Joseph Bedford: All of a sudden, Plato and Catholicism became radical, since Marxism-Leninism forbade anything that seemed idealist in favour of materialist determinism. It was the complete inverse of everything we know from French politics and political theory, which positioned the Catholic Church as the dominant antagonist. In Prague, Catholicism became the seed of radicalism.

Ines Weizman: Yes, that is completely right. I still remember very well this shielding space of the church. Although Protestant in Bach's St Thomas Church in Leipzig, we had exhilarating semi-secret debates in which we slowly discovered free speech. There are almost no traces of this incredible moment because of the secrecy of the meetings. Some of the radical speakers of then have now passed, friends have dispersed. But when I look at photographs of this time, especially of the Monday demonstrations in Leipzig, I can reconnect to this political energy then. That is also why I researched about before and after photographs of former East German cities after the reunification.

Also, much of the competition work that these Eastern European students and young architects did is all but lost. They sent in their competition entries to the West, but the West did not even recognize them as transgressive. Competition judges thought, 'What a nice submission from Budapest', but did not understand the dangerous circumstances under which these designs had been sent. Some competitions were anonymous, so those acts of transgression were not even visible, as was the case with the two dissidents Enzmann and Ettel in East Berlin, whom I mentioned. They ended up incarcerated in a high-security prison. Without recognition of their dissidence and the price they had to pay, their work went unappreciated by the jurors in West Berlin, where their proposal did not even qualify for the second round. The risks that these architects took show their anger against the regime and their commitment to the field of their practice through which they chose to speak.

Shumi Bose: In that regard, what form does dissident practice take in a setting that we perceive to be liberal and democratic?

Ines Weizman: That is very difficult to say. To a degree, the dissident needs to work on a spectrum that includes the activist. Students have asked me how to do dissident design, but of course it does not work like that. It is trying to explore the limits of the possible. I have written about the spectrum of dissidence, from gentle, discreet, almost invisible practices to outspoken ones, where others might say, 'How could you possibly do that?' But acting too audaciously could have been like driving a truck into the Berlin Wall.

Shumi Bose: That is not a dissident practice. That is a demonstration.

Ines Weizman: Exactly. My case study of the two architects who participated in the Topography of Terror competition in West Berlin was like driving a truck into the Berlin Wall. In their drawings, which they had smuggled through a network of Catholic monks from East Berlin to West Berlin, they clearly stated in capital letters that East Germany was a dictatorship. There was no subtlety anymore. They had transitioned into being activists. They could not hold it in anymore. This was not about testing the limits, but about transgressing the limits of what could be done under an obnoxious regime.

Today we are in a different place, and I am sure there is a whole spectrum available for dissident practice, especially as one totalitarian wall was followed by many more after 1989. Architects and artists are able to work much more closely with political agencies and NGOs and can collaborate in revealing human rights violations, corruption and climate crimes.

Joseph Bedford: You said that the contents of the book were less interesting in dissident action than the culture of transcribing and re-transcribing samizdat texts. Those practices of living are themselves important as a way of registering collective identity, in opposition to a dominant ideology that does not allow it. Does acknowledging that culture, or making it visible, transfer into a democratic situation? Even though we are all apparently able to dissent openly, some things are excluded from our democratic discourse.

In an earlier version of your paper, you used the phrase 'authoritarian capitalism'. That idea stuck with me, that our democracy has an authoritarian quality, in that we are not allowed to say certain things. In that case, might those practices of exchanging texts, or setting up a university in private and domestic spaces still be relevant as ways to say the things we are prohibited from saying, to dissent from the neoliberal agenda?

Ines Weizman: In the moment in which we are speaking, I know that these practices are being performed and that there is a strong critical culture among members of our profession. There is a particularly fascinating relationship between architectural practices and academic institutions, often led by young professionals who try to challenge and reflect on their architectural practice by being involved in research, design experiment, investigative work, exhibition work, interdisciplinary collaborations and public debate. With regards to dissenting from the neoliberal agenda, architecture schools and universities must be – must remain – these unique places of exploration, freedom of thought, experiment and expression.

6

Agonistic Practice

Sarah Whiting

Springboarding from Chantal Mouffe's writing on agonistic artistic practices, I would like to focus on architecture *as a practice*, and on how architectural practice can be political, specifically in agonistic terms.[1] An architectural practice differs from most artistic practices because of its scale, complexities, economies and liabilities, all of which obligate encounters with others who may or may not be sympathetic to the underlying ambitions of the project. That is, architecture requires collaborations that are not among peers or even among those who share any affinities (e.g. contractors, zoning clerks, bank lenders and, of course, clients). These collaborations are *obligatory* relationships and many of them impose constant negotiations and compromises along the way from architectural idea to built work. As such, architecture demands extreme generalism and, at the same time, extreme expertise across a spectrum that runs the gamut from aesthetics to zoning. Furthermore, architecture has a temporality that demands patience – it will never be the fast responder that other cultural players can be. Even the smallest of architecture projects takes time, and, in most circumstances, far more time than planned. Architecture is slow.

I do not foreground architecture's complicated, imbricated and protracted status either as a criticism or as an excuse – it is, simply, a given. It is a given that renders architectural practice already political if one situates the political in the realm of agonistic encounters. As political theorist Lori Jo Marso explains in *Politics with Beauvoir*, 'Without struggle, sans encounter, freedom cannot emerge … Freedom emerges or is lost within collectivity: friction, movement, cooperation, care, and struggle characterize encounters between two or more.'[2] Marso is describing generalized encounters here, but really, it is an ideal description of architectural practice, which invariably oscillates between friction and cooperation. At play, is also the imbalance that exists in almost every one of the obligatory encounters that even the most banal architectural project entails. Architects have to win over clients, banks, zoning boards, neighbours and community boards. In short, architects are almost always disadvantaged on the playing field (or battlefield – pick your metaphor). What is striking is that this political aspect to architectural practice is rarely discussed, let alone understood, by clients, by students of architecture or often by architects themselves. I would like to probe how one might practice consciously as an agonistic architect, rather than only stumbling through this terrain.

I lived until recently in Houston, a city that is well known for its generous private philanthropic support of the arts, but despite that climate there is, in Houston, a significant distinction between support of (or even interest in) architecture and the other arts. Take the home of a significant local patron of contemporary, avant-garde theatre, music and fine arts: he lives in a 20,000-square-foot faux French chateau, which is unremarkable among the houses in the city's wealthy neighbourhoods. This exceedingly intelligent philanthropist is famously progressive when it comes to the fine arts and music – how can his radically contemporary tastes in these other arts not affect his taste in architecture? I do not attribute this failure to stupidity, for he is anything but. Instead, this stifling of progressive potential in architecture results from the control that the market holds over our practices: lenders and realtors set the terms by which clients and patrons determine their options.

Architects often respond to this asphyxiating circumstance by ceding to hegemonic market desires and simply satisfying demand, rather than engaging in encounters. Or they find resistance in retreating to paper architecture, or to practicing only in the realm of installation art, two strategies that remove some of the agonistic players from this complicated practice. Other architects respond by emphasizing technical expertise – digital or material – enabling them to dominate some exchanges by commandeering expertise. One such example lies with Gehry Technologies, which developed an entire integrated project delivery software package that has now been bought out by the corporation Trimble.[3] Specialization and expertise tend to reassure, and thereby optimize marketability. All of these are examples of shirking the political, for every one of these responses is a retreat from the agonistic encounter.

Finally, and importantly, this circumstance is also why practice, understood as *building*, is often so absent from architectural education: practice within a school of architecture can be idealized because the agonistic players can be very controlled. As a design school dean, I defend this idealized model because if students were required to produce financial pro formas for their projects, as so many professionals advocate, they would be afforded very little running room for advancing ideas. But while I believe that we should enable students to design with more agency than they might be afforded in the 'real world', it is absolutely critical for schools to take on the topic of the politics of practice in academic discussions, so that students recognize, understand and anticipate the challenges to come. It is equally, if not more critical for schools to test new modes of practice and to work across media to broaden the public understanding and appreciation of design. One can draw a parallel to other professional schools – medicine, law, engineering – where students have to master precedent and practice, but where research and probing lead to new interpretations, new discoveries and new possibilities. In short, in schools we have an obligation to seed encounters that will truly be political, to return to Marso's terms above.

How might some of these seeds impact practice? I would like to draw the contours of a possible agonistic architectural practice that might help to shore up the fighting power of the architect. For architecture to be political in the agonistic terms that Mouffe lays out, it has to be *projective*. While art practices can remain at the stage of critique – 'pure' agonistic exchange – architecture has to project a possible future state, because of its permanent status, or at least its aspiration to permanence and functionality. One topic I would like to put on the table, then, is that of agonism's temporal status or maybe more simply put, its possible lifespan.

Let me first detour briefly to lay out some context, constructed from Mouffe's writings on art practices. Tellingly, Mouffe opens all of her texts on this subject with the observation that 'art occupies an increasingly central place in our societies, but can it still play a critical role?'[4] Her question is spot on in a world that co-opts criticality at an astonishing rate. Aesthetic strategies that once defined the counterculture are now regularly used to promote the conditions required by the current mode of capitalist regulation. While this diagnosis of the compromising of artistic activism may lead to philosopher Alain Badiou's nihilistic conclusion that 'it is better to do nothing than to contribute to the invention of formal ways of rendering visible that which Empire already recognizes as existent',[5] Mouffe points to some art practices that manage to have an impact despite this seemingly all-consuming condition of capitalist co-option. In her article 'Art and Democracy', published in *Open* in 2008,[6] Mouffe relies on four categories of critical art delineated by Goldsmith's Professor of Art History and Criticism, Richard Noble in his text 'Imagining the Political: Some Provisional Remarks on Art and Politics':[7]

1. art that engages critically with political reality;
2. that explores subject positions or identities defined by otherness, marginality, oppression or victimization;
3. that investigates its own political condition of production and circulation; and
4. utopian experimentation that attempts to imagine alternative ways of living, societies or communities built around values in opposition to the ethos of late capitalism.

These four categories are useful, even if today they can come across as predictable (Noble wrote his provisional remarks already almost twenty years ago). The practitioners he referenced included now familiar names as Hans Haacke, Krzysztof Wodiczko, Thomas Hirschhorn and Barbara Kruger, among others. Kruger has perhaps been the most co-opted of this group, as underscored by a recent posting on *Ploughshares's* literary blog that references the exclusive 'radical' fashion brand, Supreme: 'Supreme's skate decks and t-shirts are splashed with anti-establishment messages styled in a familiar format: a bright red rectangle surrounding a phrase presented in stark white Futura. The similarities are intentional – disliking the initial design options for his brand, [James] Jebbia turned to a book on Barbara Kruger's work for inspiration.'[8] To return to Mouffe's question, can these strategies still be critical today? It's a key question for all practitioners, and, I would argue, for architectural academia as well.

One of the great pleasures of preparing for this exchange has been reading across Mouffe's prolific output. It has offered a clear illustration of how she advances certain topics, moving them slowly through elaboration, tweaking and expansion. *Agonistics*, Mouffe's book of 2013, which has a chapter on 'Agonistic Politics and Artistic Practices', offers yet more examples of art practices, this time without referencing Noble's four initial categories, which, while helpful, are tied to a particular historic moment. *Agonistics* shifts the argument forward. What I do not know – and would like to know – is whether this shift still remains within the category of the critical, or whether her move away from Noble's categories reveals a deliberate critique on Mouffe's part regarding the limits of the critical (again we return to that question – can art still play a critical role?).

I hope it is the latter – that, rather than staying within the mode of critique, Mouffe is pushing for work that is what I would call projective in nature. The projective, as R.E. Somol and I maintained already two decades ago, takes the critical a step beyond critique by offering a model that does not just react, but additionally *acts*.[9] Architecture, I would argue, has to include but also always has to go beyond critique, for by definition, any architectural project envisions a possible world: architectural practice is always trafficking in futures. In their book *The New Spirit of Capitalism*, Luc Boltanski and Eve Chiapello extend this notion of the projective to the current state of capitalism itself (let me clarify that I am not implying that they extend Somol's and my conception of the projective, but rather, the general concept – their use of the term derives originally from management literature).[10]

Boltanski and Chiapello contend that today's world exists in a decidedly networked state, in terms of digital networks but also in terms of a more general erosion of boundaries. Their book dates from almost a quarter century ago; this dissolution of boundaries has only become more promiscuous since its publication. They note that networks are activated and briefly defined by projects and therefore the contemporary state of capitalism can be seen as a projective one – that is, as a series of projects that create a succession of fixed, if temporary, connections.[11] In short, their definition of 'project' is akin to 'catalyst' – projects create connections and impacts. The projective city, like all six cities or six models of capitalism that preceded it, following their argument, is at once an illustration or justification, as they call it, of its model of capitalism (e.g. the networked model for the projective city) and simultaneously, a critique of the model (or models) that this new phase of capitalism displaced.[12] The projective city, in short, reacts to (i.e. *critiques*) the cities that preceded it, but also acts (i.e. *projects*) by generating its own manifestation. The extension of their argument is that capitalism will continue to evolve, and that a proliferation of new networks of agonistic exchanges – 'financial markets versus countries; financial markets versus firms; multinationals versus countries; large order-givers versus small sub-contractors; world experts versus enterprises; enterprises versus temporary employees; consumers versus enterprises' – will constitute 'a new critical combination against capitalism, capable of uniting demands for solidarity and justice with those for liberty and authenticity', as Sebastian Budgen wrote in a review that he published in the *New Left Review* when the book first appeared in French.[13]

Agonistic Practice

Boltanski and Chiapello offer up a ray of hope with this analysis, although it resonates with the optimism of the very same moment when we all thought that the 'light living' of Airbnb and Uber (enabling a new generation to forgo buying vacation homes and even cars, thereby avoiding debt) was a positive advance of the neoliberal economy. The extent to which temporary employees and small sub-contractors can in fact unite to form adequate resistance to capitalism's current status is perhaps more in doubt today than it was in 1999 when their book was first published in France. Nevertheless, it does suggest the possible impact of collectivities that, like the unions that so impacted twentieth-century capitalism, might well unite to shape a new future.

The possibility of some way out, some way forward, given the forces of neoliberal capitalism is heartening, even if Boltanski and Chiapello's argument depends on a future where collectives marshal productively. Coming down to the individual scale, and returning the question of whether individual practices can play a similarly productive critical-projective role, Mouffe's chapter 'Agnostic Politics and Artistic Practices' in *Agonistics* highlights the example of the artistic practice of the Chilean artist, Alfredo Jaar. Jaar's *Skoghall Konsthall* of 2000 critiques a given reality and additionally, productively, offers a way forward. It consists of a paper museum that Jaar built for a single day for a Swedish city whose economy relied upon its paper plant; the city – Skoghall – had no cultural facilities at all. Jaar then burnt the temporary museum to the ground the following day (so the museum was open only for a day), which incited the city finally to build an actual museum, which they did seven years later (Figure 11). The *Skoghall Konsthall* project points to how temporal qualities play

Figure 11 Alfredo Jaar, The Skoghall Konsthall, 2000. Image courtesy of Alfredo Jaar.

into a project's legibility. This project, which is a literal example of paper architecture (rather than the architecture on paper mentioned above, which is not architecture built out of paper but architecture drawn onto paper) directly encounters the agnostic entities at play, rather than simply critiquing them.[14] It is a critique, yes, of the paper mill's dominance over the city and the absence of culture. It is even a violent critique, given the dramatic destruction of the piece. At the same time, the piece projected a new future for the city, one that eventually came into being. The critique, in short, went beyond the illustration of a commentary to propel a proposition: *Skoghall Konsthall* is projective.

Mouffe points to Jaar's 'profound grasp of the role that affect plays in the process of identification and of the role of passionate attachments in the constitution of political identities. ... This is where art's great power lies – in its capacity to make us see things in a different way, to make us perceive new possibilities'.[15] As Mouffe explains, referencing American philosopher John Dewey, art has the greatest intellectual impact when it reaches our intellect through our emotions or sensations. What is particularly interesting to me about Jaar, however, and most relevant for when shifting these terms from art to architecture, is his own recognition of the limits of affective artistic practices. A project Jaar did in 2005 called *Requiem for Leipzig* awed the audience instead of prompting the active discussion that he sought to instil among the viewers about the failure of the State to support culture in their society, much along the lines of the *Skoghall Konsthall* project. *Requiem* was set in an abandoned church, St. Nicholas Cathedral, in Leipzig, where Jaar slowly and dramatically lowered and raised the church's massive chandelier, illuminating and then darkening the abandoned structure's nave, accompanied by the sound of Johan Sebastian Bach's music (Bach was a cantor in Leipzig). Rather than inciting discussion, the audience was awed, lulled into absolute and reverent silence, which Jaar regarded as a failure of the project. As Edmund Burke noted in his treatise on the sublime – a term interchangeable with awe – it renders one passive (rather than inviting agonistic exchange): 'There is a wide difference between admiration and love', Burke wrote. 'The sublime, which is the cause of the former, always dwells on great objects, and terrible; the latter on small ones and pleasing; we submit to what we admire, but we love what submits to us.'[16]

> ◄ **Weizman:** *It probably was a failure if Alfredo Jaar had hoped for discussion in Philippus Church in Leipzig-Lindenau. The movements of the chandelier to me neither connect to funding cuts by the state, or the city, nor to the need for a public to speak up when actually they were respectfully entranced by the sublime performance. Jaar's performance was part of a charity initiative to raise awareness and funds for the renovation of this former church complex into what is now a remarkable site of a hotel, conference and event space in which people with and without disabilities host in a barrier-free house.*

For Jaar, a project succeeds when it fosters an encounter, an exchange, and more specifically, enables a different future. He focuses less on the event and more on the work's representation and legacy. 'There's this huge gap', he writes, 'between reality and its possible representations. And that gap is impossible to close. So as artists, we must try different strategies for representation. ... A process of identification is fundamental to create empathy, to create solidarity, to create intellectual involvement.'[17] 'Representation' is a critical term for this discussion's context, for it carries two meanings: political representation and artistic representation. For architects, representation is especially important, since we communicate through it: architects create drawings (and models, and other forms of representation) to communicate with clients, with builders, with city administrators and, more broadly, to communicate intent, whether with other architects or with a broader public. Jaar's recognition of the distance between reality and representation perfectly captures Mouffe's definition of an agonistic struggle: representations enable different constituents to enter into an engagement. As Mouffe has noted, artistic practices can create alternatives – they construct different possible subjectivities. Returning once more to Jaar's *Skoghall Konsthall* project: with it, Jaar cleverly represented a future alternative public infrastructure (the museum) through the paper, full-scale model (a representation, or model, of a building), and in so doing, offered up a representation of an alternate hegemonic order for the city. The artistic representation fostered a political representation. It enabled residents, the city government and the paper company all to envision and debate the value of a real *Skoghall Konsthall*.

◄ **Aureli:** *I cannot agree more with this point. Moreover, the majority of discussions on the politics of architecture are based on representations of architecture. To not think about representation itself as a fundamental mediating condition (for better or worse) is to entirely miss what architecture is about. Of course, this should not become an excuse to evade the implications of construction and economy, which are an integral aspect of architecture, because even in these realms representation still plays an important role.*

◄ **Weizman:** *In that sense Jaar's paper museum is also again very similar to the ambitions of the paper architects to propose designs for a different hegemonic order. On the other hand, isn't that what architectural models and representation drawings are meant to do, to represent the possibility for a different* mise en scène*?*

This work of negotiating the gap between reality and representation is the very definition of public art and is how art becomes overtly political. As Mouffe writes, 'The political, for its part, concerns the symbolic ordering of social relations, what Claude Lefort calls the *mise en scène* or the *mise en forme*, of human coexistence and this is where its aesthetic dimension lies.'[18] Architecture, I would argue, is society's *mise en scène* and *mise en forme*: it both organizes and renders manifest our political organizations, relations and (if one is optimistic) I would even say its possibilities. Architecture is one of the most public of the arts, but, as Walter Benjamin famously noted in 1937, unlike most of the arts which are experienced in states of contemplation, architecture is experienced in a state of distraction, and that state is only more extreme today, given the world of cell phones.[19] Art installations, like the *Skoghall Konsthall* project, gain attention because they are events; architecture *can* be an event at moments (a building's opening, an important occasion, etc.), but it will, very quickly, recede to a background tableau. While technology has enabled buildings to become animated (with applied media screens, as in Times Square, or with parts that move, as in the façade of Jean Nouvel's Institut du Monde Arabe), what possibilities for architecture's public engagement exist for the majority of buildings, which are static and stable?

> ◄ **Aureli:** *In Renaissance Italy (but I am sure also in other places), building ephemeral structures and choreographing events like theatrical performances and processions was often used as a blueprint for architectural projects or even urban reforms, exactly like in the case of the Skoghall Konsthall.*

In her 'Art and Democracy' text, Mouffe qualifies the creation of agonistic public spaces as having 'the objective to unveil all that is repressed by the dominant consensus'. That unveiling renders visible, and is an integral part of the critique component of the visible, but I would reiterate that architecture (in part because of its permanence, or at least its aspirations to permanence) has to go beyond the critical. Second, I would argue that the projective component has to be rendered legible in order for it to be effective.

Part of what is made legible in what Lefort referred to as the *mise en scène* and *mise en forme* are limits, borders and distinctions – in other words, the hot spots of contestation. In demarcating any space or form, architecture necessarily creates boundaries that include and exclude. It is from the exclusions engendered by these demarcations that antagonism occurs: a wall may enclose one person, but it keeps another one out; the first may be protected, while the second is exposed; and so on. The public design charrette, which has become a default means of gaining public buy-in for any project, offers a false promise of consensus for architecture with the belief that coloured pencils, magic markers, post-it notes and green and red dots can offer a common language for the public to reach consensus. Given that demarcations will never satisfy every contingency, what passes for consensus is necessarily always composed of compromises upon compromises. Rather than encouraging a healthy focus upon these contested boundaries, the charrette model replaces them with a pretence of consensus, thereby repressing antagonisms just below the surface, from whence they can erupt unproductively at any future moment.

Pointing out the heterogeneous, pluralizing aspect of language, Jean-François Lyotard reminds us that such aspirations to community consensus are near impossible, for language consists of an infinite deployment of genres of discourse and modes of phrase. Misunderstanding arises when two speakers use the same words but with different senses, or even different references. Lyotard's concept of the *différend* – that which cannot be expressed – locates that misunderstanding at the building block of communication, if you will: the phrase. To explore the *différend*, Lyotard posits the 'phrase' as an empty, operative concept, one from which all categories derive, but which itself is not determined by these categories. The *différend* ties legibility to judgement by locating the very challenge of judgement in the phrase's indeterminacy.[20]

Because of its multiple users, who range from passersby to visitors and to owners, architecture has many, many built equivalents to Lyotard's *différend*: a wall offers up a different meaning, depending on your relationship to the spaces it either contains or blocks out. An agonistic relationship is practically inevitable at the juncture of architecture's demarcations and its *différends*. Or, to be more specific, I would say that architecture's politics lie in its many *différends* and the most volatile of those are at its moments of demarcation. Architecture's demarcations – its walls, property boundaries and other hard limits – define but nevertheless also carry a multitude of meanings – they are the built equivalent of Lyotard's understanding of a phrase. The question at stake, then, becomes how might that multiplicity be productively exploited as the potential playing field for architecture's agonism?

I will offer three examples of possible directions. Dogma, a practice led by Pier Vittorio Aureli and Martino Tattara, works with representation to engage the scale, and I would say even the banality of contemporary normative practice, and tweaks it by placing the focus upon the module of repetition, shrinking the residential unit to its barest minimum so as to force collective options for living as well as for architecture. *A Simple Heart* (2002–9) places the worker at the heart of the city, countering the spectacular city of capitalist commercialism with the visibility of the worker, but also with an architecture that reorganizes the worker's life by offering both solitude and collective experience. The capitalist city cannot exist without the labours of the working class. Critiquing the contemporary city's masking of the worker, who is often forced to live in the invisible cheaper urban zones far from the centre, *A Simple Heart* projects a new organization that renders them extremely legible (Figure 12).

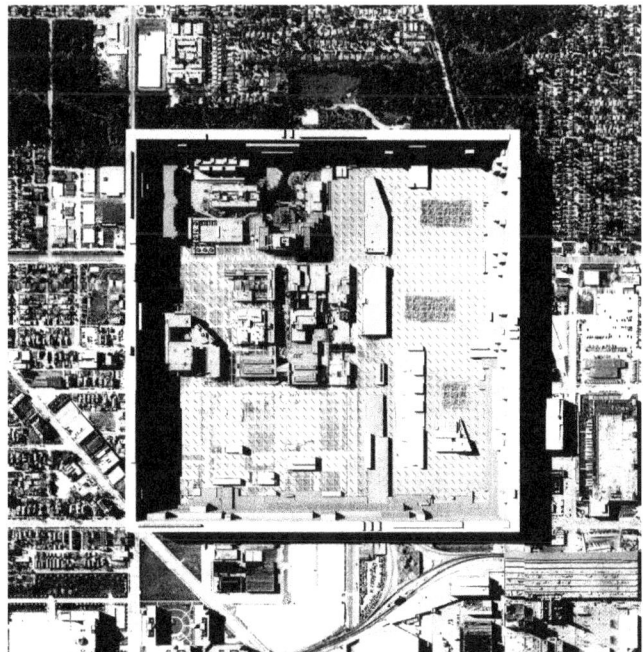

Figure 12 Dogma, Simple Heart (2002–9). Image courtesy of Dogma.

The second example is of a very different nature. Rather than opposing the capitalist commercial city, this project category appropriates neoliberal capitalism by revisiting strategies of high postmodernism. Some of these projects simply reiterate postmodernism's strategies, but others consciously try to exploit postmodern strategies of high impact legibility in order to project new possibilities. This family of projects expressly exploits current advances in graphic techniques in order to tweak the commercial control of architectural legibility. I admit to being ambivalent about this approach, as its dependence on graphic immediacy risks courting early obsolescence, but perhaps that market risk is what makes it especially relevant as a strategy for recapturing artistic practices from a capitalist stronghold.

Superkilen (Figure 13), a park in Copenhagen, is a collaborative project finished in 2012 by BIG architects, Topotek 1 landscape architects, and the artistic practice that

Figure 13 BIG, Superkilen (2012). Image courtesy of BIG and Iwan Baan.

operates under the name Superflex. Located in the Norrobro district of Copenhagen, in a neighbourhood that is home to over sixty different minority nationalities, *Superkilen* does not mask the antagonisms of these multiple constituencies, but rather positions them with, or counter to one another. It does not try to create a language that will appease all sixty groups, but instead fills the park with symbols from each of these countries. These are reconstructed familiar symbols, architectural types or literal signs from different communities: a bus sign from Iran, a sewer grate from France, a fountain from Morocco, a slide from Japan in the shape of an octopus. Some of these symbols are less benign in nature – for instance, the Jamaican boom box, which actually projects noise. The question of course is whether these signs, which were reached by consensus (or a form of consensus) by polling different constituencies, form a caricature of these different groups or whether they offer a form of identity in contrast with one another.

Finally, I will point to our own practice, WW Architecture (myself with Ron Witte), where we have deliberately focused on what might be called the *différend* between form and programme to embed a multiplicity within the demarcations of architecture. I will start by pointing to a project that is very old, 1995–6, for the IntraCenter in Lexington, Kentucky. It is for a community centre adjacent to an elementary school, in a single, small neighbourhood where 75 per cent of the population lives below the poverty line. The principal of the elementary school approached us with a programme that had everything in it – this was the mid-1990s, when the idea of responding to any project was to respond by offering programmatic complexity as the architect's solution – but here the client approached us already armed with programmatic complexity. Instead of saying that we could embody what this community looked like, or embody all of these programmes through one thing, our answer was to design a building that had a series of 'parentheses' in it – a resin-impregnated plywood wall, that would wrap through the project as a ribbon and create different zones, not necessarily corresponding to programme. The undulating walls would provide identity without fixity. The parenthetical spaces that it formed could be read as separate and overlapping areas, forming constantly different groupings of collectives that would not necessarily correspond to the building's rooms or to institutional ideas of what these collectives should be.

This productive and legible play between programme and form has carried through our work, and can also be seen in our design for the Kaihui ecological business centre outside Changsha, China. We were again faced with a client who wanted an extremely flexible programme but also one that was a legible building. This client wanted a building that could help to promote and protect the small-scale agricultural industry of the region – replete with tea fields – by introducing an enterprise that could serve as a business retreat or even wedding destination. Our answer was to offer identity and flexibility through a building that produced small, medium and large spaces that could be used for any purpose (as opposed to a Miesian universal space that cannot be easily divided for multiple simultaneous uses, or a building made up of a collection of equally sized fixed spaces that might not be amenable for uses that do not fit into that given size). Our project has a formal vocabulary of three holes, three slots and three floors that combine to create a building whose specificities of architectural form offer different possibilities of being in one space. Each space within the building always looks onto another space, which means that one is always part of several spaces at once. In short, differences are not isolated, papered over or compromised, but are instead integrated within the life of the project. Like *A Simple Heart*, *Kaihui Exchange* does offer up a singular whole, but the singularity of *Kaihui* is not a totalizing or complete form; it is a project whose legibility changes with its varied uses. Its legibility also changes from varied perspectives, as the form suggests a single block from afar but upon closer viewing comprises different parts.

None of these examples – *A Simple Heart*, *Superkilen*, the *IntraCenter* and *Kaihui* – address the complexities of financing and legalities that comprise the majority of the challenges to architecture's practice. Nevertheless, by rendering the occupation and possibilities of architecture legible and yet flexible, all make a dent in the fixity that a market driven approach to architecture tends to impose. All of these works project possibilities that do not exist on the lenders' legers of comparands; all try to advance practice by throwing a wrench into market modelling, while throwing a life jacket to architectural practice. I offer these as three different approaches to architectural politics with an understanding of the real limits of architectural practice, which does not mean we should shut down and answer that architecture can only respond through art practices or writing, but that we must find some way of practicing within the world that we have.

Notes

1 Thank you to Joseph Bedford and Jessica Reynolds for the invitation to the 'Chantal Mouffe: How Is Architecture Political' symposium organized by the Architecture Exchange at the Architectural Association on 6 December 2014. I would also like to thank Joseph, Chantal Mouffe, and Stephanie Lloyd for their comments on this text.
2 Lori Jo Marso, *Politics with Beauvoir: Freedom in the Encounter* (Durham, NC: Duke University Press, 2017), 3–4.
3 'Gehry Technologies is an AEC technology company providing leading edge solutions to the industry's most challenging projects. Our clients include some of the most recognized international architects, engineers, contractors, and owners working across the globe.' 'About', Gehry Technologies Inc., accessed 14 February 2018, https://web.archive.org/web/20180204210145/http://www.gehrytech.com/en/main/about/.

   'Trimble and Frank Gehry have recently announced their plans to enter into a strategic alliance in which Trimble will acquire Gehry Technologies to integrate digital software development and on-site fabrication techniques. As a company working in "geospatial solutions", Trimble combines software development, communication tools and services to increase productivity in the Architecture, Engineering and Construction (AEC) industry, among others. The two companies hope that their alliance will enable complex architectural designs to be realized without the construction snags that often affect such ambitious projects.' Evan Rawn, '"Geospatial Solutions" Company Trimble Acquires Gehry

Technologies', *ArchDaily*, 9 September 2014, https://www.archdaily.com/546306/trimble-acquires-gehry-technologies.
4   Chantal Mouffe, *Agonistics: Thinking the World Politically* (London: Verso, 2013), 85.
5   Alain Badiou, 'Fifteen Theses on Contemporary Art', *16 Beaver Group*, 1, https://web.archive.org/web/20130425050054/http://www.16beavergroup.org/journalisms/archives/000633.php.
6   Chantal Mouffe, 'Art and Democracy: Art as an Agonistic Intervention in Public Space', Liesbeth Melis and Jorinde Seijdel, eds., *Open 14: Art as a Public Issue: How Art and Its Institutions Reinvent the Public Dimension* (Rotterdam: NAI 010 Publishers, 2008), 6–13.
7   Richard Noble, 'Imagining the Political: Some Provisional Thoughts on Art and Politics', in *The Showroom Annual 2003/04* (The Showroom, 2005).
8   Galen Bunting, 'Supreme's Co-Option of Barbara Kruger's Oeuvre', *Ploughshares* blog (21 August 2019) https://blog.pshares.org/supremes-co-optation-of-barbara-krugers-oeuvre/
9   R.E. Somol and Sarah Whiting, 'Notes around the Doppler Effect and Other Moods of Modernism', *Perspecta* 33 (2002): 72–7.
10 'For reasons it is advisable to explain, given that the term might seem unwieldy and rather unclear, we have chosen to call the new apparatus of justification that seems to us to be being formed the "projective city". It is in fact modeled on a term that frequently crops up in management literature: project organization. This refers to a firm whose structure comprises a multiplicity of projects associating a variety of people, some of whom participate in several projects.' Luc Boltanski and Eve Chiapello, *The New Spirit of Capitalism* (New York: Verso, 2007), 105.
11 'In a reticular world, social life is composed of a proliferation of encounters and temporary, but reactivatable connections with various groups, operated at potential considerable social, professional, geographical and cultural distance. The *project* is the occasion and reason for the connection. It temporarily assembles a very disparate group of people, and presents itself as a *highly activated section of network* for a period of time that is relatively short, but allows for the construction of more enduring links that will be put on hold while remaining available. Projects make production and accumulation possible in a world, which, were it to be purely connexionist, would simply contain flows, where nothing could be stabilized, accumulated or crystallized. Everything would be carried off in an endless stream of ephemeral associations which, given their capacity to put everything in communication, constantly distribute and dissolve whatever gels in them. The project is precisely a mass of active connections apt to create forms – that is to say, bring objects and subjects into existence – by stabilizing certain connections and making them irreversible. It is thus a temporary *pocket of accumulation* which, creating value, provides a base for the requirement of extending the network by furthering connections.' Boltanski and Chiapello, *The New Spirit of Capitalism*, 104–5.
12 'Thus, the projective city serves at once to criticize "industrial" or "civic" arrangements that are deemed insufficiently flexible, and to point out those features of the connexionist world that do not conform to the justice which this world claims as its own'. Boltanski and Chiapello, *The New Spirit of Capitalism*, 522.
13 Sebastian Budgen, 'A New 'Spirit of Capitalism', *New Left Review*, no. 1 (January/February 2000): 155.
14 Thanks to Stephanie Lloyd for her observations about Jaar's Skoghall Konsthall project and how it differs from our typical notion of 'paper architecture'.
15 Chantal Mouffe, *Agonistics: Thinking the World Politically* (New York: Verso, 2013), 96–7.
16 Edmund Burke, *A Philosophical Inquiry into the Origin of Our Ideas of the Sublime and Beautiful* (Oxford: Oxford University Press, 1990; originally published in 1757), 103.

17 Alfredo Jaar, 'The Silence of Nduwayezu', http://www.youtube.com/watch?v=QRPF3inleD0&feature=related
18 Chantal Mouffe, 'Artistic Activism and Agonistic Politics', *Art and Research* 1 (2) (Summer 2007): 4.
19 Walter Benjamin 'Work of Art in the Age of its Technological Reproducibility: Third Version', trans. Edmund Jephcott et al. in *Walter Benjamin*: *Selected Writings of Walter Benjamin*, ed. Howard Eiland and Michael W. Jennings, Volume 4 1938–40 (Cambridge, MA: Belknap Press of Harvard University Press, 1996), 251–83.
20 Jean-François Lyotard, *Le Différend* (Paris: Les Editions de Minuit, 1983).

Interview

Joseph Bedford: You have been discussing the projective mode of practice for a while. Can you define it again at this moment, in relation to your more recent concept of 'engaged autonomy'?[1]

Sarah Whiting: With the projective, I have been, and I remain, startled at how it gets misinterpreted. If Bob Somol and I were to write that essay 'Notes around the Doppler Effect and Other Moods of Modernism' again we would make our points even more emphatically.[2] In it, we are clear about the fact that our use of the term *projective* is not anti-critical. Some have misconstrued it to mean anti-critical or post-critical. I have *never* used either of those terms. In order to advance architecture, critique is necessary, but we *need* to emphasize forward movement, and offer alternatives; we cannot merely content ourselves with critiques.

Engaged autonomy is an example of a strategy that emerges from a Doppler approach, for it is a way of practicing that focuses on the singular building but that also situates that building within its context. In short, engaged autonomy is about forming relationships, using architecture, within buildings and across a broader, public realm. Architectural form, space and material draw ties, relationships, to spaces within projects as well as all that extends beyond. Architecture has to engage both with the public realm, and the city.

For a project to affect the world, it has to reach beyond itself. This does not mean that it needs to resemble its context: it has to have a *relationship* with its context. Ron Witte and I have talked about our work being based on nonrepresentational legibility – that means using figuration not as a representational device, but to create relationships among rooms. 'Figure' in this sense means the figuration of space through form. Non-representational figures produce legibilities and affinities between the building and the broader context.

In the last couple of years, I have also been focused on architecture as an object – the autonomy side of engaged autonomy. Many architects have turned away from the object because of anxiety about iconic buildings based on what are called star practices. As a result, architects have been almost embarrassed to talk about architecture as form or as object. For architecture to be legible and for it to have an effect, we have to understand it as a singular object, in addition to the relationships it can forge. Many object qualities are what we would call purely architectural or disciplinary questions: only architects really focus on formal alignments, for example – columns lined up with a door opening or with a change in material. Those are object questions but they also create relationships – lining up materials can be a way of drawing a person from one room to another, or from the inside to the outside. So, disciplinary obsessions can often generate public repercussions.

Joseph Bedford: The words *projective* and *project* imply a duality of something both concrete and universal. In Italian architectural culture, when people refer to the project and the city, it seems very concrete. It is about a particular historical mode of engagement, or a certain project going on in an office. But at the same time, someone like Peter Eisenman will delineate between architects who 'have a project' and those who do not, drawing a distinction between 'project' and 'practice'. That sense of the word is more about having a coherent thread of inquiry in one's work. So, is that also the duality of autonomy and engagement, simultaneously ideal and concrete?

Sarah Whiting: Yes, exactly. To have a project is to have an ambition rather than an agenda. Eisenman has a project. He has been unbelievably consistent. Even though his work has transformed over time, and his references have changed, the ambition is the same: he uses architectural form to destabilize our expectations and generate new experiences. The same is true for Rem Koolhaas, whose ambition is very clear. Koolhaas's project has always been about the relationship between freedom and constraint. Formal or organizational definitions foster new ways of living – the experiences that his work generate are less destabilizing than Eisenman's, but they are similarly novel.

An ambition does not need to be reduced to a one-liner, but it is necessary that it be architectural. So, I absolutely agree with Eisenman that some practices have projects and others do not. Some practices simply fulfil obligations. They can do so in very elegant ways, but they are still just accomplishing the work at hand.

This is why I like teaching thesis. We start by asking 'How do you figure out what is a project?' Competitions offer good examples because you need to foreground an argument oftentimes in the concentrated time frame of a competition. Take for example the proposals for additions to the Whitney Museum of American Art: Michael Graves's submission demonstrated that he had a project. It is not one that I would embrace, but his project emerged from his architectural obsessions and ambitions. He made the Marcel Breuer building symmetrical, and he recreates the museum as a centralized institution by giving it a clear entrance. OMA had a project about redefining the museum to be a commercial entity. Renzo Piano, on the other hand, approached the Whitney Breuer addition problem as a practice. He solved the problems of needing more space in an elegant way, but not with a broader ambition.

This framework of focusing on ambitions offers a way to teach students. It asks them to look very carefully at architecture to distinguish projects from practice. Students can then also figure out where they want to be, since some may not be ready to have an ambition for the thesis – having an architectural ambition or project requires time to acquire enough knowledge to feel comfortable and confident in situating yourself within the discipline.

Jessica Reynolds: You define the criteria for a project as critique, judgement and legibility. You described architecture as an inherently political medium, and yet many architects do not have a political agenda, and some have more of an agenda than others. If a project demonstrates critique, judgement and legibility, is it necessarily political? Or, to put it another way, can I ask you whether, in your terms, it is possible that a *project* is *not political*?

Sarah Whiting: That is a good question. I agree in Mouffe's terms that architecture is always political, because it is always a form of negotiation, compromise and antagonism. At each moment it is a struggle, and there are always clear winners along the way. But while architecture is always political, the architect might not be the political agent. Instead, the agent may be the developer, the client, the council or whatever the community regulations are that determine constraints.

In order for a project to be political, I would add the criterion of ambition. We articulate our ambitions through judgement, which is how we determine what is important. For a project to be political, it also must have a form of critique. Critique has been misunderstood in an exaggerated way. A critique can be an advancing of a norm, even. It can be a very slight change. I would not call it progress, but it is an act of adding something to what exists. Judgement is figuring out the terms for what that might be, according to one's ambition. Legibility is where it goes beyond self-indulgence to become relevant to others. In fact, I am focusing my teaching at Rice University this semester on the term *relevance*. If a project does not have relevance, then it will not advance the world.

> ◀ **Aureli:** *I agree with this point. In his book* Theories and History of Architecture, *Manfredo Tafuri called this kind of critique embedded in the architectural project 'typological critique', that is to say a critique through which architects put forward new forms by revising, twisting or contradicting given architectural types.*

This comes from my frustration with public lectures by architects. They are often elaborate and incredibly intelligent, but lack any relevance to moving the world forward. That is not to imply that a project cannot be about a historical topic, but it is irresponsible to simply offer a clever observation or a series of footnotes upon footnotes in our field. In architecture, it is essential that we continue to move practice forward. That is where the discipline of architecture, its academic side, can have a political effect.

Joseph Bedford: I am interested in the topic of whether or not one moves forward, and if so, in what direction. One of the criticisms of the projective position in the mid-

2000s was that it went with the flow. It was said to have capitulated to market forces. Its thrust could just as easily align with a right-wing agenda complicit with neoliberalism and the dominance of market forces, as much as a left-wing agenda, seeking to reduce inequality and create a fairer society.

Another aspect of the projective, though, was to promote cunning. You and Bob Somol jointly wrote both your 'Doppler Effect' article and your introduction to *Log* 5 ['Okay, Here's the Plan ... '] using metaphors of game-playing. These metaphors suggest a kind of double game, both going with the flow and having a covert, progressive agenda.

Sarah Whiting: Projects can be right-wing, conservative and market driven. That does not mean that I support such projects, but I prefer engaging strong agendas, even if I disagree with them. It would be naive to assert that a project can only be one with which I would align myself. In the terms that Somol and I laid out, the projective has an aspiration to liberal critique and to dance with the market just enough to change it. In practice, one has to engage the realities of the market. But it does not only need to be sneaky. At times such engagement can be incredibly overt.

One can choose from three strategies. The first is to say that one will do the project. In that case, the agenda has to be very clear, in just the same way that politicians must be clear with their agendas. I will not vote for Jeb Bush, but at least I know what he stands for. In that regard, I would not wholeheartedly advocate a cunning approach to a project as the only way to engage.

A second strategy would be to very straightforwardly lay out how the market can take on change. For example, real estate development in Houston in the 1960s was actually very innovative under Gerald D. Hines. Today, Houston developers are very conservative and they aim for five-year profit turnarounds. I have worked with the Menil Collection, whose income comes from rent from residential and commercial properties. They are going to develop a type of residential building that is very common in Houston right now. I have been pushing for the institution to acknowledge that it will not make the profit that all the developers in Houston make. Instead, it can build according to a model that might actually end up being more profitable, because people will realize its value. It is important to have the naiveté to believe that that might be feasible.

A third strategy would be to make the developers think that they are getting everything they want, but actually incorporate little subversive things. In a lecture at Rice last semester, Michael Maltzan talked about the social housing projects he did in Los Angeles. He did certain things to comply with regulations, but which ended up being architectural features. Designing for air exhaust, they created fins that also allowed for privacy for the rooms. They would have been very easy to value-engineer out of the project, except they played an architecturally functional role, so the developer could not remove them. That may not be overly cunning, but it is a pragmatic sneakiness.

A whole spectrum of possibilities is available. I would be reluctant to advise one single strategy, because then everyone would operate in one way, and that would become a normative mode of practice again. Rather, we are in a moment of change. Several ways of pushing architecture forward are emerging, and it is healthy to encourage those multiple paths.

Joseph Bedford: This raises the question of whether the projective as an approach to practice is content-neutral. When one teaches a projective approach, is the object simply to teach formal skills, to give students the toolset and expertise to help them pragmatically manoeuvre through any project? Can one also teach topics like ethical understanding, moral values, the idea of the good life, all of which contribute to ambition and goals? Or do those factors fall outside of the purview of this approach?

Sarah Whiting: How much can you bias students' agendas or ambitions?

Joseph Bedford: Yes, exactly. Do those values simply belong to the realm of being a good citizen that one learns in one's life outside of school, or are the ethics of one's ambition a component of education?

Sarah Whiting: This is a very important point – I am glad you are raising it. Ethics of ambition must be a part of education. One must be conscious in designing a curriculum, and where students have the ability to respond. In a curriculum's earlier phases, formal techniques are important. Students have to become comfortable with the definition and design of lines and form and space. That is a good place to start: just teaching them how a line creates a boundary, which they have to define. Then we add the complexities of programming. Next comes questioning and altering programme. Then we work through the actual tools of architecture, to understand how materials, technical systems and structure work. I came into architecture without expertise in those areas, and I find myself increasingly fascinated by those forms of regulation. Michael Maltzan's talk was extremely interesting regarding how to actually work with practical components of making a building stand up and be viable.

But students cannot manipulate those dimensions of architecture until they have learned to manipulate form and programme. As educators, the models we present, and the people we bring in to lecture, have an influence on students' ethical formation. Some schools bring a whole buffet in order to let students make their own decisions. The Architectural Association in London is a good example of that. In a smaller school like Rice, we do not have the means or obligation to introduce the full spread.

All schools do have to expose students to a breadth of examples, which can be encountered in history and theory courses, in seminars and even in studio. For instance, I taught a semester on the topic of what it means to be a citizen as an architect today. We brought in speakers and had a school-wide discussion on this. Judgement was another year-long version of that. Relevance is going to be another semester. The students are very aware of my biases, and those of other members of the faculty. That does not mean that the students cannot argue with them. Our discussions on the citizen involved simple ideas: What does it mean to be active as a citizen today? Is it just voting? Is it trying to influence regulations on the urban level? Does it pertain to where one is at school, or in one's hometown? Is it global? It is important to allow for multiple ways into these problems. Schools have the obligation to teach students to adopt an ethical position. In that regard, relevance is a useful term because it does not come with the baggage of the term's *ethics* or *value*.

Jessica Reynolds: One does not encounter the same problems in paper architecture. In the same way design necessarily has an ethical component, practice does, too: welfare of construction workers, and materials and where they are sourced from.

Sarah Whiting: Or what commissions one takes.

Jessica Reynolds: Yes. These are issues that paper architects are not comfortable addressing, and do not have to address.

Sarah Whiting: That is where the divide between practice and schools is very dangerous. That does not mean that pedagogy should over-professionalize. I was at Rice for five years. Part of my job as a dean involves fundraising and development. When I deal with developers, I tell them I am very interested in practice. They hear that and think that we are going to have the students learn integrated building delivery systems. Forms of efficiency are interesting, but that is not what I mean. We are speaking past each other. It is very interesting to observe what developers hear and what the faculty hears. Faculty can feel threatened by an emphasis on practice.

Jessica Reynolds: You showed a slide to that effect when you were discussing art and politics. Political art reflects on its own modes of production and circulation. Even after it is constructed, its uses will gesture back to its making.

Sarah Whiting: Exactly. It is a big responsibility for an architect. There are moments when I become concerned that exposing students to too many of the challenges, obligations and responsibilities will cause them to flee to other fields. Figuring out how to maintain the naiveté and the optimism that fuel architecture as a possibility is important.

Joseph Bedford: In the roundtable debate at the end of the exchange, the question of truth came up from an audience member. Mouffe's reply was that, for her, truth is not an issue. You agreed, but you formulated your response in terms of situational truth, or the idea that a singular truth may be untenable. Your position was to make local connections and alliances.

Based on that relativistic position, how do you propose overcoming the baggage that comes with postmodern philosophy? Mouffe incorporates postmodern philosophy into political theory, for example, by de-essentializing Marxist teleology. Yet we are still very much within that paradigm. In architecture, terms like value and ethics elicit grimaces and suspicion.

So, on the one hand, ethics is a question of practice, but it is simultaneously a matter of the ambition that drives a project. How might one overcome the taboos that remain from the past twenty or thirty years of the discipline's engagement with theory?

Sarah Whiting: Carlos Jiménez, who is a faculty member at Rice University, was on the Pritzker Prize jury for eleven years. That is an excellent position from which to have actual influence. If an architect has specific values, they have an ethical obligation to realize those values in practice. One way of getting around the anxiety of those terms is simply not to use them. It becomes an issue of knowing one's audience and being able to serve. Architecture requires a level of concreteness, reality and durability that gestures in the direction of economy. I would also add that terms like value and ethics are slowly re-entering architectural discourse but not in the essentialist ways that defined them in pre-post-modern times.

This is why I was interested in the Boltanski and Chiapello book – *The New Spirit of Capitalism*. They shifted the discourse away from a singular focus on networks. We are all very involved with networks, whether those pertain to networks of practices, or the networked global world of architecture. Boltanski and Chiapello offer a way of freeze-framing, transcending constant fluidity and lack of fixity of networks.

We are at a moment – in many disciplines – in which we are seeing a maturation of the postmodern theoretical project, which now allows for fixity. Fredric Jameson's conception of a singular modernity is almost twenty years old.[3] The prospect of thinking beyond total fluidity without resorting to absolute truths is exciting to me.

Architecture gives us an upper hand in our obligation to act because practice forces us to reckon with concrete reality. We should be at the forefront in acknowledging that the rhetoric of total fluidity undermined our discipline. Apart from the few architects who design mobile buildings, we work in fixed media. Shifting this discourse is in our best interest.

Joseph Bedford: You suggested to Mouffe that architecture, as opposed to art, is more a viable topic for her political theory. That would be one place where that property of fixity would be intriguing. Part of your provocation was to say that you intended to go beyond artistic modes of representation, towards architectural modes of practice. Did you mean something along the lines of moving beyond surfaces or symbols towards the material and concrete?

Sarah Whiting: I would distinguish between questions of legibility and questions of representational symbolism here. In order to have an audience, legibility is very important. But that does not address issues of image and display, which point towards problems of judgement rather than legibility. Art also aspires towards permanence. I do not mean to imply that art is fleeting. But even though it is an enormous economy of trying to procure commissions from patrons and clients, it is less fraught than the economy of architecture.

Art practices still have plenty of problems pertaining to the market – I do not idealize the art field. At the same time, they do not have the same legal rules. They do not have to have a maximum of four inches of spacing for a balcony rail. Due to their professional liabilities, architects have to deal with so many obligations and restrictions. That is where I challenged her.

Architecture has to deal with the economy, technology and politics of regulation in ways that could make Mouffe's argument even more interesting. It sets up problems that are much harder than those posed by art, which does not have the same obligations.

Jessica Reynolds: Do you use precedents or examples from art in your own work?

Sarah Whiting: We definitely do. This is what I was saying about different levels of teaching: you can isolate form, programme and technique. As practitioners, we have to synthesize all of those tasks. Similarly, when defining a project, one can actually isolate an art project, which can be incredibly valuable as a provocation.

I saw the Agnes Martin show at the Tate, and I find her work remarkable not only for the grid and the order, but the qualities of low contrast and the juxtapositions. She works with colours that are very close together, lines that are very similar and patterns that are very similar.

I was fascinated to see a project inhabiting that very tight bandwidth of formal definition. Different things might provoke us at different times, but each of us always sees them through the lens of our own project or approach.

Jessica Reynolds: Should art and architecture have more of an interface? Art practice today seems much more attuned to contemporary philosophy, while the world of architecture seems out of sync.

Sarah Whiting: Yes and no. When I invite artists to give lectures at the architecture school, it can be hard to find speakers who can talk about their work in ways that go beyond the descriptive. I can anticipate which architects will talk with purpose. Some architects might just show slides and describe their work, but it is more common to find architects who will use a lecture to articulate a broader agenda than artists. Sarah Oppenheimer came to Rice as part of the semester on relevance. She is a fantastic lecturer – she situates her extraordinary work within a more expansive frame. We need to be deliberate about fostering that exchange. It is weak on both sides right now.

Joseph Bedford: Could you explain your understanding of the concept of hegemony further? I see a parallel with the cunning aspect of the projective and Mouffe's Gramscian inspired idea of hegemony as a strategy? In particular, I am also curious about your use of the idea of the 'player' with regard to hegemony as a game, and the advance of positions within a field.

Sarah Whiting: I conceptualize it as several playing fields existing at once. Again, that is where architecture would be a really interesting area of practice for Mouffe. It includes the playing field of our discipline, where one does play to win. One asserts a position within a discourse that is purely academic, but very important for advancing our discipline.

There is also the playing field of urban regulations. Another is the developer's financial gain in the market. We cannot reduce this to a question of one playing field or one domain of hegemony. It can be compared to a DJ who has several records going at once.

The political philosopher Nancy Fraser offers a great model for understanding this multiplicity. She elaborated a more productive direction from Habermas by arguing that the public sphere is not singular: we are all members of multiple public spheres that mix over each other and at times overlap. In that respect, one can choose to isolate a single playing field but one always has to be conscious that one is isolating. That was my intention in referring to Manfredo Tafuri, or Frank Gehry. Working with Gehry Technologies is a cunning, co-opting manoeuvre. Tafuri, or any mode of paper architecture, represent other ways of responding by creating their own niche. I am fascinated by people who try to engage on multiple levels. That is incredibly hard. It is similar to people who conduct instead of just playing one instrument.

Joseph Bedford: The example of Alejandro Zaera-Polo also comes to my mind, since he emphasizes cunning. On the one hand, he belongs to your generation's turn to practice but, unlike you, he is more willing to forsake the institutional disciplinary aspect in favour of pure opportunism; of what he has called the attitude of the 'sniper'. That seems to be to be a purer instantiation of hegemony as a kind of warfare. The projective, however, seems to be more of a mixture between a totally cynical form of warfare and a more utopian or idealist set of ambitions.

Sarah Whiting: Yes, the idea of the projective mode is someone who can play on all levels at once. I would not characterize it as including cynicism – it is not so much warfare as manoeuvring. Zaera-Polo's work on the politics of the envelope can be considered a project, even if he is more interested in working through practice than in intersections with academia.

Jessica Reynolds: Mouffe has always emphasized that in a democracy some forms of exclusion are necessary. On the one hand, democracy as a whole has to exclude those who challenge it, but also even within the democracy, her agonistic model advocates for local groupings and frontiers and the value of articulating identities through the 'constitutive outside' against which a group identity is understood. Do you think that the idea of the project, if it is about consistency and a degree of fixity, implies the exclusion of something outside of the project?

Sarah Whiting: For any project, one has to decide at what point to compromise for the building to be realized. That might be on a house project, where the client is pushing for more comfort, while the economic argument is to eliminate moves. Where does one hold fast, because it will undermine the project and, ideally, not alienate the client?

We are doing a master plan for an Episcopalian church and school. Episcopalians believe in reaching consensus, but what I love about the pastor we are working with is that she knows that we will probably take down an existing church building on the site. She is going through a process with a lot of talking and meetings, but she is perfectly aware that she is guiding her congregation to that decision. Some of them will resist, but that is the only way to move this project forward. Consensus is weak if it is not led by vision – that is not the same thing as forcing a direction. For a vision or ambition to move a project forward, it has to be articulated well, debated thoroughly, and advanced. But that is different from compromise that tries to please everyone, which invariably weakens any project.

So, architects should not be the ones to compromise all the time. We certainly cannot expect consensus, but the key is to make sure that the interlocutors – whether it is the client, the bank or whomever – actually understand the architectural intention, so that they can disagree with legitimacy.

I am against a cunning that will snooker clients into agreeing to something that they do not fully understand. You have to make sure that they understand. Again, both at the end and during the process, the matter of legibility and understanding is important for me.

Joseph Bedford: I would like to ask you to what degree your idea of legibility relates to the 'pop' sensibility of Robert Venturi and Denise Scott Brown, and whether legibility has to be about immediacy, speed and superficiality, or whether other deeper forms of identification can be involved including ideas about understanding and empathy – a term which you have used in other writing?

Sarah Whiting: This is where I differ from Somol who is very interested in that superficiality and immediacy. That relates to his discussion of cartoons, an intriguing topic at the moment that demands further articulation. I am wary of the immediacy of cartoons, though, because I find multiple layers of interpretation more compelling.

I am interested in the Superkilen project because of its multiple layers. Each of the signs and symbols stand for countries. Some are straightforward, like the doughnut sign for the United States to say that our crass food is actually what we all cohere around. For Japan, it has an octopus. On the one hand it is like a cartoon character – because it is not a design since it is not two-dimensional. On the other, though, it is like a goofy character. That makes it more interesting, because it opens up a variety of ways of seeing it. Superkilen borders on the simplicity of pop immediacy, but the collection of all the symbols together in one site, and their specific placement, along with the infrastructure of the park, renders it more complex.

The figures are highly legible, but they remain ambiguous in a productive way. Regarding empathy, the art historian Juliet Koss takes umbrage with my superficial use of the term, and she is right if one is considering the specific and historic use of the term. I use it to apply merely to something around which people can gather enough to have a conversation. It also implies a willingness to entertain different interpretations, approaches and interests. An open-ended, but not fully ambiguous form of legibility is productive because it allows for many interpretations, without creating a situation without limits.

It is arrogant to impose the singularity of the sign on the world. One is using commercial means and pretending to be popular, yet actually being singular and thus determinist in the interpretation of legibility.

On one pole, Somol is interested in impact, and gauges success by it. On the other, Eisenman is interested in deep, critical, close reading. Eisenman's approach, and close reading in general, are important influences on my thinking, but I aim for something in between the two of them.

The audience of architecture is not necessarily a group of people who know every reference. In good movies, some viewers might recognize the moves that the director is making, and some might be provoked by what they see. Others just watch and say, 'Those are nice colours'. Keeping all of those groups in mind is a great ambition.

Joseph Bedford: I would like to ask you about Pier Vittorio Aureli's work and that of his practice Dogma. On the one hand you share an interest in form as a means of architectural demarcation, and yet don't subscribe to the way that Dogma treats the wall surface as a blank white neutral plane. The work of WW Architects, by contrast, engages with the more patterned, coloured and optical dimension of surfaces.

Sarah Whiting: If Aureli's white walls were realized, they would certainly inspire curiosity. They are hardly neutral. His project *The Simple Heart* is incredibly smart, in that it proposes very small apartments, encouraging the use of common spaces. That is a strategic move, in line with how a developer would act, like boutique hotels that project an image of extravagance, but the rooms are as small as possible.

> ◄ **Aureli:** *I should say that in* A Simple Heart, *which was a revisitation of student housing (at the moment student welfare was being dismantled in Europe) the main idea was that the single-person thirty-sqm units were neither rented nor sold, but offered as a universal basic right (analogous to 'universal basic income') to every wage worker. This is why the scale of each quadrangle was immense.*

I would love to see what his projects would be like if they were built in the city. What would they be made of? Where would the interface between the existing city and walled world be? What is the entrance like? I would be curious about how he would resolve those details.

I find their scale provocative. We often assume that the very large scale is reserved for inadvisable commercial office space or housing projects. But I am interested in how the big scale can work in a city without becoming autonomous, miniaturized urbanism.

Planners and architects tend to theorize urban projects simply as collective neighbourhoods. The implication is that big cities are just collections of villages. Even if the world has advanced, the notion is that we still live within our little worlds, where we can walk to get our groceries and walk to school. Residents can go somewhere else, but the mentality is still populations of 3,000 to 5,000 people. That is the problem with urban politics: we have not offered models that tackle the problems and benefits of living in a city of millions of people.

Joseph Bedford: In regard to the scale of the city and planning, Aureli made clear that his inspiration is Red Vienna, a militant form enclosed within the city. He is interested in the differences between the Red Vienna housing projects and the bourgeois city. These housing projects do not have private street entrances, so their street-facing exteriors are able to present impenetrable walls. They are monumental and blank in terms of their absence of entrances at least. He suggested that such monumental exteriors, which present a kind of urban fortification, represent a kind of class solidarity and class struggle, and that representation is important because the city is otherwise largely dominated by the interests of the bourgeoisie.

◂ **Aureli:** *I am not sure I ever said that* A Simple Heart *came from the Red Vienna Hofe. As I said in my previous comment, the inspiration for* A Simple Heart *was the architecture of the college – the quadrangle – which we used as a means to critique the dismantling of the university as a form of welfare.*

Many people seeing such monumentalized exteriors would react to them as expressions of totalitarianism, but he sees them as instruments for revealing the struggle. Yet that struggle only becomes visible based on resistance to bourgeois individuation and collectivization.

This coincides with your point that we need another form of living in a large city that does not just replicate the bourgeois countryside idyll.

Sarah Whiting: One strategy would be banal repetition, which would make it very legible. Fernand Pouillon designed large-scale housing projects in Paris after the Second World War that are interesting to me because they are all of a certain language. Even though they vary enormously, they are identifiable. From the point of view of a developer they are not repetitive enough to be brilliant from a number crunching point of view. But thousands of people live in them, across the spectrum of class status.

These projects posited a different way. Those projects were built as middle-class housing, but they provide a model for extreme collective living that is not oppressively repetitive.

Jessica Reynolds: That is a more nuanced approach, but it is harder to achieve.

Sarah Whiting: It is harder to achieve, but Aureli sees this moment as one that demands stark visibility. Though Somol and Aureli both have positions that are generally seen as antithetical to each other, they nonetheless both argue for ways of amplifying legibility to a degree of exaggeration.

Joseph Bedford: That suggests a question of whether the politics of a given project are prescriptive, or if they are open to interpretation. Aureli's politics are definitive. He uses the language of class struggle, and representation becomes manifest through a collective unit in the city. Architecture is the means by which the excluded workers become visible. Of course, that gets more problematic when we take account of who the workers are in post-industrial society.

Sarah Whiting: It is not a global set of relations. The American model of post-war housing projects and superblocks is different from those of France or England. Aureli works in European and British settings, though I know he has looked at New York and Houston. The models that are most familiar to him are unfamiliar here.

Michael Speaks and others have argued that a market-driven approach distinguishes the American context, but I disagree. Acknowledging an altogether different possibility for the worker in the United States is important.

Joseph Bedford: How does the superblock figure into that formula?

Sarah Whiting: In the United States, superblocks are not state projects but are funded by private development. Even when they are linked to state money, as in public housing, they are nevertheless tied to non-state funding through insurance and other private infrastructure. Finance and property acquisition and ownership in the States is unique.

Joseph Bedford: Why would superblocks not represent class struggle, in their legibility?

Sarah Whiting: In 'The Superblock', Alan Colquhoun argues that it is all about aggregation of capital.[4] That is very different. And it is important to understand that his argument was situated in a British post-war context.

Joseph Bedford: I would like to conclude this conversation by asking you about one final subject, that of housing. On this subject, Reinhold Martin made a plea for housing during the final roundtable debate. He called it a moment of truth for architects, since that is where the state touches the ground. What did you think of his position on housing? I would imagine that this is where the two of you align with one another. Despite your disagreements during the projective debate, I would imagine that Martin's call to understand in terms of material techniques, protocols and policy aligns with the turn to practice that you, Somol and Stan Allen were pushing for.

Sarah Whiting: I agree. I am very excited by Martin's work on housing. It has been neglected as an area of theoretical articulation. A lot of interest groups have to confront one another over it, so it inevitably causes friction. It is an incredibly important, timely topic. I would have found his argument in his paper more persuasive though if he had emphasized housing more, with less of a focus on the Greeks. His discussion of Arendt is intelligent, but less urgent than his work on housing, so I would have liked to see him emphasize that more, because those kinds of questions, about the city, about public housing, but also public sidewalks, public squares or even public furniture are all things we should be focusing upon more. They are all ripe for attention.

◄ **Martin:** *Oikos = household. What could be more direct? Think about oikos as the root of both economy and ecology, and you also approach a meaningful political ecology – through the right to housing.*

Notes

1. Note: This interview was conducted while Sarah Whiting was the Dean of Rice University from 2010 to 2019. Since 2019 she has been the Dean of the Graduate School of Design at Harvard University.
2. Sarah Whiting and Robert Somol, 'Notes on the Doppler Effect: The Many Moods of Modernism', *Perspecta* 33 (2002): 72–7.
3. Fredric Jameson, *A Singular Modernity Essay on the Ontology of the Present* (New York: Verso, 2002).
4. Alan Colquhoun, 'The Superblock', in *Essays in Architectural Criticism: Modern Architecture and Historical Change* (Cambridge, MA: MIT Press, 1985), 83–103. See also Sarah Whiting, 'SUPER!' *Log* 16 (2009): 19–26.

7

The Politics of Architecture

Roundtable and Q&A

Participants: Pier Vittorio Aureli, Reinhold Martin, Chantal Mouffe, Ines Weizman, Sarah Whiting.
Moderator: Joseph Bedford

Joseph Bedford: Our discussion here together might proceed by addressing any number of questions. What weighting do we give to the representational or the material in our reflections on architecture's politics? What is architecture's relationship to consensus or order? When should we withdraw from the system and when and how do we engage it? What does it mean to be critical? What is the value of the public or public space in the politics of architecture? How can we reengage the question of housing?

But I would like to suggest that we begin with the most obvious question. Given that the advocacy of democracy is so central to Mouffe's work, I want to begin with the question of democracy. Here is a quick way to get us moving, Pier Vittorio; are you an advocate of democracy?

Reinhold Martin: Be careful, that is a trap!

Pier Vittorio Aureli: [Audience Laughs]. Yes, like anybody else in this room, of course. But democracy has been reduced to an empty ideology that can obscure aggressive, post-democratic practices. We must defend the principles of modern democracy, but we should also be aware that today, the banner of democracy has become a Trojan horse, concealing perverse strategies of winning consensus.

Martin's warning about the rhetoric that claims public space is the only space where politics occurs is a perceptive remark, but I maintain that public space is still important, even in its most traditional forms. All kinds of interested parties with ulterior motives have perverted public space. Architecture and urban design discourse often includes rhetoric that suppresses the fundamental conflicts behind this idea of space. Since the state has relinquished its role in supporting public space, it uses the phrase as jargon, even when there is no possibility of a truly political public space behind it.

I support the values we likely all share, but with certain qualifications. For example, we cannot reduce the relation between private and public to an opposition of public space versus housing in order to grasp the political dimensions of the city. A public sphere is still a worthwhile ambition, yet we often see the notion of the public sphere fetishized.

Public space makes developers very happy and this fact should signal to us that, while we should not dispose of public space, we must radically question it as a category.

Chantal Mouffe: Neither of us has mentioned the concept of the commons, but it is a popular topic today. Some people have argued that the idea of the public is necessarily reliant on the state, so we ought to abandon it in favour of the commons. As architects, what do you think of the commons? Might that ameliorate the negative conceptions of the public sphere?

Pier Vittorio Aureli: It is an interesting question. The first theorists of the commons, Antonio Negri, Paolo Virno and the post-operaist intellectuals, have been highly influential for me. In the 1990s, when the crisis of the state was becoming acute, those theorists began working on the concept of the commons. I recognize its productivity vis-à-vis the state's dismissal of public space. But these authors' fundamental theoretical mistake is to assume a mutually exclusive relationship between the commons and the public. The commons will not replace the public.

> ◀ *Aureli: Here I have to make a correction: The idea of the Common of Negri and the post-operaists is not exactly 'the commons'. The Post-operaist common is rooted in the Italian medieval tradition of the 'comune' whose best translation in English would be 'commonwealth'. According to this definition, the common is the products of the natural environment and the products of social interaction such as codes, affects, information and more in general knowledge. Historically the commons are land and resources that, especially peasants, held collectively and whose access was regulated by localized customary practices. However, both concepts have been recently mobilized in order to define a space beyond property, that is beyond the juridical binary of public and private.*

Chantal Mouffe: I agree. I propose thinking of the commons as an agonistic public, which would mean that we do not need to abandon the public.

Pier Vittorio Aureli: Within the framework of political economy, the theorists of the commons recognize how today production has led to the dissolution of the structures – oppositions between private and public, the phenomenology of production – that the modern state had built. The commons is both the main source of capital and that which is exploited by capital.

Some degree of representation would be necessary to construct a counter-project around the commons, but by definition the commons cannot be representative. This is the fundamental dilemma: the commons cannot have a form because the commons is the totality of production. In order to unify around the struggle of the commons, we need some kind of political form, but political form can only exist as a public form.

> ◀ *Aureli: Here I am referring to the 'common' rather than the commons. However, today I would not be so sure about this claim about the impossibility of representing the commons or the common. History shows us a multitude of*

examples of how commoning gave form to specific representations and even architectural and urban forms that were eradicated with the rise of the modern state and the public/private organization of space.

Sarah Whiting: This reminds me of Alexis de Tocqueville's remark that abstract terms are like empty boxes with false bottoms. They allow us to pull out and put back in anything that we want. This might bring us back to the discussion of multivalent terminology. We have these abstractions, whether they are political terms or the abstractions of the space that we form as architects in the city. They take on certain terms, but they are irreducible, and that is where the agonism lies. Abstraction is tied to agonistic struggle.

Any abstract term can be represented, so I disagree that we cannot represent the commons. But connecting terminology to the challenge of representation is key in this discussion. I find the prospect of new forms of representation spurred by these new concepts exciting, not only in regard to artistic practices, but in terms of what we do with that representation. If the discussion moves past two-dimensional representation to also engage practice, it can be propelled forward.

◀ **Martin:** *Our conversation was surprisingly silent on climate change (myself included). Earth is our commons. Only robust public institutions, and a redistributive political economy at the scale of the planet, can prevent its further enclosure, and the consequent exposure of millions – billions? – to virtually unlivable lives.*

Ines Weizman: The subject of the commons was mentioned by Pier Vittorio, Reinhold and Sarah. Sarah, you wondered what to make of the case of Superkilen Park in which the problem between the commons and the public and its embedded agonisms appears in a concrete example. You spoke about passing through the square as being like an aesthetic resonance chamber. How do we engage in such a space? How could we document and assess its working. We could photograph it from above, or take snapshots of individual objects in the square but the work of 'commoning' is not necessarily visible.

Sarah Whiting: I am ambivalent about the Superkilen Park. I regard it as a brave project, in that it resurrects postmodern modes of appropriation, while it also conveys the problematic idea that each of these sixty communities can be identified with one thing, one sign or one object. How do we deal with the representation of political groupings?

Reinhold Martin: The notion of the commons arose as a strategic move in a particular context. The context has changed, so the moves are also changing. But ultimately there is something irreducible about the problem of distinguishing the public from the commons.

When I came to Britain to study architectural history, I became interested in the tradition of the country house. This tradition corresponds directly to the enclosure of the common lands. Historicizing the problem would involve not just going back to

Italy in the 1960s or '70s, but to the enclosure of lands on which aristocrats built their estates. It draws together the transformation of agriculture in the British countryside, the urbanization of labour and other topics that Raymond Williams addresses in *The Country and the City*.[1] That book remains a wonderful reference on the poetics of these processes. Tracing that history forward demystifies them. While it is easy to accept the appearances of the supposedly dematerialized, kids-on-screens aspect of the commons as an instance of immaterial production, we must acknowledge that there is an actual historical struggle going on around the material processes of production relative to the commons.

On the subject of immaterial production, Pier Vittorio, you showed the competition for the Guggenheim Abu Dhabi. A group led by Michael Sorkin and associated with Gulf Labour ran an alternative competition which the New York group 'Who Builds Your Architecture?' has also referenced in their work addressing the exploitation of migrant construction workers.[2] These groups contest the premises on which the Guggenheim have been expanding and building, and architects' roles in perpetuating those actions. It is a counter-competition.[3] If that is hegemony, it is closer to the tradition than Ines's examples. It may not be specifically political architecture in the sense of forming a polity out of these dissident projects. But the paper project, the counter-project, constitutes a genre that many of us – certainly our colleagues who are doing activist work to challenge the profession – imagine still has a certain agency.

Furthermore, this work is quite professional. 'Who Builds Your Architecture?' conducts public and private meetings with professionals, ranging from big firms to boutique firms, working with clients that rely on enslaved or indentured labourers across the world. This is where the question of representation arises as an aspect of architecture with potential for activism. It does not have to be representation in the sense of *re-presenting* something and therefore participating in a metaphysics of presence. Instead, we might look at how to contest the premises discursively.

Regarding the literal imprisonment of dissident figures, the disappearing of the protagonists of Ines's paper is meaningful. In most cases of architectural contestation – though not in this alternative competition – and in the context of the 1980s Soviet Union, her story reminds us that certain things can and cannot be said in the public sphere at a given time. That is an extreme instance, in which there were dire consequences. But it makes clear that, in enterprises like the Guggenheim, we assume a series of factors to govern architecture's cultural-political-economic status. When we do not contest them, we allow them to hegemonically exclude other statements. So, we need ways of speaking in public that do not presume that sphere is available.

Joseph Bedford: This speaks to the topic of consensus in architecture and the possibilities of dissenting from it.

Pier Vittorio Aureli: Consensus is the fundamental problem of the whole theory of architecture and not just architecture today. I am not referring to practical consensus, in the sense of sharing space or living together. Any political form, even the most democratic, posits some level of consensus. But architecture embodies what I call 'the ideology of consensus'. This is not just practical consensus, but the conviction that stability and order are incontrovertible, and that no alternative is possible.

The reason I quoted Vitruvius, for example, is that his *Ten Books on Architecture* both starts and ends with images of conflict. In Vitruvius dedication to Augustus, he implicitly recognizes that Augustus came to power to pacify the empire. The last image of the text is the siege of Marseilles, the last polis in the Mediterranean, which symbolizes the possibility of architectural knowledge being used to win a conflict. The last part of the *Ten Books* is about war machines. In between these two images of conflict, Vitruvius's rhetoric is entirely concerned with what Leon Battista Alberti called *aedificatoria*, an idea of building that exceeds just building buildings, to develop an ethos of suppressing conflict to achieve stability. The line from Vitruvius to Le Corbusier is evident. Until recently, architectural theory has always enacted this rhetoric of reconciliation.

Chantal Mouffe: You say consensus, but why would you not say order?

Pier Vittorio Aureli: It is not just order. The theorists of modern architecture already considered order to be too aggressive a word. So, authors subtly evoked order and stability by referring to peaceful coexistence. Architecture is full of representations of cities in which everything is peaceful and smooth. Manfredo Tafuri called this problem 'architectural ideology'. Architects only began to question the mandate of architecture in the 1960s, and only since the 1970s have we been discussing critical practices in architecture.

Ideas like these always arise outside of institutions. Within what I call 'labour-intensive architecture' – architecture that is produced by big practices – the ideology of consensus is still strong. A very important, intelligent Italian architect, Stefano Boeri, offers an astonishing example of this. In the 1970s, Boeri was involved in political struggle. I am not critiquing him as a person, but as an architect his practice represents the phenomenon of the ideology of consensus. He is one of the few architects with a real engagement with politics. He can speak about how to be an architect and also a political agent within institutions. A few years ago, Hines, one of the biggest real estate developers in the world, commissioned him to design residential towers in Porta Nuova, Milan, a former working-class district. Its location near the central station attracted a lot of real estate interest. Boeri is an astute, subtle intellectual, yet he designed two high-rise, luxury apartment buildings. Beyond gentrification, it is an almost military occupation of the city. Evidently, the only way to create consensus was to clad the tower with trees. It is the least subtle solution I can imagine, and it is striking that someone with his theoretical background felt it necessary to adopt this consensual strategy just to perform his role as an architect.

Sarah Whiting: Chantal, you critique architecture for reproducing consensus as well. Your agonistic model of politics implies a respect for the adversary, but does it not also imply that one thinks that one is right?

Chantal Mouffe: Yes, in that one wants to win.

Sarah Whiting: One wants to win because one thinks one is right, and believes that others will buy in. Thinking as an architect, a level of consensus is obligatory to the hubris that goes with any architectural proposition of constructing something that will organize other people's lives. To what degree can one believe in consensus knowing there is another potential battle down the road that an adversary might win? We all traffic in consensus, whether in politics or architecture, but we have to parse degrees of consensus.

Chantal Mouffe: Yes, one wants to win over a majority. But reconciliation is the way to achieve consensus. Winning against adversaries is important, but that is a matter of convincing opponents. I reject the idea of absolute truth, so being right is not relevant. I would not describe a project as constituting consensus just because its author thinks it is good or because people identify with it.

Sarah Whiting: It is a temporary consensus. The people trying to persuade others acknowledge that they are not the only ones who are right, but that they are convinced that they have a good proposition. I am not trying to advocate for truth, but persuasion and consensus are operative parts of our field.

Reinhold Martin: Yes, but arriving at consensus might be difficult. Referring to our starting point about the question of democracy, we might find some consensus about what a democratic architecture might look like today. But I would say that, today, arriving at a consensus on what a socialist architecture might look like would be much harder. Even getting the question on the table is difficult.

That is the question that Ines's protagonists posed. They were appealing to human rights protocols strategically, but they identified as socialists. As I have been learning from Daniel Talesnik about the example of how the Red Bauhaus became diasporic.[4] In addition to Ernst May, it included several other dissidents. Hannes Meyer had a group around him, which is the reason he was expelled from the Bauhaus. That movement travelled to Chile and to Mexico, with effects that have been invisible to history so far.

> ◄ **Weizman:** *See Thomas Flierl, 'Migrant with a Conflicted Sense of Home: Hannes Meyer after the Bauhaus', in* Dust and Data. Traces of the Bauhaus across 100 years*, ed. Ines Weizman (Leipzig: Spector Books, 2019), 420–35, and Daniel Talesnik, Tibor Weiner's Architectural Design Curriculum in Chile (1946–7) in the same publication.*

We are now performing the effort of recovering these kinds of projects. It is historical research projects of these kinds that allow us to ask, without being kicked out of the room, is there a socialist architecture? Has there ever been, or could there ever be one? Where I teach and work, asking questions such as these are very difficult.

Chantal Mouffe: We published *Hegemony and Socialist Strategy* in the 1980s. If we were going to write it today, we would not write it in a socialist mode. In that moment, the battle we were waging was to redefine socialism and radical democracy.

Reinhold Martin: Yes, and vocabularies and counter-vocabularies are important. But returning to concrete examples, one of the reasons that housing is meaningful is that it raises the spectre of the state in its various dimensions vis-à-vis the public. It prompts us to study issues like who is paying for it, who owns the land and other structural questions, without settling for an outdated, nostalgic, state-dominated model.

The modern form of the state, classically, is only one scale of hegemonic production. The thing we call China is not just the Chinese state government, but a series of articulations that people like Giovanni Arrighi have argued constitute a global model that is potentially counter-hegemonic to those sanctioned by the United States after the Cold War.

Architects are traveling around the world and reproducing this apparatus, and it would help us to think about what it is that architects are reproducing. Alternatively, what counter-models might we imagine that would constitute legitimate successors – with or without the vocabulary – of historically socialist projects?

Joseph Bedford: I would like to bring in questions from the audience.

Audience Member 1: Can we approach consensus through the lens of norms rather than truth? Chantal said agonism does not belong to the Left because it has no norm. It guarantees the legitimacy of various positions. For architecture, this is attractive because it implies a kind of formalism. But if we have no norm, how do we escape the accusation of relativism? As Reinhold Martin was just asking, can architecture be radically political without norms and without militancy?

Sarah Whiting: Chantal referred to moments of fixity, as Luc Boltanski and Eve Chiapello also describe in *The New Spirit of Capitalism*.[5] Every project offers up its own provisional norm. I get nervous when you brush off formalism. We always must attend to form in discussions of how architecture engages politically. Not to do so is to pretend that we do not traffic in limits and delineations. The fact that we have allowed the term form to become associated with particular aesthetics does not mean we should not use the term. Suggesting norms is a way to make a proposition with the assumption that someone else will understand it, whether it produces consensus or not. Even if it does not establish a new norm, it at least projects a moment for advancing our field.

Joseph Bedford: Is your question about what visions of the good life are driving us?

Audience Member 1: Red Vienna conveys a formal strategy. We cannot abandon form, since it is integral to architecture. But the political elements of Red Vienna are not reducible to the domain of formalism. I am concerned that we are discussing agonism only on that formal register. The experience of form becomes an aspect of inhabiting the city, but what are the politics that motivate engaging formally? What were the architects and builders of Red Vienna actually trying to do?

Pier Vittorio Aureli: Red Vienna is a unique situation. First of all, the promoters, social democrats, were renegades compared with the more orthodox Marxists. Traditional Marxists have always despised social democrats because they accept liberal democracy as the grounds for class struggle. The projects manifest that conflict. The social democrats had to consent to the given rules, which they could not change because they were only in power in the city and not at the level of the state. They found profound motivation in the class they represented, despite having opponents on all sides. They had to accept the adversarial nature of the struggle, and they exploited that enmity as a way to reinforce their project.

In that sense, it was an alternative to people like Hannes Meyer's strategies for socialist architecture. Meyer wanted to completely engineer socialist life. He would organize everything according to the principles of socialism. In Red Vienna, the form of the project itself conveys the struggle. This is an architectural project that escapes both the totalizing aspirations of realist socialism, and the value-free relativism of 'acupuncture architecture', or small-scale, negligible interventions.

Ines Weizman: Red Vienna was a municipal project and it was workable and successful in the scale in which it was designed and managed by its planners, architects and city bureaucrats. Also Hannes Meyer's collective housing projects in Dessau-Törten houses could be considered successful as experiments that sit within other housing typologies and housing concepts. I cannot agree more that the totalizing aspirations of the real-existing socialist regime flattened the pluralism and diversity that is needed in thinking the collective city and urban life. And I like when Chantal says that in the 1980s *Hegemony and Socialist Strategy* was aiming to redefine socialism and radical democracy. It was also a task for rethinking planning and architecture in these terms.

Audience Member 2: The dimension of time within architecture has remained in the background. We have discussed its spatial dimensions, but one of the things that the system of neoliberal capitalism does so well is to produce perpetual, immediate crises, in order to deny the possibility of fundamentally restructuring social power relations. Chantal said that there is no revolutionary architecture. By means of its duration, architecture preserves the power structures already in place. Housing is often the best place to look at this. Forms of revolutionary architecture – for example, the invention of the terrace row in Britain, or the reconstruction of Paris under Napoléon III and Haussmann – inevitably lapse into formulas over time. In that sense, architecture is more about these formulas than about building. Yet socialism in architecture has neglected to address housing. Would you attribute that blind spot to Friedrich Engels's *The Housing Question*, which principally implicated housing?[6]

Reinhold Martin: Yes. Anecdotally, a small New York division of a Marxist group called Platypus hosted a panel a couple of years ago called 'Ruins of Modernity: The Failure of Revolutionary Architecture in the Twentieth Century'.[7] They invited Peter Eisenman, Bernard Tschumi, Joan Ockman and me. It took place in a room at NYU that was designed by Roche Dinkeloo.

They asked us, is there a revolutionary architecture? My reply was, yes, we are in it now, for the reasons you point out. Eisenman was oblivious to the implications of that, but he felt the need to disagree. So, I am agreeing with you completely. But for those of us who object to this state of affairs, then, the question is what a counter-revolutionary architecture could be. For me, housing is the place where architects tend to look for politics, or at least for social responsibility. It is where society most traditionally enters into architectural education. For example, at Columbia we have a housing studio, one of the few remaining, and students typically design projects that are appropriately sober and responsible.

> ◀ **Martin:** *To clarify: By 'revolutionary architecture' I mean in this case the architecture of the neoliberal counter-revolution. This counter-revolution was and remains no less fierce than any of its vanguardist cognates, a cruel irony that was made palpable by the postmodern setting.*

When you mention time, you are implying a sharper edge related to historicity. Architects have tended to repeatedly build according to the same models, with slight differences each time. For Engels, housing was not really a solution to anything. It was more or less superstructural, and what was at stake were the relations of production. That was the housing question Engels was debating with Pierre-Joseph Proudhon over property. At issue was the relationship between ownership and collectivity, as well as conceiving of the house as a site for the production of class consciousness. That intuition remains one of the ghosts, following Jacques Derrida, that continues to haunt us. Architecture, specifically, has not escaped the spectres of Marx and Engels.

Chantal Mouffe: Reinhold, when I said, 'there is no such thing as a revolutionary architecture', I was quoting you. It is dependent on context. You need to clarify those remarks.

Reinhold Martin: Yes. That was from a piece I wrote on Occupy Wall Street, where the call was for a revolution.[8] I was asking what the role of architecture was in the context of organized dissent. The day after the revolution will always come – not just literally, but also in the imagination. How do we imagine the institutions of a new society? Thinking this way is a little more conservative than traditional revolutionary models. I argue that monuments to neoliberalism are, in fact, revolutionary. They are the infrastructures that are meant to sustain the neoliberal revolution. In its temporality, architecture always operates through deferral and perpetuation.

◄ **Martin:** *Architecture tends to become necessary the day after the (political) revolution, after the smoke has cleared. My perspective is therefore historical in a double sense: in noting the failure of most avowedly 'revolutionary' architecture, which tends to miss its mark by arriving too early or too late, while also recognizing this untimeliness as an asset. Thinking in the future perfect tense, an architecture adequate to revolutionary change will only have become necessary after the fact. What will that architecture be?*

Ines Weizman: I agree that housing has been a blind spot. Pier Vittorio critiqued Boeri for approaching housing as simply building marketable apartments, not as a part of the city. I think it is not enough to just address a 'housing problem'. Provision alone is not sufficient. Housing is about urban life, infrastructures of culture, education and leisure. So housing is also always a question of thinking about the city at different scales.

Reinhold Martin: Boeri participated in an event that we held in Venice about housing. He claimed that project in Milan is about post-sustainable ecological practice. The practical, political dimension to this, though, is that historically we have seen environmentalist discourse used to conceal deeper forms of contestation. Richard Nixon set up the Environmental Protection Agency in the United States deliberately to split the left, to create friction between the anti-war movement and the civil rights movement and provide a channel for the less radical ecologists. Our response could be to say that this will always be about housing, in the sense that the planet itself is an *oikos* that is being contested in the current moment. We need to discuss it, and not pretend that we will reach a harmonious resolution.

Audience Member 3: I would like to ask about other parts of the world. Chantal, does your agonistic approach apply to non-Western spaces? How can we in, for instance, Latin America, Asia, Turkey, India or Japan use an agonistic approach?

Chantal Mouffe: First of all, Latin America is not really a non-Western society. In fact, my model is very popular in Latin America. Cristina Fernandez de Kirchner, the president of Argentina, said that she is a fan of my work. Later, I learned that she had been accused of not being democratic on the grounds of not trying to build consensus. Her response was to strike back by referring to my work. She did so in order to help her argue that democracy is not about consensus but dissensus!

I have a student from Lebanon who is trying to frame Lebanese politics in terms of agonism. I am interested, but I am circumspect. My understanding of agonism stipulates democratic institutions. I insist on agonism as a consequence of my criticism of what I call the post-political situation, in which there is no difference between centre-right and centre-left. Where some might say that this is good for democracy, I argue that it is dangerous because it paves the terrain for right-wing populism. I began my reflection on populism in Austria, and then moved to studying France. People regarded Britain as a counterexample, because this is the birthplace of Third-Way politics, where right-wing populism does not exist. At the time that was true, but all of the conditions were ripe in the UK for its development. Now we have it, with the rise of the UK Independence Party.

In general, populism attenuates the vigour of democracy by making it overly consensual. In some cases, though – and here I am thinking of Tunisia – the problem is not to inject greater agonism. Tunisia needs more grounds for consensus. I do not mean to imply that this is a recipe, that too much consensus requires more agonism, and vice versa. In the absence of a basic consensus, people need to institute some framework to establish it. It entirely depends on context. If basic democratic institutions do not exist, then agonistic politics are not possible.

Audience Member 4: Referring to Ines' work on the Russian paper architects, the Moscow critic Anatole Rappaport wrote an essay titled 'Fantasy versus Utopia'.[9] Rappaport described these architects' work not as utopian but as an architecture of fantasy. This suggests two lines of thought to me. First, what opportunities for imaginative freedom arise out of fantasy, if it is not beholden to the programmatic form of a utopian project? Second, the concept of utopia has not yet been addressed by this panel. What form can a political programme take in architecture if it is not utopian? Architecture produces ideal forms to accord with utopia as an image of power. Rephrasing the proverb, 'Man proposes, God disposes', we might say that architects propose, but it is power that disposes. Power creates laws, which are translated into walls. Following from Pier Vittorio's critique of the ideology of consensus, what other activities can architects undertake, which are not utopian, and do not simply fulfil an existing consensus?

Reinhold Martin: Rather than asking about utopia on the level of ideal cities and authoritarian plans we might pose the question on a more discursive register. In Michel Foucault's sense of discourse, we would ask how the term functions to enable certain thoughts and foreclose others. That outlook would spur us to seek ways of conjuring what I call 'utopia's ghost'.[10] By that I mean not utopia itself, in some reified form, but instead, the glimmer of structural change. It makes that possibility thinkable and allows us to have a substantive political argument about what constitutes this or that concrete possibility in this or that situation. In place of an idealist conception of utopia, I would substitute a materialist one that approaches utopia through actual possible actions. For example, as teachers, we have the ability to go back through the tradition that we know and to globalize it by rereading the documents. The previous question was completely right. We have to interrupt the Eurocentrism of our conversation. Many other examples do not fit our mould.

The failure of utopia, the end of history, and all of that are problems for the Anglo-American sphere, but they are not questions in most of the world. In postcolonial societies, master plans are structurally necessary to get out from under the yoke of colonial power.

For various reasons, that is why they are often regarded as the end of the status quo. In early twentieth-century India, the colonized population appropriated the techniques of the British. The colonial powers intended the relocation of the capital from Calcutta to New Delhi, to quell the contestation of colonial rule in Calcutta. So, while the planning and building of the new capital was a colonialist project, the subsequent planning of housing, universities, hospitals and infrastructures of all kinds in the 1950s and 1960s was nationalist and anti-colonial. They carried out those projects in a dramatically modernist, heroic way. Today might call them utopian. The ideals were more or less socialist, or at least social democratic. Many of the protagonists of those projects were architects who were later mislabelled critical regionalists. The buildings and plans were problematic in a number of ways, and we could analyse those issues. But to simply rule them out as not available to the historical imagination, which is to say, the imagination of the future is an absolutely brutal and inexcusable act, pedagogically and discursively.

Joseph Bedford: Please allow me to bring this roundtable to a close. Despite all of our discussion about the necessity of dissensus, I would say that we have reached a surprising degree of consensus during this roundtable. All of us agree that there is a great degree of relevance and applicability of the model of agonism and the idea of hegemony to architectural thought and practice, and we agree on the importance of housing for the politics of architecture, and we mostly agree that there is some value in maintaining at least the built legacy of public spaces if not the current concept of the public, and we agree that there are difficulties with the idea of replacing the public with the commons.

There are still disagreements I am sure, between the respective personal politics of each of us, and subtle differences between different positions on concepts like form, representation, symbolism and materiality, and so on, but we will be able to unpack these differences as we take the exchange further both in our follow-up conversations and in print.

Notes

1 Raymond Williams, *The Country and the City* (London: Chatto and Windus, 1973).
2 On Gulf Labor and Who Builds Your Architecture?, see the websites https://gulflabour.org/ and http://whobuilds.org/
3 http://www.nexthelsinki.org/#about
4 Daniel Adolfo Talesnik, *The Itinerant Red Bauhaus, or the Third Emigration* (New York: Dissertation, Columbia University, 2016).
5 Luc Boltanski and Eve Chiapello, *The New Spirit of Capitalism* (London, New York: Verso, 2005).
6 Friedrich Engels, *The Housing Question* (Atlanta: Pathfinder Press, 1997). Originally published as a pamphlet in 1887.

7   Ruins of Modernity: The Failure of Revolutionary Architecture in the Twentieth Century, NYU Kimmel Center, New York, 7 February 2012. https://platypus1917.org/2012/12/19/2-7-13-ruins-of-modernity/
8   Reinhold Martin, 'Occupy: The Day After', *Places Journal* (December 2011) https://placesjournal.org/article/occupy-the-day-after/
9   Anatole G. Rappaport, 'Fantasy versus Utopia', in *Nostalgia of Culture: Contemporary Soviet Visionary Architecture*, ed. Mikhail Belov (London: AA, 1988).
10 Reinhold Martin, *Utopia's Ghost: Architecture and Postmodernism, Again* (Minneapolis, MN: University of Minnesota Press, 2010).

8

Architecture's Challenges to Chantal Mouffe

Joseph Bedford

A Summary of the Exchange

The four representatives of architecture in the intellectual exchange with Chantal Mouffe that took place in the context of the Architecture Exchange, Pier Vittorio Aureli, Reinhold Martin, Ines Weizman and Sarah Whiting, each put forward a specific set of issues, many of which overlapped with one another, that helped to deepen the understanding of the political nature of architecture. Through the exchange that unfolded in the pages of this book, the reader will have observed a number of key positions which each participant holds. Some were more concerned with the vocation of the scholar and others with the vocation of the practitioner. Some were more concerned with architecture as a kind of generic, background infrastructure, and some were concerned with the singular potential of architectural design. Some were concerned with the political potential of architectural knowledge, and representation, and the relative distance or autonomy it has from practice, and some advocated for architects to collapse that distance in order to be more effective political agents. Some were concerned to think at a global or planetary scale, and others to think at the scale of the city or the building. And some saw a fruitful connection between architecture and the idea of the public realm and others less so.

One of the central issues discussed in the exchange was that which we could refer to simply as type. "Type," here, can be understood as a name for the ideal, model or standard, of which multiple buildings or building parts are made in their image. The topic of type in architecture can also name the many typical particulars that result from a standard. Both Reinhold Martin and Pier Vittorio Aureli understood what they referred to as 'universal urbanization' as a phenomenon of architectural typification, as that force of architecture which governs the social body through what Michel Foucault called 'bio-politics'; the reach of politics into the management of the life of the population itself. For Martin, the power of type in architecture has been a matter of 'the repetitions of the social: the small, technical rituals by which we are governed'. And the 'iterative spatial techniques ... include[ing] standardized unit and building types, construction modules, Taylorized furniture arrangements, factory-made fixtures, design standards calibrated to the measurements of statistically "average" or "normal" bodies, and, eventually, prefabricated modular building components'. If power in industrialized, mass society, is biopolitical power, then universal urbanization is today's new 'governing hegemony', as Martin put it.

> ◄ **Martin:** *Here and below, we should avoid conflating urbanization with biopower. Neither is universal, but in different ways. By 'urbanization', I mean a more circumscribed process than do, say, Neil Brenner and Christian Schmid, who speak of 'planetary urbanization' in a Lefebvrian sense. By any measure, half the world's population does not live in cities.*

One potential response to this insight about the power of architecture through its repetitious spatial techniques was to 'historicize' those very techniques (Martin) or to forensically 'map' 'analyse' and 'study' the concrete production of architecture (Aureli). That is, one response, for those in the field of architecture who are aware of this power, is to produce forms of disciplinary knowledge. Martin described this response as 'concrete' and 'patient' pedagogical work. Presumably, for Martin, the idea behind such a call for greater knowledge would be that eventually such knowledge would lead to changes in the formulas and models behind those standardized units of architecture built across the globe.

This topic of 'universal urbanization', of course, as Martin and Aureli discussed it, can be seen to map directly on to the problematic of the 'rise of the social' which was diagnosed by both Hannah Arendt and Michel Foucault, and which has always been a central issue in Mouffe's work. For Foucault and Arendt, one of the central problems of political modernity has been the triumph of the realm of the social and private life in which populations are reproduced and managed (*oikonomia*) like a large household (*oikos*) and thus without resort to the public realm of political action which stood beyond the realm of the social.

> ◄ **Martin:** *Again, per Arendt the sprawling 'rise of the social' is associated with the domestic, managerial oikos, and not with the public, political polis. So the term 'urbanization' can mislead. But whatever we choose to call it, I certainly wouldn't want to describe this zone as a 'sea' in which float 'islands' of typologically legible – and therefore politically salient – architecture. That writes off the political topology of the household, which was my point.*

Yet where Martin accepted the universal urbanization that the rise of the social has produced, and wagered that 'the social ... can inaugurate a political topology' of its own, Aureli resists urbanization, describing it as the dominating 'sea' against which monumental architectural 'islands' can be constructed and that reassert the political realm of action.[1] And where Martin spoke through the voice of the scholar, directing his patient pedagogical work towards the raising of planetary consciousness and seeking to avoid formal short-cuts to problems that he viewed as much larger and more complex in scale, Aureli spoke as the architect, imagining the difference that the particular design of a built project can make. And so correspondingly, where Martin spent much of his intervention in the historical scene of ancient Greece, examining how the historical spaces of the public realm and its distinction with the private realm might have themselves informed the very theoretical categories by which we think politics today, Aureli spent a great deal of time examining examples of what he labelled 'politically explicit architecture' whose singular instances of design played a role in the political rearticulations of their time. The first example, that of Palladio's villas, which Aureli offered, was more clearly the work of a single author, and was also more conservative in its politics. The second example, that of the housing of Red Vienna, was the result of a more complicated mixture of architectural design and municipal policy, and it was also, and perhaps not uncoincidentally, more progressive in its politics.

Red Vienna has clearly been the favoured model for Aureli in his own work with his practice Dogma, and in his book, *The Possibility of an Absolute Architecture*, in which he argued, drawing upon Mouffe's work, for the role of formal delineation in architecture as a means to institutionalize agonistic conflict in the city. Aureli has been in full agreement with Mouffe that the political should not be subordinated to reason or morality, but articulated as the highest principle of collective social organization. He has explicitly deployed Mouffe's work when writing that the task of politics in architecture is to 'transform conflict into coexistence without exaggerating, or denying, the reasons for the conflict itself' and that: 'By clearly exposing their limits, architectural parts confront each other and form an agonistic plurality, becoming a site where judgement through difference is again possible.'²

◄ **Aureli:** *In all my work there is a distinct separation between my own writings and the work of my practice. I do not use my writings to support the architecture of my practice. In this sense, Red Vienna is not a model for my practice, but a relevant case study in the more general question of a policy about public housing.*

The topic of type was also tied to a second central topic of the exchange, that of scale, because for Martin, it is the planetary scale of today's capitalism that has rendered the functions of localized places, buildings, or cities, in particular countries somewhat obsolete in their political potentiality. He questioned whether it is possible today to construct the kinds of consciousness (or identification) needed to support political progress in localized spaces and places under the logic of abstraction that pertains to globalization. In short, the question being debated was whether the building or the city are the appropriate vehicle for the construction of 'consciousness' of economic relations or the 'identification' of the worker today? For Martin, the answer appears to be 'no'. For Aureli it is 'perhaps'.

◄ **Martin:** *Looking back, nowhere did I argue that the global supersedes the local as a site of politics. The politics of scale is much more kaleidoscopic than that. In highlighting an international (or planetary) division of labour intimately woven into the clothes we all wear, I only want to concretize scalar abstractions like 'local' and 'global'. Today's language of 'supply chains' does the opposite: it* *fetishizes the interests of those being supplied, at the expense of those doing the supplying.*

◄ **Weizman:** *I would argue that the architectural project is a medium of political work in all the stages of conceiving, commissioning, designing, building and making it part of a community, and aiming to reach consensus. The architectural project is a constant negotiation between and about political and social forces on an institutional and organisational level and through space. This conflict even remains part of a building's life, well beyond its planning stage, or its completion. As I have argued elsewhere, large-scale social housing needs to include a certain management of care and maintenance to keep this conflictual dynamic alive.*

Mouffe herself has argued that identification and consciousness raising should be understood as beginning at the local scale and enlarging through 'chains of equivalence' to a global scale. Yet for her, identification should not focus upon economic relations or the identity of the worker alone, but on all forms of identification equally. For Martin and Aureli, by contrast, the identity of the worker remains primary, though Martin argues that a larger planetary scale needs to be in play in order to understand the conditions of the worker in today's globalized division of labour, and Aureli imagines that worker solidarity can be constructed through architectural form at the scale of the building and city. Of course, Mouffe's prioritization of the local above the global comes not from a preference for the possibility of architecture, which necessarily operates at the scale of particular places, but rather from what her critics have called her 'historicist' philosophical position which refuses to universalize its applicability beyond its given Western starting point. Though, here we can also add that Aureli shares this architectural preference for the local scale of intervention with the second architectural practitioner in the exchange, Sarah Whiting; who, like Aureli, has argued for her own kinds of idea of discreteness; that of 'the project'.

◄ **Aureli:** *I would like to highlight the way that the idea of 'project' is used in the Italian and Anglo-Saxon contexts. In Italian 'progetto' does not simply address the architectural scale, what Aldo Rossi in his book* The Architecture of the City *calls the 'urban artifact' but a more general strategy that unites policy, urbanism and architecture. In the English-speaking context, 'project' seems to address the architect's imagination or a specific approach. For me, and in all my work, this difference in the use of the term 'project' is crucial.*

Despite their disagreements over matters of history versus practice, pedagogy versus architectural form, or the global scale versus the local scale, Martin and Aureli agreed entirely, as did others in the exchange, about the idea that housing was indeed the central front of architecture's politics. Unsurprisingly, Martin insisted upon understanding housing in terms of the 'scaled measurements, statistically derived norms, and regulatory parameters' by which the social is today managed, where Aureli tried to position housing as a moment of municipal politics whose architectural, stylistic and monumental characteristics could play an equal political role to aspects of policy such as taxation, rent and amenities. Yet Martin nonetheless agreed that today's housing projects, such as those in Harlem, constitute powerful symbols of a certain political moment of truth today – witnessed in the resistance of so many housing tenants to gentrification and displacement.

◀ **Martin:** *By housing I mean public or social housing. New York is among the few US cities where public housing has not been demolished under neoliberal legislation. In an ironic twist on Aureli's argument, behind that legislation (HOPE VI) was the Congress for the New Urbanism, who used architecture's formal and stylistic characteristics to promote privately developed, less dense, racially coded, 'neotraditional' streetscapes in place of modernist public housing. Blithely, these architectural humanists thereby withdrew the right to housing of thousands of mostly African-American residents in cities like Chicago, New Orleans, Baltimore (see HBO's The Wire, Season 3), etc.*

Another central topic to the exchange, placed on the table primarily by Sarah Whiting, was that of the political terrain of architectural practice itself. Here Whiting was self-conscious of her 'challenge' to Mouffe to consider the 'imbricated status' of architectural practice, with its legal and regulatory constraints, its economics, its expansive scale, its wide-ranging forms of expertise, and especially so when contrasted to the practices of artists. As Whiting put it, artists:

> do not have the same legal rules. They do not have to have four inches for a balcony rail. Due to their professional liabilities, architects have to deal with so many obligations and restrictions. That is where I challenged her. Architecture has to deal with the economy, technology, and politics of regulation in ways that could make her work even more interesting.

Whiting's challenge was in effect the challenge of the 'turn to practice' against the Derridean 'Il n'y a pas de hors-texte' that defined Mouffe's intellectual starting point and her claim, going back to *Hegemony and Socialist Strategy*, that there is no non-discursive realm that matters to politics. It echoes the challenge made by Whiting's former colleague Stan Allen to Mark Wigley – the Derridean theorist of architecture – that 'if you understand architecture exclusively as a form of discourse, it is very easy to forget about the specificity of building and begin to compare architecture to other discursive practices: writing, film, new media, computers, and so on'.[3] And if you do so, you lose site of the 'specific opportunities presented by architecture's material and instrumental properties'.[4]

The term 'discourse,' Mouffe and Laclau insisted in 1985, was not just about language but included every level of reality from actions, institutions and material things. As they put it: 'the practice of articulation … cannot consist of purely linguistic phenomena; but must instead pierce the entire material density of the multifarious institutions, rituals and practices through which a discursive formation is structured.'[5] They insisted at that moment that all the non-linguistic aspects of the world are equally identifiable as part of discourse – giving the example of 'blocks, pillars, slabs, and beams'.[6] Yet there was always a sense that, if all these architectural elements were part of a Wittgensteinian 'language game', they were so because for them they constituted 'differential positions' in a signifying network. Blocks, pillars, slabs and beams had no essential positive content of their own, if they did it was irrelevant to the symbolic universe of politics if no antagonism resulted from these material properties. The philosophical starting point of Mouffe's discourse theory thus appears to have annulled the very material and instrumental properties of architecture that Whiting's generation argued distinguish it from other media – and Whiting's generation had argued as much against the Derridians in the generation above them. It is something of the material and instrumental properties of architecture that lay behind the 'imbricated status' Whiting emphasized and which she views as distinguishing architecture from art.

Aureli joined Whiting in highlighting the politics of practice, though he emphasized the degree to which this imbrication was ultimately with capitalism, because architects, for Aureli, are subject to the power and patronage, and forced by the market into the position of both workers and mini-capitalists in their increasingly stiff competition with other professions for status and market share. Like Whiting, Aureli emphasized that technical competence is central to maintaining the political agency of the architect. This was for him all the more so given that architects have been losing this form of competence during the postmodern rise of an alternate architectural disciplinary domain rooted in education and artistic practice. Yet Aureli also clearly remained committed to both a knowledge of form and a knowledge of ethics and politics, and would likely admit that it is the domain of the discipline that has been the domain within which such knowledge has thrived as it has been constructed in educational environments and through a wider sphere of architectural representations such as books and unbuilt projects.

Aureli might have tried to counter Martin's suspicion that the paradigm of Red Vienna risked an 'essentialism, in which all forms of withdrawal and fortification ... are justifiable' and that its power lay in the consciousness-raising capacities of its monumentality, by arguing against this 'Red Vienna myth' that it was in fact – and much like his example of the Sao Paolo collective USINA – the very participation of architects among other local municipal actors that makes progressive architecture so politically effective. Yet Aureli would still likely admit that it is a knowledge of form, ethics and politics that architects bring to such participation, as much as technical knowledge.

Whiting and Aureli thus could also be seen to be in close agreement certainly in terms of their interest in form and its capacities to delineate the distinction between the inside and the outside. Where they might differ, however, is in terms of their respective understanding of the architectural project and whether it is idealist or concrete.

Whiting's theorization of practice did not intend to leave behind the gains of knowledge generated within the relatively 'autonomous' domain of architectural representation and architectural education from the 1960s to the 1990s. Rather, she defends what she calls an 'idealized model' of architectural education as the space for architects to think politically *about practice*. In this respect, 'the project' as a key to her theoretical position has an idealist side *as well as* a concrete side. The domain of practice is not sufficient to sustain the creation of 'projects' in Whiting's terms. Practice has to be guided by a consistent ambition in order for it to constitute a project, and the space of architectural representation and education more often than not, is what helps to formulate, shape and guide the consistency of ambitions. It is in such projects, in Whiting's terms, that architectural knowledge is advanced and it is in architectural knowledge that the future potentialities for architecture's politics exists.

What Whiting *did* resist in her theorization of practice was the idea of critique in architecture being absolutely negative and oppositional. On the surface of things, Whiting and Mouffe may appear to have been in agreement. Mouffe believes that she is also committed to a 'projective' approach insofar as she has argued that *rearticulating identities* and *positing the social* is an absolutely crucial moment within the struggle for hegemony; that simply resisting and negating the social are not enough. Yet Whiting's 'challenge' to Mouffe is evident here in that she argued that Mouffe's preference for artistic practices constitutes a limitation of her thought and would prevent her from fulfilling her theoretical interests in the idea of the positive moment of *rearticulation* of *identities* and of *positing the social*. This is so for Whiting because unlike architecture, artistic practices tend to remain at the level of the temporary, the symbolic and the representational. For her, artistic practices lack the pretence to permanence that makes architecture such a powerful tool in forming the moment of positive rearticulation. In this sense, the limitation to Mouffe's ability to think the positive moment of rearticulation, is tied to her limitation in thinking the material and concrete, and her difficulty engaging with the significance of architecture.

The challenge for Mouffe to consider architectural practice and not just artistic practice is also ultimately a challenge regarding what 'space' could mean for politics if it is treated as more than merely a metaphor. Spatial images repeat throughout Mouffe's writing when she evokes *'levels'* 'constitutive *outsides*', '*sedimentation*', 'discursive *surfaces*', 'common symbolic *spaces*' and 'nodal *points*' but critics, particularly in geography, have long challenged her and Laclau on the lack of concrete spatial thinking in their work.[7] And indeed Mouffe herself has acknowledged that for her 'interest in artistic practices … [is] on the abstract level' because 'artistic and cultural practices are' as she put it 'where forms of subjectivity are established'. Thus, Mouffe's frequent use of the phrase 'common symbolic space' to describe that which transforms antagonism into agonism and which renders the enemy as an adversary, has been less, for her, the symbolic nature of concrete spaces, than simply the idea of a symbolic domain, where the word 'space' is merely a metaphor that could easily be substituted by words like 'realm', 'sphere', 'area' or 'context'.

The concrete 'space' which mattered most in the exchange was 'public space', named as such in order to signal that it is in that space that politics appears in a more visible, representational and instituted way. Here Mouffe's relation to the idea of the public was a key point of contention. Ultimately, while she has been a highly informed reader of Foucault's understanding of the 'rise of the social' and the historical displacement of public space by the private in industrialized society, she remained closer to Hannah Arendt in her resistance to the rise of the private realm and the eclipse of public spaces of representation. When Mouffe writes of 'levels' in her work, or of a hierarchy or structure that exists between the realm of the private and the realm of the public that is more closely linked to traditional political institutions of the state or the public sphere, she holds on to the idea of the public as potentially primary realm of the political. This at least was the point of contention that Martin sought to probe in his paper.

Martin's principal challenge to Mouffe was that in her use of the concept of the public, she returns to an essentialism that she herself claims to have gone beyond, and that she fails to take the wager of pluralism to its ultimate end point in abandoning even the structures of representation and the levels that exist between private and public. That is, Martin accused Mouffe of not following through her post-structuralist theoretical starting point to its final conclusion, which for him would lead her to the abandonment of any nostalgia for privileged spaces of representation that could harbour positive meaning. For Martin, the underlying assumption of this challenge was that the very idea of representation *is* essentialist.

Yet for Mouffe, being as much a reader of Schmidt as a reader of Foucault, taking such a position would lead to abandoning democracy and to leaving the liberal impulse of modernity unconstrained by the civic and sovereign logic of the political. Her agonistic model aims instead at there being a necessary tension between freedom and equality within democracy. Without the constraints of institutionalized spaces of representation and agonistic conflict, one would have liberty in a merely negative form.[8]

A final complication to the debate over the public was the discussion of the common that arose primarily in the round table, and the question of how the idea of the common is different from that of the public and whether the common is a more useful concept that helps overcome some of the perceived problems of hierarchy and representation baked into the concept of the public. The idea of the common has been advanced most recently by Antonio Negri and Michael Hardt as a possible substitute for the public.[9]

Yet here Martin, Mouffe and Aureli were in some agreement that the idea of the 'common' should be questioned, because it appears to assume *a priori* in a quasi-naturalistic manner that certain domains of land, air, water, information, knowledge, language and so on are from the outset common to all, and thus universally owned and collective. While the common appears to promise the possibility of a spontaneous solidarity based on the recognition of nature and a shared basis of natural life, it involves a loss of the political within its conceptual architecture, and a loss of historical social and symbolic understanding. In contrast to the concept of the commons, Martin admitted, in the end and in spite of his challenge to Mouffe's use of the idea of the public in her work, that the idea of the public should remain on the table as a topic by which architects might think through how architecture is political. As he argued, speaking to his own vocation as a historian, this was not least of all because the historical legacies of a world structured by the idea of the public remains with us today and has its potential uses.

◀ **Martin:** *Consistent with the defence of public housing, above, I do not accept the wholesale substitution of an anarchistic 'commons' for the social democratic or socialist 'public'. Rather than take refuge in an uncritical, bygone statism, I have long argued instead that the left ought imaginatively to reinhabit and reanimate the ruins of the state and its institutions left behind by neoliberalism – both metaphorically and actually – by, for example, renovating and rebuilding public housing and the policies that support it.*

Finally, and returning to the thread within the debate that relates to the assessment of critical practice, Ines Weizman's defence of dissident practices as a viable part of architecture's political tool box could also be said to hinge upon the larger thematic of the critical versus the projective.

First of all, the dissident for Weizman is not a historical figure relegated to the other side of the iron curtain during the cold war, but is an active possibility of practice in the capitalist West, whenever one is force to simply say 'no'. There is always a moment of dissent that appears in any architectural practice. For example, when architects have to decide whether to take the job or not. Most participants in the exchange agreed upon this and most of them recognized that architects engage in moments of dissent when they extract themselves from the imbricated status as professionals entangled within capitalism and act instead as individual citizens with civic responsibilities and ethical conscience. Such moments of saying 'no' and shifting roles from being compromised professionals to becoming ethical citizens are moments of refusal and withdrawal.

Yet, secondly, while such moments of refusal are real and important, there are, for Weizman, many registers of dissidence. Even the historical dissidents of the soviet bloc did not in the end *only* or *simply* withdraw negatively and refuse participation. She found rather that many of those registers were either based in subversive tactics that engage more directly than one would think, or were quite visible and part of a public and political realm. And similarly, the moment of saying 'no' in architectural practice in the West has multiple registers, including possibilities of subversion and more public and political forms of refusal that constitute positive acts as much as negative ones.

Finally, and to bring this book to a close, the question of when to withdraw into a purely negative mode of critique ultimately intersected with a question that is increasingly upon everyone's lips today in regard to democracy, which is whether or not we in the West *do* still live in democracies today. Mouffe has said that her agonistic model presumes the existence of a functioning democracy as its background and therefore it does not apply to places where democratic institutions do not function or are not present, for example, in non-democratic states such as former Eastern Bloc countries during soviet rule or in China or North Korea today. Yet the question can be raised – and was raised by Weizman – as to whether Western democracies have slipped into something better labelled as 'neoliberal authoritarianism'. Weizman's point here is similar to that raised many times by other theorists, such as the late Mark Fisher who argued in his book *Capitalist Realism* that the constraining of individual liberty had become stronger within the decentralized neoliberal form of government than it had ever been in the supposedly centralized model of authoritarian states.[10] If the post-political situation brought about by neoliberal forms of managerialism has in fact finally displaced democratic institutions, then does Mouffe's agonistic model apply anywhere?

If the West today is actually not that dissimilar to the Soviet Bloc during the cold war, as Weizman implies, then why would the political strategies of those contexts not apply. On the one hand, those strategies involved the various forms of dissidence that Weizman has analysed, but they also, crucially, revolved around philosophical models that were very different from the sceptical philosophies of post-structuralism which were Mouffe's starting point. Dissidents in the Soviet Union often appealed to humanistic philosophies of truth that had at their core roots in philosophical anthropologies and phenomenology. Weizman's framing of the dissident moment of refusal was in short precisely attached to 'truth', or to a conception of human nature, by which the dissidents formed their judgements of the present regime. If the West has entered or is entering a period of systematic institutional breakdown and if its democratic procedures are failing, then perhaps philosophies of truth – those which Vaclav Havel[11] once appealed to – might be as crucial to political strategy in the West today as anti-essentialist philosophy once appeared to be in the 1960s.

Notes

1 Pier Vittorio Aureli, *The Possibility of an Absolute Architecture* (Cambridge, MA: MIT Press, 2011), xi.
2 Ibid., 42.
3 Stan Allen, 'Untitled Article', *Assemblage* 41 (April, 2000): 8.
4 Ibid., 8.
5 Mouffe and Laclau, *Hegemony*, 109.
6 Ibid., 108.

7 For the debate in geography critical of Mouffe and Laclau's conception of space, see Doreen Massey, 'Politics and space/time', *New Left Review* 196 (1992): 65–84; David Howarth, 'Reflections on the Politics of Space and Time', *Angelaki* 1, no. 1 (1993): 43–57; and Michael Reid, 'The Aims of Radicalism: A Reply to David Howarth', *Angelaki* 1, no. 3 (1996): 181–4.
8 Isaiah Berlin, 'Two Concepts of Liberty', in *Four Essays on Liberty* (Oxford: Oxford University Press, 1969), 118–72.
9 As Antonio Negri and Michael Hardt in their 2009 book *Commonwealth* put it, 'By the "common" we mean, first of all, the common wealth of the material world – the air, the water, the fruits of the soil, and all nature's bounty – which in classical European political texts is often claimed to be the inheritance of humanity as a whole, to be shared together. We consider the common also and more significantly those results of social production that are necessary for social interaction and further production, such as knowledges, languages, codes, information, affects, and so forth.' Antonio Negri and Michael Hardt, *Commonwealth* (Boston: Belknap Press, 2009), vii.
10 Mark Fisher, *Capitalist Realism: Is There No Alternative* (London: Zero Books, 2009), 19–20.
11 Vaclav Havel, Living in Truth: *22 Essays* (London: Faber & Faber, 1987)

Afterword

Chantal Mouffe

I have argued that recognizing the role of cultural-artistic practices in the construction of a hegemony helps us to visualize the role that architectural practices play in the construction, reproduction and transformation of a hegemony. I think that in our exchange there was a general agreement on the fact that in order to address the question 'how to envisage a critical architecture?' it was necessary to acknowledge that the social is always discursively constructed, and that architecture has a political dimension. But there were different views with respect to the strategies to be followed to orient this political dimension in a critical direction.

As I have made clear, the strategy that we have advocated since *Hegemony and Socialist Strategy* is one of critical engagement with institutions in order to transform them. The hegemonic strategy is a strategy of disarticulation and re-articulation; you need to disarticulate a certain hegemony, but you also need to create something new. This is, I think, what Reinhold Martin asserted when he said that we always need to ask the 'day-after' question.[1] It is not enough that we negate, and believe that better things will automatically arise. This is why in my answer to Sarah Whiting's question I insisted that critique is never a purely negative moment. When I speak of critique, it is always in the sense of a double movement of disarticulation and re-articulation; that is the strategy of the war of position. It is something that takes place in a multiplicity of agonistic spaces because the agonistic struggle requires envisaging an alternative. This is what agonism is about: the moment of disarticulation of a given hegemony in order to make a proposal for establishing a different one. It can take place in many different areas, but there are privileged points around which a given hegemony is structured.

It seems to me that this strategy is particularly suited to architectural practices. I cannot really think of architectural practices that would correspond to the strategy of exodus. In architecture one is always dealing with representation, construction and mediation, which are precisely the things that the exodus strategy rejects. I cannot imagine architecture without this dimension. So, I think that when one is trying to envisage the possibility of a critical architecture, it should be under the mode of the strategy of 'engagement with', and not the strategy of 'exodus from'. Reinhold Martin once wrote in a piece he sent to me that there is no 'revolutionary architecture',[2] and I believe that he is right; you are not going to achieve revolution through architecture. Of course, architectural practices can contribute to making transformations in a hegemonic formation, but their role in revolution is difficult to imagine. Envisaging critical architectural practices according to a counter-hegemonic approach implies a process of disarticulation and re-articulation.

I agree with Reinhold Martin when he says that housing is an important terrain, because I see housing as one of those nodal points in the hegemonic structure that is definitely central to envisaging a critical architecture. I like what Pier Vittorio Aureli said about Red Vienna. I think Red Vienna is definitely an example of an agonistic architecture, and of course the question of housing was central to the development of Red Vienna. It demonstrates that housing is a privileged space for architectural practices to contribute to the counter-hegemonic struggle.

With respect to Pier Vittorio Aureli's question about architecture always being political, I feel that we have a basic agreement. Architecture always has a political dimension, in the sense that it contributes to reproducing or establishing a hegemonic order, but it is not always political in the sense of being critical, or as an attempt to disarticulate an existing hegemony. Architectural practices can either contribute to sustaining or reproducing an existing hegemony or attempting to disrupt it. I agree that there is always a dimension of consensus within architectural practices, in the sense that even in a counter-hegemonic way what is at stake is the creation of a different kind of consensus. There is always this aspect of consensus-conflict because architectural practices organize our common life. For a counter-hegemonic architecture, the dimension of consensus is there in order to disarticulate one form of consensus and create another form of consensus around different values and different ways of organizing our common life. There is always this element of consensus, and I think that although we say it in different ways we agree on this point.

Concerning what Sarah Whiting said about Lyotard, even if I do find his work and idea of *différend* very interesting, this is not what I mean by agonism. The *différend* has got more to do with antagonism. At some point, Whiting said that the *différend* requires or automatically implies agonism, but I believe that what it implies is antagonism. Given the situation we are in, with the ever-present possibility of antagonism, the whole question of agonism is: how are we going to organize our life so that we can live together, instead of killing each other? That is really what is at stake in agonism. So, the *différend* for me is what we call antagonism. Agonism is not automatically the consequence of the *différend*; it is an answer to the challenge posed by the existence of the *différend*.

I must say that I am rather suspicious of the idea of dissidence proposed by Ines Weizman because, though she gave a very interesting paper, the practices she refers to do not resonate with my understanding of agonism. Of course, one is entitled to use agonism in different ways, but I do not see the struggle of the dissidents in the USSR as a form of agonism because dissidence does not engage with institutions and the state. Dissidence resonates more with the strategy of exodus, even if it is not exactly the same. It is not something that corresponds to the idea that I have of a strategy of 'engagement with' against neoliberal hegemony understood in terms of a war of position. Practices of dissidence are certainly important practices of resistance, but this is not what I have in mind when I think of agonistic practices. Agonistic practices require the existence of some democratic institutions; agonism is a struggle within democratic institutions in order to establish a different hegemony. We cannot think about the struggles of the dissidents in the USSR in terms of agonistic struggles; it is a different kind of politics. For the same reason, I do not think that struggles like the one against Mubarak in Egypt are agonistic. You cannot have agonistic struggle under a dictatorship. In order to have an agonistic struggle, in my understanding of the term, you have to have some democratic institutions.

I would like to make a final comment. I feel that in our debate there was a tendency to collapse radical democracy and agonistic democracy, and I think that it is important to clarify this issue and spell out the difference between radical democracy and the agonistic model of democracy. These two terms cannot be used indistinctively as it is sometimes the case, because they refer to different aspects of my reflection. In *Hegemony and Socialist Strategy,* criticizing the class-reductionism dominant in the Marxist tradition, we argued for a new understanding of the socialist project in terms of a radicalization of democracy. We advocated for the creation of a chain of equivalences among democratic demands, in order to extend the democratic principles to a wider set of social relations. Radical democracy, as we envisaged it, is clearly a political project, to be distinguished from other political projects, like the social democratic or the neo-liberal ones. The agonistic model of democracy, however, is something different. It is an analytical approach, formulated as an alternative to the aggregative and deliberative models. While scrutinizing the discussion among liberal-democratic theorists and realizing the limitations of the consensual understanding of democracy, I became aware that neither the aggregative nor the deliberative models allowed us to visualize the possibility of a hegemonic politics. To give account of the ineradicability of antagonism and of the hegemonic nature of politics, a different approach was needed. How to envisage democracy within the framework of our hegemonic approach? How to conceive democracy in a way that allows in its midst a confrontation between conflicting hegemonic projects? The agonistic model of democracy is my answer to those questions and I see it as providing the analytic framework necessary to visualize the possibility of a democratic confrontation between hegemonic projects. Asserting the constitutive character of social division and the impossibility of a final reconciliation, the agonistic perspective recognizes the necessary partisan character of democratic politics. By envisaging this confrontation in terms of adversaries and not in terms of a friend/enemy mode that might lead to civil war, it allows such a confrontation to take place within democratic institutions. Nonetheless, the agonistic model does not take sides in this confrontation, and it is erroneous to believe it favours the radical democratic project. One thing is to create the conditions for a hegemonic confrontation, a completely different one is to determine its outcome. This outcome will be the result of the political struggle between forces vying for hegemony, and nothing guarantees the victory of one project over another.

Regarding this issue, it might be useful to say a word about my position in the discussion about 'left ontologies'. Soon after the publication of *Hegemony and Socialist Strategy* we clarified that it was a mistake to believe that there was a causal link between the ontological approach developed in the book and the political project of radical democracy advocated in the last chapter. To be sure, post-structuralist insights, by allowing us to criticize the shortcomings of the essentialist approach, played a crucial role in our reformulation of the socialist project, but those insights could also be used by theorists with very different political objectives. There is no direct route from ontological postulates to specific political positions, and these are always the result of ethico-political decisions. The existence of an agonistic model of democracy in no way guarantees that the radical democratic project will be chosen. To put it in another way, while the critique of essentialism is a necessary condition to visualize the agonistic struggle and the possibility of the radical democratic project's success, it is not a sufficient condition. Indeed, starting from the same ontological premises, different hegemonic projects can be envisaged and the outcome of the agonistic struggle is never pre-determined. Everything depends on the result of the hegemonic struggle and the state of the contending forces.

Notes

1 Reinhold Martin, 'Occupy: The Day After', *Places Journal* (December, 2011) https://placesjournal.org/article/occupy-the-day-after/
2 Ibid.

Bibliography

By Chantal Mouffe

Mouffe, Chantal, and Anne Showstack Sassoon, 'Gramsci in France and Italy – A Review of the Literature', in *Economy and Society* 6, no. 1 (1977): 31–68.
Gramsci, Antonio, and Chantal Mouffe, *Gramsci and Marxist Theory* (London: Routledge & Kegan Paul, 1979).
Mouffe, Chantal, 'Introduction: Gramsci Today', in *Gramsci and Marxist Theory* (London: Routledge & Kegan Paul, 1979), 1–18.
Mouffe, Chantal, 'Hegemony and Ideology in Gramsci', in *Gramsci and Marxist Theory* (London: Routledge & Kegan Paul, 1979), 168–205.
Laclau, Ernesto, and Chantal Mouffe, 'Socialist Strategy: Where Next?', in *Marxism Today* 25, no. 1 (January 1981): 17–22.
Laclau, Ernesto, and Chantal Mouffe, *Hegemony and Socialist Strategy: Towards a Radical Democratic Politics* (UK: Verso Books, 2001). (Originally published in 1985.)
Mouffe, Chantal, 'Rawls: Political philosophy without politics', in *Philosophy and Social Criticism* 13, no. 2 (1987): 105–23. Reprinted in *Universalism vs Communitarianism*, edited by David Rasmussen (United States: MIT Press, 1990), 217–37, and in *The Return of the Political* (UK: Verso, 1993), 41–60.
Laclau, Ernesto, and Chantal Mouffe, 'Post-Marxism without Apologies', in *New Left Review* 166, no. 11–12 (1987): 79–106.
Mouffe, Chantal, 'Hegemony and New Political Subjects: Toward a New Concept of Democracy', in Cary Nelson and Lawrence Grossberg eds., *Marxism and the Interpretation of Culture* (UK: University of Illinois Press, 1988), 89–104.
Mouffe, Chantal, 'American Liberalism and Its Critics: Rawls, Taylor, Sandel and Walzer', in *Praxis International* 8, no. 2 (July 1988): 193–206. Reprinted with a new title 'American Liberalism and Its Communitarian Critics', in *The Return of the Political* (UK: Verso, 1993).
Mouffe, Chantal, 'Radical Democracy: Modern or Postmodern?', in *Social Text*, no. 21 (1989): 31–45.
Mouffe, Chantal, 'Rawls: Political Philosophy without Politics', in David Rasmussen ed., *Universalism vs. Communitarianism: Contemporary Debates in Ethics* (United States: MIT Press, 1990), 217–37.
Mouffe, Chantal, 'Radical Democracy or Liberal Democracy?', in *Socialist Review* 20, no. 2 (April-June, 1990): 57–66. Reprinted in Mouffe, Chantal, 'Radical Democracy or Liberal Democracy?' in David Trend ed., *Radical Democracy: Identity, Citizenship and the State* (London and New York: Routledge, 1996), 1–25.
Mouffe, Chantal, 'Pluralism and Modern Democracy: Around Carl Schmitt', in *New Formations*, no. 14 (Summer, 1991). Reprinted in *The Return of the Political* (UK: Verso, 1993), 117–35.
Mouffe, Chantal, 'Democratic Citizenship and the Political Community', in Miami Theory Collective eds., *Community at Loose Ends* (Minneapolis: University of Minnesota Press, 1991), 70–82. Reprinted in Mouffe, Chantal, ed., *Dimensions of Radical Democracy* (UK: Verso, 1992).

Mouffe, Chantal, 'Citizenship and Political Identity', in *October* 61, *The Identity in Question* (Summer, 1992): 28–32.

Mouffe, Chantal, ed., *Dimensions of Radical Democracy: Pluralism, Citizenship, Community* (London: Verso, 1992).

Mouffe, Chantal, 'Democratic Politics Today', in *Dimensions of Radical Democracy: Pluralism, Citizenship, Community* (London: Verso, 1992), 1–17.

Mouffe, Chantal, 'Democratic Citizenship and the Political Community', in *Dimensions of Radical Democracy: Pluralism, Citizenship, Community* (London: Verso, 1992), 225–40.

Mouffe, Chantal, 'Feminism, Citizenship and Radical Democratic Politics', in Judith Butler and Joan Scott eds., *Feminists Theorize the Political* (London: Routledge, 1992), 369–85.

Mouffe, Chantal, 'On the Articulation between Liberalism and Democracy', in *The Return of the Political* (London: Verso Books, 1993), 102–16. Originally presented as a paper at *'The Legacy of C.B. Macpherson'* conference (Canada, Toronto: October, 1989).

Mouffe, Chantal, 'Towards a Liberal Socialism', in *The Return of the Political* (London: Verso Books, 1993). Originally presented at 'The World Congress of the International Political Science Association' (Argentina, Buenos Aires: July 1991, and edited and reprinted in Mouffe, Chantal, *The Return of the Political* (London: Verso, 1993)).

Mouffe, Chantal, 'Toward A Liberal Socialism', in *Dissent* 40, no. 1 (Winter, 1993).

Mouffe, Chantal, 'Introduction: For an Agonistic Pluralism', in *The Return of the Political* (London: Verso Books, 1993), 1–9.

Mouffe, Chantal, 'Radical Democracy: Modern or Postmodern?', in *The Return of the Political* (London: Verso Books, 1993), 9–23.

Mouffe, Chantal, 'American Liberalism and Its Communitarian Critics', in *The Return of the Political* (London: Verso Books, 1993), 23–41.

Mouffe, Chantal, 'Rawls: Political Philosophy without Politics', in *The Return of the Political* (London: Verso Books, 1993), 41–60.

Mouffe, Chantal, 'Democratic Citizenship and the Political Community', in *The Return of the Political* (London: Verso Books, 1993), 60–74.

Mouffe, Chantal, 'Feminism, Citizenship and Radical Democratic Politics', in *The Return of the Political* (London: Verso Books, 1993), 74–90.

Mouffe, Chantal, 'Towards a Liberal Socialism', in *The Return of the Political* (London: Verso Books, 1993), 90–102.

Mouffe, Chantal, 'Pluralism and Modern Democracy: Around Carl Schmitt', in *The Return of the Political* (London: Verso Books, 1993), 117–35.

Mouffe, Chantal, 'Politics and the Limits of Liberalism', in *The Return of the Political* (London: Verso Books, 1993), 135–55.

Mouffe, Chantal, 'For a Politics of Nomadic Identity', in George Robertson ed., *Traveller's Tales: Narratives of Home and Displacement* (UK: Routledge, 1994), 103–13.

Mouffe, Chantal, 'Political Liberalism: Neutrality and the Political', in *Ratio Juris* 7, no. 3 (December 1994): 314–24.

Mouffe, Chantal, 'Democracy and Pluralism: A Critique of the Rationalist Approach', in *The Cardozo Law Review* 16, no. 5 (1994–1995): 1533–1545.

Mouffe, Chantal, 'Democracy and Pluralism: A Critique of the Rationalist Approach', in *The Cardozo Law Review* 16, no. 5 (1994–1995): 1533–1545. Originally written as a paper given at the *Benjamin N. Cardozo School of Law* (2 November 1994). It was revised and reprinted in *Democracy and Difference* (Princeton: Princeton University Press, 1996), 245–56, and reprinted in revised form as 'Democracy, Power and "The Political"', in *The Democratic Paradox* (New York: Verso, 2000).

Mouffe, Chantal, 'The End of Politics and the Rise of the Radical Right', in *Dissent* 42, no. 4 (1996): 498–502.
Mouffe, Chantal, 'Deconstruction, Pragmatism and the Politics of Democracy', in Simon Critchley, Jacques Derrida, Ernesto Laclau, and Richard Rorty eds., *Deconstruction and Pragmatism* (UK: Routledge, 1996), 1–13.
Mouffe, Chantal, 'Democracy, Power, and the "Political"', in Seyla Benhabib ed., *Democracy and Difference: Contesting the Boundaries of the Political* (Princeton: Princeton University Press, 1996), 245–56. (Revised and reprinted edition of the paper *Democracy and Pluralism – A Rationalist Critique*.)
Mouffe, Chantal, 'Radical Democracy or Liberal Democracy', in David Trend ed., *Radical Democracy: Identity, Citizenship and the State* (UK: Routledge, 1996), 1–25.
Mouffe, Chantal, 'Ethics and the Question of Space, the Environment and Architecture', Lecture at the Architectural Association, 17 November 1997.
Mouffe, Chantal, 'Wittgenstein. Political Theory and Democracy', *paper presented at a conference at the University of Bielefeld* (January 1996). Developed and reprinted in *The Democratic Paradox* (New York: Verso, 2000), 60–80.
Mouffe, Chantal, 'Carl Schmitt and the Paradox of Liberal Democracy', in *The Canadian Journal of Law and Jurisprudence* 10, no. 1 (January 1997): 21–33.
Mouffe, Chantal, 'Decision, Deliberation, and Democratic Ethos', in *Philosophy Today* 41, no. 1 (Spring, 1997): 24–30.
Mouffe, Chantal, 'The Radical Centre – A Politics without Adversary', in *Soundings* 9 (Summer, 1998): 11–23. Revised and reprinted as 'A Politics without Adversary?', in *The Democratic Paradox* (New York: Verso, 2000), 108–29.
Mouffe, Chantal, 'Deliberative Democracy or Agonistic Pluralism?', in *Science Research* 66, no. 3 (Fall, 1999): 745–58.
Mouffe, Chantal, ed., *The Challenge of Carl Schmitt* (UK: Verso Books, 1999).
Mouffe, Chantal, 'Introduction: Schmitt's Challenge', in *The Challenge of Carl Schmitt* (UK: Verso Books, 1999), 7–18.
Mouffe, Chantal, 'Carl Schmitt and the Paradox of Liberal Democracy', in *The Challenge of Carl Schmitt* (UK: Verso Books, 1999), 38–54.
Mouffe, Chantal, 'Ten Years of False Starts', in *New Times* 9 (1999).
Mouffe, Chantal, 'Rorty's Pragmatist Politics', in *Economy and Society* 29, no. 3 (2000): 439–53.
Mouffe, Chantal, 'For an Agonistic Model of Democracy', in Noel O'Sullivan ed., *Political Theory in Transition* (London: Routledge, 2000). Reprinted in *The Democratic Paradox* (New York: Verso, 2000), 80–108.
Mouffe, Chantal, *The Democratic Paradox* (London: Verso Books, 2000).
Mouffe, Chantal, 'Which Ethics for Democracy?', in Marjorie Garber, Beatrice Hanssen, and Rebecca Walkowitz eds., *The Turn to Ethics* (London and New York: Routledge, 2000), 85–94.
Mouffe, Chantal, 'Every Form of Art Has a Political Dimension', in *Grey Room*, no. 2 (Winter, 2001): 98–125.
Mouffe, Chantal, 'Democracy – Radical and Plural', interview in *CSD Bulletin* 9, no. 1 (2001): 10–13.
Mouffe, Chantal, 'Response to Bruce Robbins', in *Grey Room*, no. 5 (Fall 2001): 118–19.
Mouffe, Chantal, 'Which Kind of Public Space for a Democratic Habitus?', in Jean Hillier, Emma Rooksby ed., *Habitus: A Sense of Place* (London: Ashgate, 2001), 93–100.
Mouffe, Chantal, and Jürgen Trinks. *Feministische Perspektiven* (Germany: Turia and Kant, 2002).

Mouffe, Chantal, 'Die Fundamente des Politischen', in Bazon Brock and Gerlinde Koschik ed., *Krieg und Kunst München* (Germany: Wilhelm Fink, 2002), 55–63.
Mouffe, Chantal, 'For an Agonistic Public Sphere', in Okwui Enwezor ed., *Democracy Unrealized: Documenta 11, Platform 1* (Germany: Hatje Cantz, 2002), 87–97. Reprinted in Lars Tønder, and Lasse Thomassen, ed., *Radical Democracy: Politics between Abundance and Lack* (Manchester: Manchester University Press, 2005).
Mouffe, Chantal, 'Which Public Sphere for a Democratic Society?', in *Theoria: A Journal of Social and Political Theory* 99 (2002): 55–65.
Mouffe, Chantal, 'Wittgenstein and the Ethos of Democracy', in Chantal Mouffe and Ludwig Nagl ed., *The Legacy of Wittgenstein: Pragmatism or Deconstruction* (London: Peter Lang, 2002), 131–9. (Developed from a conference in London in 1999.)
Mouffe, Chantal, *Politics and Passions – The Stakes of Democracy* (London: Centre for the Study of Democracy, 2002).
Mouffe, Chantal, 'Civil Society beyond Liberalism and Communitarianism', in Emil Brix and Peter Kampits eds., *Zivilgesellschaft Zwischen Liberalismus und Kommunitarismus Passagen* (Germany: Passagen Verlag, 2003), 81–91.
Mouffe, Chantal, 'Untitled', in *Parallax* 9, no. 3 (2003): 61–5.
Mouffe, Chantal, 'Le Politique et la Dynamique des Passions', in *Les 20 ans du College International de Philosophie Paris* (France: Presses Universitaires de France, 2004), 179–92.
Mouffe, Chantal, 'Pluralism, Dissensus and Democratic Citizenship', in Fred Inglis ed., *Education and the Good Society* (London: Palgrave Macmillan, 2004).
Mouffe, Chantal, 'Til Varnar Agreinings Likani um Lydraedi', in *Hugur* 16 (2004): 44–60.
Mouffe, Chantal, 'The Limits of Liberal Pluralism: Towards an Agonistic Multipolar Order', in Andras Sajo ed., *Militant Democracy Utrecht* (Netherlands: Eleven International Publishing, 2004), 69–80.
Mouffe, Chantal, 'Some Reflections on an Agonistic Approach to the Public', in Bruno Latour and Peter Weibel eds., *Making Thing Public: Atmospheres of Democracy* (Cambridge, MA: MIT Press, 2005), 804–7.
Mouffe, Chantal, 'The "End of Politics" and the Challenge of Right-Wing Populism', in Francisco Panizza ed., *Populism and the Mirror of Democracy* (UK: Verso Books, 2005), 72–98.
Mouffe, Chantal, 'Agonistic Public Spaces, Democratic Politics and the Dynamics of Passions', in *Thinking Worlds: The Moscow Conference on Philosophy, Politics, and Art* (Moscow; Berlin: Interros Publishing Program, Sternberg Press, 2005), 95–104.
Mouffe, Chantal, 'The Limits of John Rawls's Pluralism', in *Politics, Philosophy & Economics* 4, no. 2 (2005): 221–31.
Mouffe, Chantal, *On the Political* (London: Routledge, 2005).
Mouffe, Chantal, 'Schmitt's Vision of a Multipolar World Order', in *South Atlantic Quarterly* 104, no. 2, (April 2005): 245–51.
Mouffe, Chantal, 'Which Public Space for Critical Artistic Practices?', in Shep Steiner and Trevor Joyce eds., *Cork Caucus: on Art, Possibility, and Democracy* (Frankfurt am Main: Revolver Verlag, 2006), 149–71. (Originally presented as a paper at the Cork Caucus conference: July 6, 2005).
Mouffe, Chantal, 'Artistic Activism and Agonistic Politics', in *Art and Research* 1, no. 2 (Summer, 2007): 4.
Mouffe, Chantal, 'Cultural Workers as Organic Intellectuals', in Stephan Schmidt-Wulffen ed., *The Art as Public Intellectual* (Vienna: Schlebrugge, 2008), 150–60.

Mouffe, Chantal, 'Art as an Agonistic Intervention in Public Space', in Liesbeth Melismas and Jorinde Seijdel ed., *Open 14: Art as a Public Issue: How Art and Its Institutions Reinvent the Public Dimension* (Amsterdam: NAI Publishers, 2008), 6–14.
Mouffe, Chantal, 'Which World Order: Cosmopolitan or Multipolar?', in *Ethical Perspectives* 15, no. 4 (2008): 453–67.
Mouffe, Chantal, 'Democratic Politics and the Dynamics of Passions', in José María Rosales, Kari Palonen and Tuija Pulkkinen eds., *The Ashgate Research Companion to the Politics of Democratization in Europe: Concepts and Histories* (Italy: Ashgate, 2008), 89–100.
Mouffe, Chantal, 'Democracy in a Multipolar World', in *Millennium* 37, no. 3 (May 2009): 549–61.
Mouffe, Chantal, 'The Limits of John Rawls' Pluralism', in *Theoria: A Journal of Social and Political Theory* 56, no. 118 (2009): 1–14.
Mouffe, Chantal, 'Politique et Agoniste', in *Rue Descartes* 67, no. 1 (2010): 18–24.
Mouffe, Chantal, 'An Agonistic Approach to the Future of Europe', in *New Literary History* 43, no. 4 (2012): 629–40.
Mouffe, Chantal, *Agonistics: Thinking the World Politically* (New York: Verso, 2013).
Mouffe, Chantal, 'What is Agonistic Politics', in *Agonistics: Thinking the World Politically* (New York: Verso, 2013), 1–18.
Mouffe, Chantal, 'Which Democracy for a Multipolar Agonistic World', in *Agonistics: Thinking the World Politically* (New York: Verso, 2013), 19–42.
Mouffe, Chantal, 'An Agonistic Approach to the Future of Europe', in *Agonistics: Thinking the World Politically* (New York: Verso, 2013), 43–64.
Mouffe, Chantal, 'Radical Politics Today', in *Agonistics: Thinking the World Politically* (New York: Verso, 2013), 64–84.
Mouffe, Chantal, 'Agonistic Politics and Artistic Practices', in *Agonistics: Thinking the World Politically* (New York: Verso, 2013), 85–106.
Mouffe, Chantal, 'Conclusion', in *Agonistics: Thinking the World Politically* (New York: Verso, 2013), 107–28.
Mouffe, Chantal, 'Interview with Chantal', in *Agonistics: Thinking the World Politically* (New York: Verso, 2013), 129–46.
Mouffe, Chantal, 'Democracy, Human Rights and Cosmopolitanism: an Agonistic Approach', in *The Meaning of Rights: The Philosophy and Social Theory of Human Rights* (Cambridge: Cambridge University Press, 2014), 181–92.
Mouffe, Chantal, *For a Left Populism* (UK: Verso Books, 2018).

About Chantal Mouffe

Barker, Rodney, 'Book Review: The Return of the Political', in *The British Journal of Sociology* 47, no. 2 (1996): 370–1.
Barrett, Michele, 'Ideology, Politics, Hegemony: From Gramsci to Laclau and Mouffe', in Slavoj Zizek ed., *Mapping Ideology* (London: Verso, 1994), 235–65.
Bauman, Zygmunt, 'From Pillars to Post', in *Marxism Today* (February 1990): 20–5.
Bayart, Jean-François, 'Review of The Democratic Paradox', in *Critique Internationale* 12 (2001): 85.
Bertram, Benjamin, 'New Reflections on the "Revolutionary" Politics of Ernesto Laclau and Chantal Mouffe', in *Boundary* 22, no. 3 (Autumn, 1995): 81–110.
'Book Review of The Return of the Political' in *Constellations* 3, no. 1 (April 1996): 115–35.

Boucher, Geoff, 'Crop Circles in the Postmarxian Field: Laclau and Mouffe on Postmodern Socialist Strategy', in *The Charmed Circle of Ideology: A Critique of Laclau and Mouffe, Butler and Žižek* (Melbourne: Re-Press, 2009), 77–127.
Breckman, Warren, 'The Post-Marx of the Letter: Laclau and Mouffe between Postmodern Melancholy and Post-Marxist Mourning', in *Adventures of the Symbolic: Postmarxism and Democratic Theory* (New York: Columbia University Press, 2013), 183–216.
Brockelman, Thomas, 'The Failure of the Radical Democratic Imaginary', in *Philosophy & Social Criticism* 29, no. 2 (2003): 183–208.
Butler, Judith, 'Review of Poststructuralism and Postmarxism: The Philosophy of the Limit by Drucilla Cornell' and 'Beyond Emancipation by Ernesto Laclau', in *Diacritics* 23, no. 4 (Winter, 1993): 2–11.
Butler, Judith, Ernesto Laclau, and Slavoj Zizek, eds., *Contingency, Hegemony, Universality: Contemporary Dialogues on the Left* (London: Verso, 2000).
Camargo, Ricardo, 'Rethinking the Political: A Genealogy of the "Antagonism" in Carl Schmitt through the Lens of Laclau-Mouffe-Žižek', in *The New Centennial Review* 13, no. 1 (Spring, 2013): 161–88.
Carpentier, Nico, and Bart Cammaerts, 'Hegemony, Democracy, Agonism and Journalism', in *Journalism Studies* 7, no. 6 (2006): 964–75.
Clegg, Sue, 'The Remains of Louis Althusser', in *International Socialism* 53 (Winter, 1991): 57–78.
Cloud, Dana, 'Socialism of the Mind – The New Age of Post-Marxism', in *After Postmodernism – Reconstructing Ideology Critique* (London: Sage, 1994), 222–51.
Cohen, Jean L., and Andrew Arato, 'Excursus on Gramsci's Successors: Althusser, Anderson, and Bobbio', in *Civil Society and Political Society* (Cambridge, MA: MIT Press, 1992).
Connolly, William E., 'Review Essay – Twilight of the Idols (Under Consideration – Chantal Mouffe's the Return of the Political)', in *Philosophy Social Criticism* 21, no. 3 (1995): 127.
Cornell, Drucilla, 'Socialism or Radical Democratic Politics?: On Laclau and Mouffe', in *Law and Revolution in South Africa: UBuntu, Dignity, and the Struggle for Constitutional Transformation* (New York: Fordham University Press, 2014), 34–44.
Dahlberg, Lincoln, 'Radical Democracy', in Benjamin Isakhan and Stephen Stockwell eds., *The Edinburgh Companion to the History of Democracy: From Pre-History to Future Possibilities* (Edinburgh: Edinburgh University Press, 2015), 491–501.
Dallmayr, Fred, 'Hegemony and Democracy: On Laclau and Mouffe', in *Strategies* 1 (1988): 29–49.
Davidson, Alastair, 'Review of Dimensions of Radical Democracy', in *The Australian and New Zealand Journal of Sociology* 29, no. 3 (1993): 404–5.
Eagleton, Terry, *Ideology: An Introduction* (New York: Verso, 1991).
Fowler, Justin, 'Agonism, Consensus, and the Exception: On the Newest Monumentalists', in Lei Qu, Chingwen Yang, Xiaoxi Hui and Diego Sepúlveda eds., *The New Urban Question: Urbanism beyond Neo-Liberalism. 4th Conference of International Forum on Urbanism Conference Proceedings* (Amsterdam/Delft: International Forum on Urbanism, 2009), 627–36.
Fukuyama, Francis, 'Book Review – The Return of the Political', in *Foreign Affairs* 73, no. 5 (1994): 144.
Geras, Norman, 'Post-Marxism?', in *New Left Review* 163 (May/June 1987): 40–82.
Geras, Norman, 'Ex-Marxism without Substance: Being a Real Reply to Laclau and Mouffe', in *New Left Review* i, no. 169 (May/June 1988): 34–61. (Reprinted in Geras, Norman, 'Ex-Marxism without Substance', in *Discourses of Extremity – Radical Ethics and Post-Marxist Extravagences* (New York: Verso, 1990), 127–68.)

Gies, Lieve, 'Review of The Democratic Paradox', in *Political Quarterly* (2008).
Harris, David, *From Class Struggle to the Politics of Pleasure* (London: Routledge, 1992).
Jacobs, Thomas, 'The Dislocated Universe of Laclau and Mouffe, An Introduction to Post-Structuralist Discourse Theory', in *Critical Review* 30, no. 3–4 (2018): 294–315.
Jorgensen, Marianne W., and Louise J. Phillips, 'Laclau and Mouffe's Discourse Theory', in *Discourse Analysis as Theory and Method* (London: Sage, 2002), 24–60.
Kapoor, Ilan, 'Deliberative Democracy or Agonistic Pluralism? The Relevance of the Habermas-Mouffe Debate for Third World Politics', in *Alternatives: Global, Local, Political* 27, no. 4 (2002): 459–87.
Lloyd, Moya, and Adrian Little, 'Introduction', in *The Politics of Radical Democracy* (Edinburgh: Edinburgh University Press, 2009).
Marchart, Oliver, *Post-Foundational Political Thought: Political Difference in Nancy, Lefort, Badiou and Laclau* (Edinburgh: Edinburgh University Press, 2007).
Marchart, Oliver, 'Institution and Dislocation: Philosophical Roots of Laclau's Discourse Theory of Space and Antagonism', in *Distinktion: Scandinavian Journal of Social Theory* 15, no. 3 (2014): 271–82.
Martin, James, 'Introduction: Democracy and Conflict in the Work of Chantal Mouffe', in James Martin ed., *Chantal Mouffe: Hegemony, Radical Democracy, and the Political* (London: Routledge, 2013), 1–13.
McLennan, Gregor, 'Post-Marxism and the "Four Sins" of Modernist Theorising', in *New Left Review* 218 (1996): 53–74.
McRobbie, Angela, 'Post-Marxism and Cultural Studies', in Larry Grossberg, Cary Nelson, and Paula Treichler eds., *Cultural Studies* (New York and London: Routledge, 1992), 719–30.
Miessen, Markus, and Nikolaus Hirsch, eds., *The Space of Agonism: Markus Miessen in Conversation with Chantal Mouffe* (London: Sternberg Press, 2013).
Miklitsch, Robert, 'The Rhetoric of Post-Marxism: Discourse and Institutionality in Laclau and Mouffe, Resnick and Wolff', in *Social Text* 45 (Winter, 1995): 167–96.
Miliband, Ralph, 'The New Revisionism in Britain', in *New Left Review* 150 (1985): 5–26.
Miller, David, 'Review of Dimensions of Radical Democracy', in *American Political Science Review* 87, no. 4 (1993): 1003–4.
Mouzelis, Fred, 'Ideology and Class Politics: A Critique of Ernesto Laclau', in *New Left Review* 112 (1978): 45–61.
Mouzelis, Nicos, 'Marxism or Post-Marxism?', in *New Left Review* 1, no. 167 (January February, 1988): 107–25.
Mouzelis, Nicos P., 'Marxism versus Post-Marxism', in *Post-Marxist Alternatives: The Construction of Social Orders* (London: Palgrave Macmillan, 1990), 20–41.
Neve, Gorden, 'Review of The Democratic Paradox', in *Democratization* 9, no. 2 (2002): 175–8.
Norris, Andrew, 'Against Antagonism: On Ernesto Laclau's Political Thought', in *Constellations* 32, no. 1 (2006): 111–34.
Osborne, Peter, 'Radicalism without Limit?' in *Socialism and the Limits of Liberalism* (New York: Verso, 1991), 201–25.
Phillips, Anne, 'Book Review – Dimensions of Radical Democracy: Pluralism, Citizenship, Community', in *Sociology* 27, no. 2 (1993): 358–9.
Pugh, Jonathan, 'On the Political: by Chantal Mouffe', in *Area* 39, no. 1 (2007): 130–1.
Robinson, Andrew, and Simon Tormey, 'Is "Another World" Possible? Laclau, Mouffe and Social Movements', in *The Politics of Radical Democracy* (Edinburgh: Edinburgh University Press, 2009), 133–58.
Roche, Maurice, 'Book Review: Dimensions of Radical Democracy', in *The British Journal of Sociology* 44, no. 1 (1993): 180–1.

Roskamm, Nikolai, 'On the Other Side of "Agonism"- "The Enemy," the "Outside," and the Role of Antagonism', in *Planning Theory* 14, no. 4 (2015): 384–403.
Rummens, Stefan, 'Book Review: On the Political (Thinking in Action Series)', in *Tijdschrift Voor Filosofie* 68, no. 4 (2006): 830–2.
Rummens, Stefan, 'Democracy as a Non-Hegemonic Struggle? Disambiguating Chantal Mouffe's Agonistic Model of Politics', in *Constellations* 16, no. 3 (2009): 377–91.
Rustin, Michael, 'Absolute Voluntarism – Critique of a Post-Marxist Concept of Hegemony', in *New German Critique* 43 (1988): 147–73.
Schaap, Andrew, 'Aboriginal Sovereignty and the Democratic Paradox', in *The Politics of Radical Democracy* (Edinburgh: Edinburgh University Press, 2009), 52–72.
Schaap, Andrew, 'Political Theory and the Agony of Politics', in *Political Studies Review* 5, no. 1 (2007): 56–74.
Sim, Stuart, ed., *Post-Marxism: A Reader* (Edinburgh: Edinburgh University Press, 1998), 45–55.
Sim, Stuart, 'An Intellectual Malady'? The Laclau – Mouffe Affair (I)', in *Post-Marxism: An Intellectual History* (London: Routledge, 2000), 12–34.
Sim, Stuart, '"Without Apologies": The Laclau – Mouffe Affair (II)', in *Post-Marxism: An Intellectual History* (London: Routledge, 2000), 34–48.
Sim, Stuart, 'Introduction', in *Reflections on Post-Marxism: Laclau and Mouffe's Project of Radical Democracy in the 21st Century* (Bristol: Bristol University Press, 2022), 84–98.
Sim, Stuart, ed., *Reflections on Post-Marxism: Laclau and Mouffe's Project of Radical Democracy in the 21st Century* (Bristol: Bristol University Press, 2022).
Smith, Anna Mari, *Laclau and Mouffe: The Radical Democratic Imaginary* (London: Routledge, 1998).
Sim, Stuart, and Philip Goldstein, eds., 'Ernesto Laclau and Chantal Mouffe: The Evolution of Post-Marxism', in *Reflections on Post-Marxism: Laclau and Mouffe's Project of Radical Democracy in the 21st Century* (Bristol: Bristol University Press, 2022), 84–98.
Sparks, Chris, 'Book Review: The Return of the Political', in *History of Political Thought* 15, no. 1 (1994): 147–50.
Squires, Judith, Chantal Mouffe, and Anne Phillips, 'Dimensions of Radical Democracy', in *Feminist Review* 44 (1993).
Stavrakakis, Yannis, 'Book Reviews of On the Political', in *The Political Quarterly* 77, no. 2 (2006): 306–7.
Strickland, Donna, 'Worrying Democracy – Chantal Mouffe and the Return of Politicized Rhetoric', in *JAC* 19, no. 3 (1999): 476–84.
Tønder, Lars, and Lasse Thomassen, eds., *Radical Democracy: Politics between Abundance and Lack* (Manchester: Manchester University Press, 2005).
Tormey, Simon, 'Ernesto Laclau (1935–) and Chantal Mouffe (1943–)', in Jon Simons ed., *From Agamben to Zizek – Contemporary Critical Theorists* (Edinburgh: Edinburgh University Press, 2010), 144–60.
Torfing, Jacob, *New Theories of Discourse: Laclau, Mouffe, and Žižek* (London: Blackwell, 1999).
Torfing, Jacob, and David Howarth, eds., *Discourse Theory in European Politics: Identity, Policy and Government* (London: Palgrave Macmillan, 2005).
Townshend, Jules, 'Laclau and Mouffe's Hegemonic Project: The Story So Far', in *Political Studies* 52 (2004): 269–88.
Townshend, Jules, 'Discourse Theory and Political Analysis' A New Paradigm from the Essex School?', in *The British Journal of Politics and International Relations* 5, no. 1 (2016): 129–42.

Tully, James, 'Review of The Democratic Paradox', in *Political Theory* 30, no. 6 (2002): 862–4.
Wenman, Mark Anthony, 'Laclau or Mouffe? Splitting the Difference', in *Philosophy & Social Criticism* 29, no. 5 (September 2003): 581–606.
Wiley, James, 'The Impasse of Radical Democracy', in *Philosophy & Social Criticism* 28, no. 4 (2002): 483–8.
Wingenbach, Edward C., *Institutionalizing Agonistic Democracy: Post-Foundationalism and Political Liberalism* (London: Ashgate Publishing, 2011).
Wood, Ellen Meiksins, *The Retreat from Class: A New 'True' Socialism* (New York: Verso, 1999).
Yamamoto, Arata D., 'Why Agonistic Planning? Questioning Chantal Mouffe's Thesis of the Ontological Primacy of the Political', in *Planning Theory* 16, no. 4 (2017): 384–403.
Yamamoto, Arata D., 'The Enemy within the Dangers of Chantal Mouffe's Figure of the Adversary to the Democratic Task of Agonistic Planning', in *Planning Theory* 17, no. 4 (2018): 551–67.

Select Bibliography

Adams, Ross Exo, *Circulation & Urbanization* (London: Sage, 2019).
Allen, Stan, 'Untitled Article', in *Assemblage* 41 (Cambridge, MA: MIT Press, April 2000).
Arendt, Hannah, *The Human Condition* (Chicago: University of Chicago Press, 1998).
Aristophanes, 'The Assemblywomen', in Jeffrey Henderson ed., *Three Plays by Aristophanes: Staging Women* (New York: Routledge, 1996).
Aureli, Pier Vittorio, *The Possibility of an Absolute Architecture* (Cambridge, MA: MIT Press, 2011).
Benjamin, Walter, 'Work of Art in the Age of Its Technological Reproducibility: Third Version', in Howard Eiland and Michael W. Jennings eds., *Walter Benjamin: Selected Writings of Walter Benjamin*, Volume 4 1938–1940 (Cambridge, MA: Belknap Press of Harvard University Press, 1996), 251–83.
Birignani, Cesare, *The Police and the City: Paris, 1660–1750* (PhD. diss., Columbia University, 2013).
Blau, Eve, *The Architecture of Red Vienna 1919–1934* (Cambridge MA: MIT Press, 1999).
Boltanski, Luc, and Eve Chiapello, *The New Spirit of Capitalism* (New York: Verso, 2007).
Budgen, Sebastian, A New 'Spirit of Capitalism', in *New Left Review*, vol. ii (Paris, January/February 2000), 149–56.
Burke, Edmund, 'Succession and Uniformity', in *A Philosophical Inquiry into the Origin of Our Ideas of the Sublime and Beautiful* (Oxford: Oxford University Press, 1990). Originally published in 1757.
Cacciari, Massimo, *L'arcipelago* (Milan: Adelphi Edizioni, 1997).
Cavelletti, Andrea, *La Città biopolitica. Mitologie della sicurezza* (Milan: Bruno Mondadori, 2005).
Colquhoun, Alan, 'The Superblock' in *Essays in Architectural Criticism: Modern Architecture and Historical Change* (Cambridge, MA: MIT Press, 1985), 83–103.
Le Corbusier, 'La Guerre? Mieux vaut Costruire', in *Plans* 6 (June 1931): 65–7.
Deleuze, Gilles, 'The Rise of the Social', foreword to Jacques Donzelot, *The Policing of Families* (New York: Pantheon, 1979), ix–xix.
Engels, Friedrich, *The Housing Question* (New York: International Publishers, 1997). Originally published as a pamphlet in 1887.

Esposito, Roberto, *Living Thought: The Origins and Actuality of Italian Philosophy* (Stanford, CA: Stanford University Press, 2012).
Fisher, Mark, *Capitalist Realism: Is There No Alternative* (London: Zero Books, 2009).
Flierl, Thomas, 'Migrant with a Conflicted Sense of Home: Hannes Meyer after the Bauhaus', in Ines Weizman ed., *Dust and Data. Traces of the Bauhaus across 100 Years* (Spector Books: Leipzig, 2019), 420–35.
Forsén, Björn, and Greg Stanton, eds., *The Pnyx in the History of Athens: Proceedings of an International Colloquium Organized by the Finnish Institute at Athens, 7–9 October 1994* (Helsinki: Foundation of the Finnish Institute at Athens, 1996), 126.
Forsén, Björn, and Greg Stanton, eds., *The Pnyx in the History of Athens: Proceedings of an International Colloquium Organized by the Finnish Institute at Athens, 7–9 October 1994* (Helsinki: Foundation of the Finnish Institute at Athens, 1996), 806–7.
Foucault, Michel, *The Birth of Biopolitics: Lectures at the Collège de France, 1978–1979* (New York: Palgrave Macmillan, 2008).
Fraser, Nancy, and Axel Honneth, *Redistribution or Recognition? A Political-Philosophical Exchange* (New York: Verso, 2003).
Fukuyama, Francis, *The End of History and the Last Man* (New York: Free Press, 1992).
Giannetto, Raffaella Fabiani, 'Medici Gardens', in *Medici Gardens: From Making to Design* (Philadelphia: Pennsylvania University Press, 2008), 10–87.
Hardt, Michael, and Antonio Negri, *Empire* (Cambridge, MA: Harvard University Press, 2000).
Hardt, Michael, and Antonio Negri, *Empire Multitude: War and Democracy in the Age of Empire* (New York: Penguin, 2004).
Hardt, Michael, and Antonio Negri, *Commonwealth* (Cambridge, MA: Belknap Press of Harvard University Press, 2009).
Jameson, Fredric, *A Singular Modernity Essay on the Ontology of the Present* (New York: Verso, 2002).
Kristeva, Julia, 'A New Type of Intellectual: The Dissident', in Toril Moi ed., *The Kristeva Reader* (Oxford: Blackwell Publishers, 1986), 292–301.
Kurg, Andres, 'Architects of the Tallinn School and the Critique of Soviet Modernism in Estonia', in *The Journal of Architecture* 14, no. 1 (2009): 85–108.
Landrum, Lisa, 'Before Architecture: Archai, Architects and Architectonics in Plato and Aristotle', in *Montreal Architectural Review* 2 (2015): 6.
Lyotard, Jean-François, *Le Différend* (Paris: Les Editions de Minuit, 1983).
Marso, Lori Jo, *Politics with Beauvoir: Freedom in the Encounter* (Durham, NC: Duke University Press, 2017), 3–4.
Martin, Reinhold, 'Public and Common(s)', in *Places Journal*, https://doi.org/10.22269/130124
Martin, Reinhold, *Utopia's Ghost: Architecture and Postmodernism, Again* (Minneapolis, MN: University of Minnesota Press, 2010).
Martin, Reinhold, 'Occupy: The Day After', in *Places Journal*, https://placesjournal.org/article/occupy-the-day-after/
Patočka, Jan, 'The Spiritual Person and the Intellectual', in *Living in Problematicity* (Prague: OIKOYMENH, 2007).
Rabeneck, Andrew, 'The Place of Knowledge in Construction', https://www.academia.edu/30231811/The_Place_of_Knowledge_in_Construction
Rappaport, Anatole G., 'Fantasy versus Utopia', in Mikhail Belov ed., *Nostalgia of Culture: Contemporary Soviet Visionary Architecture* (London: AA, 1988).
Rossi, Aldo, *The Architecture of the City* (Cambridge, MA: MIT Press, 1984).
Somol, R.E., and Sarah Whiting, 'Notes around the Doppler Effect and Other Moods of Modernism', in *Perspecta* 33 (Cambridge, MA: MIT Press, 2002), 72–7.

Bibliography

Staten, Henry, *Wittgenstein and Derrida* (Oxford: Basil Blackwell, 1985).
Stratford, Helen, 'Enclaves of Expression: Resistance by Young Architects to the Physical and Psychological Control of Expression in Romania during the 1980s', in *Journal of Architectural Education* 54, no. 4 (London: Routledge, 2001): 218–28.
Streeck, Wolfgang, *Buying Time: The Delayed Crisis of Democratic Capitalism* (New York: Verso, 2017).
Summerson, John, *Georgian London* (London: Pleiades books, 1945).
Talesnik, Daniel Adolfo, *The Itinerant Red Bauhaus, or the Third Emigration* (Dissertation, Columbia University, 2016).
Daniel, Talesnik, 'Tibor Weiner's Architectural Design Curriculum in Chile (1946–47)', in Ines Weizman ed., *Dust and Data. Traces of the Bauhaus across 100 Years* (Spector Books: Leipzig, 2019).
Teyssot, Georges, 'Figuring the Invisible', in *A Topology of Everyday Constellations* (Cambridge, MA: MIT Press, 2013), 31–82.
Torfing, Jacob, and David Howarth, eds., *Discourse Theory in European Politics: Identity, Policy and Government* (London: Palgrave Macmillan, 2005).
Toscano, Alberto, 'Factory, Territory, Metropolis, Empire', in *Angelaki* 9, no. 2 (London: Routledge, 2004): 197–216.
Ventura, Angelo, 'Considerazioni sull'agricoltura veneta e sull'accumulazione originaria del capitale nei secoli XVI e XVII', in *Studi Storici*, no. 3–4 (Roma: Fondazione Istituto Gramsci,1969): 674–722.
Weizman, Ines, *Iron Curtain, Plastered Walls: The Architectural Transformation of Former East German Cities* (Dissertation: Architectural Association, 2005).
Weizman, Ines, 'Citizenship', in *The SAGE Handbook of Architectural Theory*, C. Greig Crysler, Stephen Cairns and Hilde Heynen eds. (London: Sage, 2012), 107–20.
Weizman, Ines, 'Dissidence through Architecture', in *Perspecta* 45 (2012): 27–38.
Weizman, Ines, ed., *Architecture and the Paradox of Dissidence* (Milton Park: Routledge, 2014).
Weizman, Ines, ed., *Dust & Data: Traces of the Bauhaus across 100 Years* (Leipzig: Spector Books, 2019).
Weizman, Ines, 'Als die Architekten die Revolution verließen. Regimekritiker und Dissidenz in der DDR und Osteuropa vor 1989', in Nina Gribat, Philipp Misselwitz, and Matthias Görlich eds., *Vergessene Schulen. Architekturlehre zwischen Reform und Revolte um 1968* (Leipzig: Spector Books, 2017), 291–306.
Weizman, Ines, *Documentary Architecture Dissidence through Architecture*, *Arquitectura Documental* (Santiago de Chile: ARQ Editiones, 2020).
Whiting, Sarah, and Robert Somol, 'Notes on the Doppler Effect: The Many Moods of Modernism', in *Perspecta* 33 (2002): 72–7.
Whiting, Sarah, 'SUPER!', in *Log* 16 (2009): 19–26.
Williams, Raymond, *The Country and the City* (London: Chatto and Windus, 1973).
Žižek, Slavoj, 'The Leninist Freedom', in *On Belief* (Milton Park: Routledge, 2001), 115.

Index

A
Agonism 9, 16, 17, 20, 23, 50, 61, 71, 85, 97, 101, 104, 109, 145, 161
Althusser, Louis 2, 65
Antagonism 8, 9, 13–16, 105
Archizoom 27
Arendt, Hannah, 59–65, 67, 73, 134
Artistic practices 18, 31, 32, 109–17

B
Badiou, Alain 111
Barry, Charles, and Augustus Pugin 24
BIG 56, 118, 131, 138
Birignani, Cesare 36
Boeri, Stefano 140
Boltanski, Luc and Eve Chiapello 112, 128

C
Cacciari, Massimo 51
Cerdà, Ildefons 36
Colquhoun, Alan 134
Commons 70, 137–8
Consensus 14, 17, 33–5, 44, 47–50, 61, 116, 131, 139–41

D
Da Vinci, Leonardo 52
Delamare, Nicolas 36
Deleuze, Jacques 17, 64
Democracy 20, 51, 59, 107, 136, 162
Derrida, Jacques 2, 6, 15, 22
Discourse 4, 6
Dissidence 85, 86, 95, 97, 99–101, 139, 161
Dogma 117, 132

E
Eisenman, Peter 123, 132
Engels, Friedrich 65, 144
Enzmann Christian, and Bernd Ettel 92–4, 106
Esposito, Roberto 51

F
Filippov, Mikhail and Nadezhda Bronzova 88, 91
Fisher, Mark 158
Foucault, Michel 62, 69, 72, 73, 150
Fraser, Nancy 21, 130
Freud, Sigmund 30
Fukuyama, Francis 80

G
Galimov, Iskander 89–91
Giddens, Anthony 20
Globalization 27–9
Gramsci, Antonio 2, 18, 19, 26, 31, 42, 79, 97
Graves, Michael 123

H
Habermas, Jürgen 17, 23, 30
Hardt, Michael 19, 28, 55, 62, 70
Havel, Vaclav 158
Hegemony 15, 24, 130
Heidegger, Martin 16, 68
Honneth, Axel 21
Housing 44, 53, 55, 64–5, 75, 79, 125, 134, 145, 152

J
Jaar, Alfredo 113–15
Jacobs, Sam 56
Jacques-Germaine Soufflot 24
Jiménez, Carlos 128

K
Kabakov, Ilja 94
Kirpichev, Vladislav 88
Koolhaas, Rem 123
Koss, Juliet 131
Kristeva, Julia 86

L
Lacan, Jacques 2, 7
Laclau, Ernesto 2, 4, 61

Index

Latour, Bruno 61
Le Corbusier 35
Lefort, Claude 18
Liberalism 3, 13–14
Loos, Adolf 105
Lyotard, Jean-François 116

M
Maltzan, Michael 125
Marso, Lori Jo 109
Mouffe, Chantal
  Agonistics 22, 112–13
  'Art and Democracy' 111
  For a Left Populism 25
  Hegemony and Socialist Strategy 2–3, 15, 21, 27, 31, 84–5, 103, 142–3, 153, 162–3
  Making Things Public 60
  On the Political 7, 18, 20, 30

N
Nationalism 30–1
Negri, Antonio 19, 28, 55, 61, 62, 64, 70, 138
Neoliberalism 20, 25
Noble, Richard 111

O
Occupy Wall Street 76–7
Oppenheimer, Sarah 129

P
Palladio, Andrea 37, 38
Patočka, Jan 87
Piano, Renzo 123
Piranesi, Giovanni Battista 27
Plato 22
Political, The 8, 13, 15, 47, 55
Projective 78, 80, 111, 112, 122
Public Space 17

R
Rabeneck, Andrew 43

Rancière, Jacques 29
Red Vienna 39–41, 50, 53, 71, 73, 82, 133, 143, 151
Rossi, Aldo 26, 152
Rowe, Colin 51

S
Saussure, Ferdinand de 2, 4, 6
Schmidt, Carl 8, 60, 68
Socialism 21, 80, 85, 103–4, 143
Somol, R.E. 56, 112, 132
Speaks, Michael 134
Staten, Henry 14
Stratford, Helen 88
Streeck, Wolfgang 21
Summerson, John 49
Superstudio 26

T
Tafuri, Manfredo 26, 76, 81, 124
Tronti, Mario 51, 61

U
Ungers, O.M. 51
Urbanization 36–38, 150

V
Ventura, Angelo 39
Venturi, Robert 56, 131
Vesely, Dalibor 87, 100
Virno, Paolo 137
Vitruvius 34, 35, 140

W
Weiwei, Ai 105
Witte, Ron 118, 122
WW Architecture 118

Z
Zaera-Polo, Alejandro 130
Žižek, Slavoj 85

www.ingramcontent.com/pod-product-compliance
Lightning Source LLC
Chambersburg PA
CBHW052125300426
44116CB00010B/1783